# Happy Days

# Happy Days

## IMAGES OF THE PRE-SIXTIES PAST IN SEVENTIES AMERICA

Benjamin L. Alpers

RUTGERS UNIVERSITY PRESS

*New Brunswick, Camden, and Newark, New Jersey*

*London and Oxford*

Rutgers University Press is a department of Rutgers, The State University of New Jersey, one of the leading public research universities in the nation. By publishing worldwide, it furthers the University's mission of dedication to excellence in teaching, scholarship, research, and clinical care.

Library of Congress Cataloging-in-Publication Data

Names: Alpers, Benjamin Leontief, 1965– author.
Title: Happy days : images of the pre-sixties past in seventies America / Benjamin L. Alpers.
Other titles: Images of the pre-sixties past in seventies America
Description: New Brunswick, New Jersey : Rutgers University Press, [2024] | Includes bibliographical references and index.
Identifiers: LCCN 2023018240 | ISBN 9781978830530 (paperback) | ISBN 9781978830547 (hardback) | ISBN 9781978830554 (epub) | ISBN 9781978830578 (pdf)
Subjects: LCSH: United States—Civilization—1970– | Popular culture—United States—History—20th century. | Mass media and history—United States. | Nostalgia in mass media. | Nineteen seventies.
Classification: LCC E169.12 .A3759 2024 | DDC 973.92—dc23
LC record available at https://lccn.loc.gov/2023018240

A British Cataloging-in-Publication record for this book
is available from the British Library.

References to internet websites (URLs) were accurate at the time of writing. Neither the author nor Rutgers University Press is responsible for URLs that may have expired or changed since the manuscript was prepared.

♾ The paper used in this publication meets the requirements of the American National Standard for Information Sciences—Permanence of Paper for Printed Library Materials, ANSI Z39.48-1992.

rutgersuniversitypress.org

*To my parents*

*Paul Alpers (1932–2013)*

*and*

*Svetlana Alpers (1936–)*

*who introduced me to the study of the past*

*and with whom I experienced the Seventies*

# CONTENTS

# Happy Days

# Introduction

In 1979, the writer Joan Didion published *The White Album*, her second collection of essays. It came more than a decade after *Slouching towards Bethlehem*, which had established Didion's reputation as a leading practitioner of the "New Journalism." Published in 1968, *Slouching towards Bethlehem* collected essays that Didion had written throughout the Sixties and was largely devoted to understanding what was happening to American society and culture during that tumultuous decade. Its famous title essay was a critical portrait of young people in San Francisco during 1967's "Summer of Love."

*The White Album* collects pieces written in the years after the publication of *Slouching.* Most of the material was thus written in, and largely concerns, the Seventies. And yet the book is haunted by the Sixties, by Didion's continuing desire to understand what that decade meant and how it changed her home state of California, in particular, and America, in general. Considerations of the Sixties form bookends to the collection. The long title essay, which also serves as the first of the book's five sections, is dated 1968–1978, and focuses on the bitter end of the Sixties in Los Angeles, where Didion lived during that decade. And the book's fifth and final section is entitled "On the Morning after the Sixties."

In "On the Morning after the Sixties," which was, as the title suggests, written on January 1, 1970, Didion attempts a kind of instant retrospective on that decade. But rather than think about the Sixties themselves, or even speculate what the Seventies might hold, Didion looks back to a past *before* the 1960s: "When I think about the Sixties now I think about an afternoon not of the Sixties at all, an afternoon early in my sophomore year at Berkeley, a bright autumn Saturday in 1953."[1] Though "On the Morning after the Sixties" is dedicated to an understanding of its title decade, it largely focuses on the 1950s. Didion suggests that the Fifties, the decade that formed her as an adult, "a peculiar and inward time," left her ill-prepared for the decade that now lay between her and that formative time. It is telling that Didion, who had risen to fame as a chronicler of the Sixties as they were happening, looked to the pre-Sixties past in her very first effort to think about that decade retrospectively. It would be a move that many other American writers and thinkers in the 1970s would also make.

The Seventies is often thought of as a decade marked by peculiarly intense nostalgia for the past. Indeed, the idea that nostalgia characterized the 1970s goes right back to the early years of that decade. "Nostalgia may prove to be the overriding emotion of the Seventies," the *New York Times* theater critic Clive Barnes noted in a January 1971 review of the Broadway revival of *No, No, Nanette*, "with remembrance of things past far more comfortable than the realization of things present."[2] Just a few months later, Gerald Clarke drew similar conclusions in an essay in *Time* magazine on the meaning of nostalgia: "Without question the most popular pastime of the year is looking back. . . . We seem not so much to be entering the new decade as backing away from it full astern."[3] And the reputation of the 1970s as the decade of nostalgia has continued to this day.

Yet Joan Didion's look back to the Fifties in "On the Morning after the Sixties" is not nostalgic in its tone. Didion is not an author prone to nostalgia. The Fifties shaped her and must be reckoned with if she is to understand the Sixties as she enters the Seventies. The decade in which she went to college, Didion argues, made her permanently ill-equipped for the times to come. But Didion does not long for the Fifties or even present them as particularly attractive. She turns to the Fifties not to escape her 1970 present, but merely to better understand that present and her relationship to the changes in American life that had taken place in the ensuing decade. The intellectual move that Didion made on the morning after the Sixties would be mirrored by many other Americans in the 1970s and is the subject of this book. Americans in the 1970s frequently looked back to times before the tumultuous 1960s to grapple with the changes that had recently taken place in American life. And though nostalgia was, indeed, one of the modes in which they did so, it was not the only one.

This project grew out of a blog post. In 2013, the film *American Graffiti* celebrated its fortieth anniversary. A surprise hit for its young director, George Lucas, who was previously known only for *THX 1138* (1971), a cold, art-house science fiction piece that attracted more critical attention than audience affection, *American Graffiti*'s excellent box-office performance would eventually allow Lucas to make *Star Wars* (1977), the success of which quickly overshadowed *American Graffiti*'s. Though *American Graffiti* was an enormous hit in 1973, by 2013 it had become something of a historical curiosity. So I thought it would be interesting to revisit the film for the Society for U.S. Intellectual History's *U.S. Intellectual History Blog*, which I was editing at the time.[4]

Though I did not see *American Graffiti* in its initial theatrical run, I'm old enough to remember its cultural impact in the 1970s. It helped spur that decade's fascination with 1950s youth culture. I knew—or at least thought I knew—that it had spawned *Happy Days*, one of the biggest television hits of the 1970s, which, like *American Graffiti*, starred Ron Howard and prominently featured high-school-aged characters hanging out in a diner. And I remembered seeing *American Graffiti* for the first time, probably toward the end of the 1970s, in one of the many repertoire film theaters in my hometown of Berkeley, California. I liked the film at the time. Its characters were about the age I was when I saw it, though they lived in a time and place that felt quite distant.

It was only when I revisited the film and wrote that blog post about it decades later that I realized that the setting of *American Graffiti* was much closer than I had imagined it to be. Though I thought of *American Graffiti* as a "fifties film," it is actually set late in the summer of 1962, just three years before I was born and a little over a decade and a half before I saw it for the first time. And the film takes place in George Lucas's hometown of Modesto, just ninety miles or so from Berkeley. I'm pretty sure that none of this would have been unknown to me in high school when I first saw the film. But in 2013, the peculiarity and significance of this really struck me: How could a place and time so close to my own have become an object of nostalgia, not only for people of my age but also for people who were alive at the time that *American Graffiti* was set?

Studying and thinking about the film only heightened my interest in this question. Though *American Graffiti* was released in 1973, only eleven years after its story took place, it was marketed as a nostalgia film. Its poster asked: "Where Were You in '62?" And film critics like Roger Ebert, who, unlike me, could actually answer that question, also noted how distant that time felt even in the early 1970s.[5]

Of course, it was no great mystery why 1962 felt so distant from 1973. In between those two dates "the Sixties" happened. *American Graffiti* was a deeply autobiographical project for George Lucas. In the actual summer of 1962, the summer after Lucas himself graduated from high school, a near fatal accident led him to leave behind a passion for cars and drag racing and, eventually, to devote himself, instead, to film. But 1962 was also a moment before the 1960s became the Sixties. President Kennedy's assassination was a little over a year away. And though several thousand American military personnel were already in Vietnam, that conflict does not weigh at all on the characters in *American Graffiti*, who are instead focused on deciding whether or not to leave their hometown, family, and friends to go to college far away. But the film is haunted by the changes that are to come, though this only becomes explicit in an end-credit sequence in which a crawl reveals the fates of the characters, many of whose lives will be terminated or disrupted by the Vietnam War.

As I grappled with *American Graffiti*, I began to notice other instances in which 1970s American culture seemed to turn to the pre-Sixties past in order to understand the changes that had taken place during that turbulent decade. Some of these, like *American Graffiti* itself, seemed to fit into the category of nostalgia. Television shows like *Happy Days*, *Laverne & Shirley*, and even *The Waltons* could be read as expressing a kind of longing for the past. These works seemed to instantiate the notion that the Seventies were an era dominated by nostalgia.

But, as Joan Didion's assessment of her experience of the 1950s suggests, Americans' engagements with the past during the Seventies did not always take the form of nostalgia. Commemorations of the American

Revolution's Bicentennial, which were seen as a great success in 1976, despite nearly constant, and often valid, criticism of the federal government's planning for it in the years leading up to it, were certainly celebratory. But they tended to be less about nostalgia for the past than they were about locating a sense of national purpose in the country's founding moment that might, in turn, become a resource for a nation that again found itself in a time of social and political turbulence. Alex Haley's *Roots* (1976) was one of the most successful works to grapple with the past created during the Seventies, spawning both its ABC miniseries adaptation (1977), which became the most popular television program of all time, and the nationwide phenomenon of people, especially Blacks, searching for their families' roots. And yet, it would be hard to argue that *Roots*, a harrowing tale of a Black family's passage through American slavery to freedom, was in any simple way a nostalgia piece. Bicentennial programs and *Roots* looked to the past to understand and renew the present without wishing for a return to that past.

And sometimes the relationship to nostalgia was deeply complicated by Seventies works themselves. The explosion of neo-noir cinema in the decade was certainly, in part, a reflection of a wave of nostalgia among filmmakers and cineastes for Hollywood's glorious past. But the cynical, psychologically and socially critical depictions of America in classic film noir were attractive to Americans in the 1970s precisely because they raised questions about America in the past that seemed relevant again to Americans in the present. The great neo-noirs of the 1970s— whether set in the past like Roman Polanski's *Chinatown* (1974) or the present like Robert Altman's *The Long Goodbye* (1973)—frequently featured protagonists who were based on the hard-boiled private eyes of classic noir, but who were less capable than their classic noir forebears of standing apart from the rot of the world around them. Films like *Chinatown* and *The Long Goodbye* explored an old model of American masculinity and found it wanting.

In the midst of engaging with the readers of the *U.S. Intellectual History Blog* about my *American Graffiti* post and thinking about these other examples of Seventies Americans grappling with the pre-Sixties past, I offhandedly mentioned to a friend that someone should write a book about this. Although I was between projects at the time, it took me a few weeks to realize that I wanted to tackle this myself. I knew immediately that I wanted to take an essayistic approach to this project. Though I think that the Seventies were a moment in American life in which public culture grappled with the past in distinctive ways, I thought that I neither could nor should discuss those engagements with the past comprehensively. I felt that these many, parallel 1970s forays into the past were driven by different impulses and reached different conclusions. The historian Daniel Rodgers has argued that during the last quarter of the twentieth century, the past seemed both more immediate and more fractured to Americans.[6] In a sense I was charting the beginnings of what Rodgers has called the Age of Fracture. Nostalgia is certainly one of the modes in which Americans in the Seventies dealt with the pre-Sixties past, but I did not want my book to focus on nostalgia alone.

This book has four chapters, each an exploration of a set of 1970s attempts to grapple with the pre-Sixties past. The first is on images of the Fifties in the Seventies, with a special focus on the image of "greasers," a once rebellious, working-class subculture that enjoyed a new popularity in the 1970s. Although images of greasers featured prominently in Elvis Presley's television special *Elvis* (1968; usually referred to as his "comeback special"), the Fifties-revival singing group Sha Na Na (which was formed in 1969), the musical *Grease* (1971), the film *The Lords of Flatbush* (1974), and a variety of other cultural productions, the image of the greaser reached its 1970s apotheosis in the character of Arthur Fonzarelli, better known as "Fonzie" or "The Fonz," in the hit ABC sitcom *Happy Days* (1974–1984). In their apparently "safe" and nostalgic images of pre-Sixties rebellion, these Seventies greasers have frequently been read as essentially conservative figures, visions of a kind of alternative to a true counterculture, a quaint sort of rebellion that, at least in retrospect, seemed culturally unthreatening. But as I worked on the figure of the greaser in the 1970s, I soon encountered many less "safe" and conservative appropriations of this image, including the gay leather scene and early punk rock. Punk's appropriation of the greaser was, like the more culturally mainstream versions of him, quite directly a response to the Sixties. Bands like the Ramones and zines like *Punk* self-consciously rejected values that they associated with the Sixties counterculture and invoked the Fifties as a moment when rock 'n' roll was truly rebellious. Though some critics of the punk scene felt that this, too, was just another form of cultural conservatism, musicians and artists associated with it attempted to create a new, post-Sixties kind of cultural rebellion by reappropriating and celebrating images of Fifties rebellion.

My second chapter concerns 1970s neo-noir movies and the figure of the hard-boiled private investigator within them. I knew from having taught a course on film noir for over a decade that the Seventies played an important and peculiar role in the history of film noir. French film critics first began to use the term "film noir" in the summer of 1946, when they saw an interesting, new tendency within the raft of Hollywood movies from the first half of the 1940s that played for the first time in France following liberation and the end of World War II. French critics saw elements of existentialism and surrealism in these dark, often cynical, crime films. And they also reminded these critics of the great French poetic realist films of the 1930s, a style of filmmaking that was associated with the period of the Popular Front and that had essentially ended with the fall of France in 1940. As Hollywood continued to produce the sort of movies that the French called "noir," a sophisticated critical discourse about "film noir" developed in France. But the term took a while making its way into anglophone film criticism. The first American journal article about film noir would not be published until 1972. This essay, Paul Schrader's "Notes on Film Noir," was originally written as screening notes to a series of film noirs that were part of the first Los Angeles Film Exposition (1971). At the time, Schrader was a twenty-five-year-old recent film school graduate who was about to shift his career focus from film criticism to screenwriting and later directing.

Schrader is the central figure in my chapter on neo-noir for a variety of related reasons. First, "Notes on Film Noir" is, among other things, a reflection on the Seventies and their relationship to the 1960s. Schrader sees the fatalism and hopelessness of classic noirs of the 1940s and 1950s as reflecting the dashed radical hopes of pre–World War II American culture. Schrader, correctly as it turns out, predicted that American audiences in the 1970s would grow more interested in noir, precisely because American culture found itself in a similar moment: "As the current political mood hardens, filmgoers and filmmakers will find the *film noir* of the late Forties increasingly attractive. The Forties may be to the Seventies what the Thirties were to the Sixties." In "Notes," Schrader set the terms of American critical discussions of noir. And in his screenplays of the 1970s such as *The Yakuza* (1974), *Taxi Driver* (1976), and *Rolling Thunder* (1977), he helped forge the emergent Seventies genre of *neo*-noir. The central character in all three of these screenplays is a man who has returned from war (World War II in the case of *The Yakuza*; Vietnam in the case of the other two films), but who finds himself utterly out of place in the world of America in the 1970s. Each of their stories climaxes in a vast act of vengeful violence. Though, in each case, the film's antagonists are defeated, there is some question as to whether these acts of violence represent a successful and perhaps even admirable kind of masculine reassertion or whether we should instead read them as themselves reflecting the brokenness of the films' protagonists and the world in which they find themselves. Seventies neo-noirs are full of such male protagonists who are presented as bearers of masculine values that are no longer common in American culture. And like the three films written by Paul Schrader, many other Seventies neo-noirs end in acts of violence that arguably represent a violation of those values. In addition to tracking Schrader's views on and use of neo-noir, I look at a parallel strain of 1970s neo-noir characters that are more directly based on the hard-boiled detectives on the 1940s, such as Robert Altman's Raymond Chandler adaptation, *The Long Goodbye* (1973).

My third chapter concerns the celebration of the Bicentennial of the American Revolution in 1976. President Johnson had begun planning for the national celebration of the Bicentennial by creating the American Revolution Bicentennial Commission (ARBC) in 1966. Upon taking office three years later, President Nixon treated ARBC as a political opportunity for his own benefit and the agency soon became mired in controversy, leading to its dissolution in 1973 and the creation of the American Revolution Bicentennial Agency (ARBA), which was to be focused on fostering local celebrations around the country rather than creating a single, national celebration. To the surprise of many, when the Bicentennial finally rolled around in July 1976, the celebrations were seen as a great success. In the last decade or so, historians like Tammy Gordon and Rick Perlstein have seen, in the patriotic outpouring around these decentralized celebrations, a kind of anticipation of Reaganism, with its emphasis on renewing love of country and devolving power to states and localities. My chapter, however, is focused on the largely contentless nature of the sense of unity that ARBA helped forge. Americans of all political stripes, including the political radicals who formed the People's Bicentennial Commission, could find things worth celebrating in the story of the nation's founding. But the social and cultural divisions that flowed from the 1960s made creating any sort of consensus vision of the meaning of the American Revolution essentially impossible.

Two films from the 1970s that deal, in very different ways, with the Founding and the Bicentennial nicely illustrate this state of affairs: the musical *1776* (1972) and *Nashville* (1975). Despite being a well-made adaptation of a popular, Tony Award–winning musical that had premiered on Broadway just three years earlier, *1776* received generally negative reviews from major film critics and largely failed to find an audience. The musical celebrates the members of the Continental Congress as great, but humorously ordinary and flawed, men, a vision of the founders that seemed, by 1972, to entirely please neither conservatives nor liberals. Its politics reflected a kind of vital-center liberalism that was also fading into the past. The musical acknowledges that slavery is a great evil, but presents the Continental Congress's unwillingness to denounce it as prudent and necessary. The musical also stresses the need for the nation to pull together in times of war, even if the war is going badly. In 1969, when the show was a Broadway hit, this message seems to have resonated more than it did when the film appeared in 1972, as the nation's attitude toward the Vietnam War continued to sour and the domestic divisions over it increased.

In contrast, the more cinematically challenging *Nashville* both received praise from many critics, who considered it a masterpiece, and achieved success at the box office in 1975. Themes of patriotism run throughout Altman's film, which is set in the very near-future Bicentennial year of 1976. While *1776* attempted to create a coherent, celebratory narrative of the United States' revolutionary past, reflections on that past in *Nashville* are presented with a studied ambivalence. The film begins with the recording of a seemingly serious, Bicentennial-themed song, "200 Years," that *Nashville* largely plays for laughs. But in its conclusion, the film seems to affirm the thesis of that song: that what truly holds this country together is shared tragedy. In both its ambivalent presentation of patriotism and its affirmation of a kind of downbeat, but nevertheless potentially unifying, national identity, *Nashville* seemed to resonate with the public mood more successfully than *1776* had.

The fourth and final chapter of *Happy Days* looks at two books from the Seventies that grapple with the history of slavery and its meanings for Americans in the present day: Alex Haley's *Roots* (1976) and Octavia Butler's *Kindred* (1979). In tracing his family back, through slavery, to eighteenth-century Gambia, Haley argued that a history often seen as unrecoverable could in fact be uncovered. And though archives assisted Haley in his search for his family's roots, the key to its success, Haley suggested, lay in African oral traditions. The seeds of his search came from stories that his older relatives had told him, when he was just a boy, about his family's distant past, including an African ancestor who was the first in his family to be enslaved and brought to America. And much of the information he eventually gathered on that ancestor, Kunta Kinte, would come from a griot, who told Haley details about his ancestral family when the author visited Gambia. Ripped from an almost Edenic existence in his home country, Kunta Kinte never forgets his family's history in Africa and teaches it to his daughter, Kizzy, who, in turn, teaches it to her progeny, all the way down to the relatives who told it to Haley himself. In telling his family history, Kunta Kinte is carrying on a cultural tradition of oral history that Haley depicts as an important part of his ancestor's upbringing in Gambia. And these tellings and retellings of the family's history form a crucial motif in the centuries-long saga that is *Roots*. Haley suggests that, properly understood, Black family histories are both recoverable and heroic. His family's rich cultural roots in Africa were interrupted by the horrors of slavery. Now, centuries later, Haley can reconnect with them thanks in large measure to a tradition of historical storytelling, in which, in writing *Roots*, Haley, too, took part. While slavery maims Haley's ancestors—for example, half of Kunta Kinte's foot is cut off in punishment for trying to escape and Kizzy is raped by her enslaver—understanding that difficult history is liberating. Just as he has recovered a fuller sense of his identity through that understanding, Haley suggests that his readers can as well.

In 1979, just three years after the appearance of *Roots*, Octavia Butler would publish *Kindred*, a novel that also explores Black family history and the relationship of the present to the past under slavery. Like

*Roots*, *Kindred* suggests that the history of slavery is absolutely crucial to Black identity. And, in a sense, it also indicates that that history is at least partially recoverable. Both books suggest that knowledge of the Black past can have a profound impact on the 1970s present. *Roots* takes its story all the way up to Haley himself and his search for his family's past, making the book the final product of all those generations of the oral transmission of the story of Kunta Kinte. *Kindred*, on the other hand, makes the impact of the era of slavery on the present more direct and brutal. And it suggests that the story of a Black family's passage through slavery cannot be as easily reconstructed nor as simply triumphant as Haley makes it in his book. Neither Haley nor Butler felt entirely at home in the dominant strains of Black politics in the Sixties. If *Roots* offers an optimistic alternative to them, *Kindred* might be read as a pessimistic one.

Finally, *Happy Days* concludes with a brief afterword in which I discuss the discomfort on the part of many professional historians during the Seventies about the nature of American culture's interest in the past. Even as interest in the past seemed to be growing in intensity during that decade, interest in the formal study of history was lagging. High school students felt that history was the least "relevant" subject, enrollments in history courses in college declined, and the history profession faced its first major jobs crisis since the beginning of the post–World War II boom in higher education. These historians' contemporary reactions to the way American public culture dealt with the past in the 1970s help sharpen our sense of what was distinctive about that engagement.

This book's explorations of the past in 1970s public culture illuminate the peculiarly intense, yet multivalent, meanings that Americans found in the past during that decade. The first major academic monograph on America in the 1970s, originally published just two years after that decade concluded, bears the title *It Seemed Like Nothing Happened*. Its title was intended ironically. Its author, Peter N. Carroll, saw the decade as one of enormous and significant change, as Americans confronted what felt like an endless series of political, social, and economic crises and searched for new ways forward. But the title was apt, as, after the Sixties, so full of social and cultural change and (often dashed) hopes, the Seventies felt to many Americans like a time of drift. Looking backward, to times before the transformations of the Sixties, was

one of the ways in which Americans responded to the perceived doldrums of the Seventies. Carroll recognized this, but, like many before
and after him, emphasized nostalgia and positive feelings of connection
as the guiding impulses of these looks backward. I hope that this book
will complicate that picture of what Americans in the 1970s saw when
they turned to the past.[7]

# 1

## "Where Were You in '62?"

### The Long Fifties and Nostalgia in Seventies Culture

Any study of the relationship of Americans in the 1970s to the American past needs to grapple with the issue of nostalgia. From very early in that decade, cultural critics saw the 1970s as an era peculiarly steeped in nostalgia. And for nearly all these critics, this was not a good thing. The image of the 1970s as a peculiarly nostalgic time survived that decade and lives on today. But while nostalgia was certainly an important way in which Americans in the 1970s viewed their nation's past, it was far from the only way. This was even the case with American attitudes toward the period that has come to be most associated with nostalgia in the Seventies: the 1950s.

From the very start of the 1970s, American cultural critics noted a growing public fascination with the Fifties. And many of these critics did not like what they saw. Popular representations of the 1950s were often dismissed as escapism, as mere nostalgia. The popularity of movies and television shows set in the 1950s, which critics felt failed to reflect the real complexities of that earlier time, suggested to some that Americans in the 1970s were unwilling to face the problems of their own time. In the wake of the changes in American life brought about by the Sixties, the cultural politics of nostalgia for the Fifties seemed obviously conservative. And the fascination with the Fifties seemed to be part of a larger wave of nostalgia that overtook America in the wake of the Sixties. This largely negative view of the place of the Fifties in 1970s American culture has lasted into the twenty-first century.

This chapter will argue that the Fifties played a more complicated role in 1970s culture than the fiercest critics of nostalgia have suggested. Popular interest in the Fifties certainly represented a response to the problems of the Seventies present. The Sixties, especially the five turbulent years following the assassination of President Kennedy, had transformed the country in many ways. Thinking about the time immediately before these changes was an important part of coming to terms with them. Casting the Fifties in a simply positive light could certainly turn these explorations of the past into escapist nostalgia. But nostalgia was not the only lens through which 1970s American popular culture saw the Fifties.

After describing some highlights of Fifties revivalism in the Seventies, this chapter will look at contemporary critics of nostalgia in the Seventies. It will then explore in greater detail some of the texts most associated with Seventies nostalgia for the Fifties: the musical *Grease* (1971), the movie *American Graffiti* (1973), and the television show *Happy Days* (1974–1984). (Though *American Graffiti* is set in the summer of 1962, it is, rightly, seen as movie about what historians call the "long 1950s." The film presents its setting as a world that is about to go through enormous changes.) I will argue that each of these texts had a more complicated relationship to the 1950s than mere nostalgia.

All these texts feature as key characters what retrospectively came to be known in the Seventies as "greasers": white teenage boys sporting ducktail haircuts, wearing jeans and leather jackets, and often riding on motorcycles or in hot rods.[1] While clearly imagined as a rebel in the context of the 1950s, from the vantage point of the 1970s, the greaser's rebellion could be seen in a variety of different ways. Despite appearing to present these characters as quaint figures ripe for nostalgia, both *Grease* and *American Graffiti* go out of their way to present them as subtly tragic, especially in light of the political upheavals that lay just around the corner from the setting of these works. The character of Arthur Fonzarelli, better known as "Fonzie" or "The Fonz," who moved from a supporting role to a central figure in *Happy Days* over the course of its first few seasons, presented a domesticated version of the greaser, who was ultimately unthreatening not only to Seventies audiences, but even to the adults in the Fifties story world of the show. And unlike equivalent characters in other Seventies texts (and images of similar rebels from texts produced in the 1950s), Fonzie lacks the alienation usually associated with greasers.

Having looked at these texts generally associated with nostalgia for the Fifties, the chapter will then explore two cultural spaces in which the image of the greaser took on quite different, more countercultural meanings: the gay leather scene and the emerging world of punk rock. Though perhaps more grounded in nostalgia than either punk musicians or critics promoting them liked to admit, punk's appropriation of the iconography of Fifties youth culture was not merely backward facing. Rather, punk artists and critics sought to use the materials of youth culture from before the Sixties to move beyond what they saw as the inauthentic, naïve, and calcified place of the legacy of Sixties popular culture in the Seventies. By the end of the decade, even Ellen Willis, a critic who was both suspicious of nostalgia for the past and much less hostile to the Sixties than the punk scene itself, began to see merit in punk rock and its cultural project.

Finally, the chapter concludes by returning to the theme of nostalgia itself and two scholars who, as the Seventies came to a close, questioned, in different ways, the place of nostalgia in American culture: the sociologist Fred Davis and the historian Christopher Lasch. While Davis and Lasch were, in different ways, too quick to discount the significance of nostalgia in Seventies culture, their concerns about the relationship of mass culture to the lived experience of ordinary Americans ironically echoed many of the themes of putatively nostalgic Seventies images of the Fifties. Though Seventies nostalgia for American youth culture of the long Fifties was a real phenomenon, American popular culture in the Seventies—even works like the musical *Grease* that are still most often seen as mere nostalgia—grappled with the Fifties in ways that were not merely nostalgic.

## Fifties Revivals in the 1970s

A growing interest in the popular music of the Fifties was already under-way at the end of the 1960s. Elvis Presley, whose career had been lan-guishing in a series of musical films that grew steadily worse as their musical numbers became ever more perfunctory, made an extraordinary return to form in December 1968 with a television special entitled sim-ply *Elvis*. Though the show featured a number of newly composed songs, including the gospel-tinged finale "If I Can Dream," at its heart was a celebration of Elvis's Fifties musical past. Along with surviving mem-bers of his original band, Elvis, clad entirely in black leather, performed live versions of many of his old hits, including "Heartbreak Hotel," "Jail-house Rock," and "Love Me Tender," while joking with his bandmates about the old days in the studio and on the road. Even *Elvis*'s more con-temporary production numbers thematized the singer's musical past: one celebrated the gospel roots of rock 'n' roll; another told a fictional story of a rock 'n' roller trying to make it traveling around the South. Elvis's television special was an enormous hit and immediately brought new life to his career, leading to its being known ever since as his "come-back special."

Younger performers, too, harkened back to the Fifties as the Sixties came to a close. At Columbia University, which had become the site of some of that decade's most famous student protests, the a cappella group the Kingsmen decided to start performing music of the Fifties in 1969. Soon they renamed themselves "Sha Na Na." By the middle of that year, they were playing Woodstock and, thanks to the film of that festival, gained international fame in 1970. Wearing period haircuts and gold lamé suits that recalled a famous outfit worn by Elvis in the Fifties that he later revived for his comeback special, Sha Na Na were poised between loving tribute and parody. But to the extent that they were the latter, the fun they were having at the expense of the recent past was entirely good-natured.

As the Seventies began, the popular interest in the Fifties only seemed to intensify. In early 1971, the musical *Grease* opened in Chicago. A year later it began an off-Broadway run in New York, before moving to a series of Broadway theaters later that year. *Grease* would become the single big-gest Broadway hit of the decade. The show would play uninterrupted on

Broadway until 1980, setting what was then a record for longest Broadway run.

As *Grease* was finishing its year in Chicago, television producer Garry Marshall was filming a pilot for a situation comedy set in the 1950s. Originally entitled *New Family in Town*, Paramount initially turned the show down, instead recycling the pilot for an episode of the anthology series *Love American Style* entitled "Love and the Television Set," which aired early in 1972.

Later that year, George Lucas, one of the young directors associated with what critics were already calling "the New Hollywood," was starting production on his second film. In marked contrast to the coldly dystopian science fiction of his debut, *THX 1138* (1971), this new film would be a warm, nostalgic, and semi-autobiographical look at youth culture in his hometown of Modesto, California, before most of the changes we associate with the Sixties had taken place. Set in the summer of 1962, the year Lucas himself graduated from Modesto's Thomas Downey High School, *American Graffiti* would be the first enormous hit of Lucas's incredibly successful career. The 1962 of *American Graffiti* was very much part of what we might think of as the long Fifties, before the arrival of the Beatles, before the Kennedy assassination, before Vietnam became a national issue, before the counterculture left its mark. To emphasize this fact, the soundtrack of *American Graffiti*, which crucially set the film's mood, was drawn from the entire early rock 'n' roll era; the film opens with Bill Haley & His Comets' "Rock around the Clock" (1954), one of the first hit rock 'n' roll records.

So successful was *American Graffiti* that Paramount rethought its decision not to proceed with Garry Marshall's *New Family in Town*, whose pilot just happened to star the lead actor in *American Graffiti*, Ron Howard. Premiering in January 1974, the sitcom was retitled *Happy Days* and initially featured "Rock around the Clock" as its theme music. *Happy Days* would enjoy only modest success until it began to focus on the character of Arthur "The Fonz" Fonzarelli (Henry Winkler) and was paired with its spin-off show *Laverne & Shirley*, which had become a hit from the moment it went on the air in January 1976. From 1976 through 1978, *Happy Days* and *Laverne & Shirley* would occupy two of the top three slots in the national television ratings.

*Grease, American Graffiti*, and *Happy Days* were only the most successful products of a much broader fascination with the Fifties. Fifties clothing grew in popularity, college kids held "sock hops," and advertisements for the soft drink 7 Up featured a young Mandy Patinkin playing the Teen Angel, a ghostly version of a greaser. In 1972, in the face of these cultural trends, both *Newsweek* and *LIFE* magazines ran features on Fifties nostalgia.[2]

## Critics of Nostalgia and Fifties Revivalism

From early in the 1970s, American cultural critics identified the growing importance of nostalgia as a disturbing trend. *New York Times* theater critic Clive Barnes began his January 20, 1971, review of the revival of the 1925 musical *No, No, Nanette* with a prediction about the young decade: "Nostalgia may prove to be the overriding emotion of the Seventies, with remembrance of things past far more comfortable than the realization of things present."[3] Barnes was not alone in this sense. From very early in the decade, the American media declared that nostalgia was one of the hallmarks of Seventies culture. In the May 3, 1971, issue of *Time* magazine, in an essay entitled "The Meaning of Nostalgia," Gerald Clarke wrote, "Without question the most popular pastime of the year is looking back. . . . We seem not so much to be entering the new decade as backing away from it full astern."[4]

Nostalgia was observed in both American culture and American politics. "The Boom in Nostalgia Turns Junk into Junque," proclaimed a *New York Times* headline in August 1970, over a story about the sudden collectability of the detritus of earlier generations.[5] And in January 1970, *Time* magazine named "The Middle Americans" their "Man and Woman of the Year." Having explained that Richard Nixon was himself a Middle American and that the collective political power of Middle Americans had gotten him elected, *Time* went on to suggest that the worldviews of these politically ascendant Middle Americans were essentially rooted in the past:

Americans of different generations inhabit the same continent. but they exist in different eras. The American mind is, in effect, stretched out over several decades. The radical young dwell in a projection of the '70s. The values of many of their fathers are the ethics of the Depression, of World War II or the later '40s. In the imagination of his ideals, the Middle American glimpses cracked snapshots through a scrim: a khaki uniform, trousers gathered at the waist; a souvenir samurai sword; a "ruptured duck"; a girl with Betty Grable hair and hemline; the lawn of a barely remembered house. The ideological order that he sees is a civics-book sense of decency.

*Time*'s sense, at the very dawn of the decade, that nostalgia was only for the old would soon fade, as would its quite positive account of nostalgia's political effects. Indeed, in the early 1970s, the word "nostalgia" tended to be used critically; even in January 1970 *Time* had made a point of noting that the politics of those Middle Americans were not "merely grounded upon nostalgia."[6]

As the decade progressed and the political ferment over Vietnam gave way to the economic and political crises of the first half of the 1970s, nostalgia's importance in American culture seemed to grow and critics' concerns about it intensified. The popular television show *The Waltons*, which had begun in 1971, and the hit movie *The Sting* (1973), which would eventually win seven Oscars, including Best Picture, were set during the nation's greatest economic crisis, the Great Depression of the 1930s. While the tough resiliency of the Walton family in the face of poverty was quite different from the joyful con games successfully played by *The Sting*'s protagonists, both painted extraordinarily positive portraits of Americans surviving difficult times. In early 1974, a movie adaptation of *The Great Gatsby* appeared. Starring Robert Redford as Gatsby and Mia Farrow as Daisy, the film was widely criticized for lacking any emotional connection to its characters or the feel of the novel, while caring deeply about the details of the material culture of the 1920s. A "a superficially beautiful hunk of a movie," complained Roger Ebert in the *Chicago Sun-Times*.[7] The filmmakers, wrote Vincent Canby in the *New York Times*, "treated the book as if it were an illustrated encyclopedia of the manners and morals of the nineteen-twenties."[8] "The automobiles," noted Canby, "are stunning."[9] But audiences flocked to *Gatsby*. "Like disenchanted adults leafing through the family album of a happy childhood, Americans today are dosing themselves with nostalgia," wrote

Anatole Broyard in a book review published in August 1973, in the midst of the Watergate hearings. "Nostalgia was becoming a national cult," the historian Rick Perlstein has more recently noted about this period.[10]

Within this larger wave of nostalgia, fascination with the Fifties seemed especially common and, to many, especially disturbing. Critics dismissed Fifties nostalgia as foolish, simplistic, and fundamentally conservative, a naïve form of escapism that both misunderstood the Fifties and sought to evade the world created by the Sixties. By the middle of the Seventies, both Fifties nostalgia and this critique of Fifties nostalgia seemed pervasive.

Writing in 1976, the historian Douglas Miller and the journalist Marion Nowak began *The Fifties: The Way We Really Were*, one of the first attempts at a comprehensive social and cultural history of that decade, with an invocation of Fifties nostalgia and its utter failure to capture the truths about that decade. After surveying the many aspects of what they ironically called "THE FABULOUS FIFTIES!" that had been celebrated during the first half of the Seventies in movies, music, and fashion, Miller and Nowak argue that such "excessive, sentimental nostalgia" usually represents an attempt to escape "times of perceived crisis." Fifties nostalgia was a "pleasant distraction" from "the traumas of the Sixties and Seventies." "One imagines the past," write Miller and Nowak, "and so overlooks the present." The real Fifties, Miller and Nowak suggest, were far darker and less pleasant than Seventies popular culture imagined them to be. They were "essentially a humorless decade," "tired, dull, cautious, and anxious."[11]

To a great extent, the scholarship on the image of the Fifties in the Seventies has accepted this critique and refined it. Daniel Marcus's study of images of the Fifties and Sixties in American politics since the 1980s begins with a chapter about the image of the Fifties in the Seventies. Marcus quotes many contemporary cultural critics in the late Sixties and early Seventies who saw the revival of Fifties culture as either a "way to stave off the present" or as nostalgia designed to "temper the divisions of the Sixties." In part because of its emphasis on rock 'n' roll, Marcus argues, Fifties nostalgia was centered overwhelmingly on images of white, middle-class teenagers. Of particular importance was the image of the greaser, whom Marcus presents as a deeply conservative figure, unlike some other available stereotypes of Fifties adolescent masculinity like the beatnik. Though less explicitly political than invocations of the Fifties in later decades, the Seventies view of the Fifties, according to Marcus, was nonetheless essentially conservative and escapist.[12]

While Marcus is correct about the general centrality of white, middle-class experiences to Seventies images of the Fifties and the particular importance of the figure of the greaser, he is wrong to see these images as simply examples of uncritical nostalgia, as expressions of a longing to escape the world wrought by the Sixties. While the Fifties could certainly be invoked in such a spirit—and, as Marcus argues, would frequently be during the 1980s and 1990s—1970s representations of the Fifties were more ambivalent. Though conservative in some ways, they were also frequently critical of the period they depicted. For Jim Jacobs and Warren Casey, who created the musical *Grease* (1971), or George Lucas, who wrote and directed the film *American Graffiti* (1973), exploring the long Fifties becomes, among other things, a powerful, if indirect, way to process the changes that had taken place during the Sixties. Jacobs, Casey, and Lucas were all themselves children of the Fifties, whose fictional creations were deeply autobiographical. But though these projects were, in that sense, personal, they had enormously broad appeal. As noted above, *Grease* would become the longest-running show ever on Broadway. *American Graffiti* would become one of the biggest surprise cinematic hits, recouping its production costs faster than any other film in Hollywood history.

The hit television show *Happy Days* (1974–1984) comes closer to the simple, escapist celebration of the Fifties of which Seventies popular culture is so often accused. In Fonzie, it featured a character who would become both the most famous Seventies greaser and the one whose air of rebellion was most domesticated. *Happy Days* was even more male-centered than *Grease* or *American Graffiti* had been. The female peers of *Happy Days'* male protagonists were largely reduced to ciphers, especially in the early seasons. Yet it only leapt to its greatest popularity after its female-centered, working-class spin-off *Laverne & Shirley* (1976–1983) joined it in ABC's Tuesday night lineup.

While both *Grease* and *American Graffiti* had grown out of their creators' experiences of the youth culture of the long Fifties, *Happy Days* grew more out of its creators' appreciation for Fifties television. Michael Eisner, then an executive with ABC, and Tom Miller, who was in production at Paramount, were moved to develop the show out of a sense of nostalgia for the family situation comedies of that era. Eisner's favorite show was *Mama* (1949–1957); Miller's was *Father Knows Best* (1954–1960). Though Eisner and Miller wanted to recapture the atmosphere of Fifties television, the idea of actually setting the show in the Fifties was apparently producer Garry Marshall's, though both Miller and Eisner quickly warmed to the concept.[13] Of course, *Happy Days*' audiences were as aware of the conventions of old-fashioned situation comedies as its creators were. Old episodes of shows like *Leave It to Beaver* (1957–1963) and *Ozzie and Harriet* (1952–1966), in syndication after new episodes had stopped appearing, were still playing on American television in the 1970s. Much of the nostalgia being peddled by *Happy Days* was not so much for a simpler time as it was for an older form of situation comedy.

Taken together, these 1970s visions of the Fifties indicate a more complicated picture than the stereotype of the "Fabulous Fifties" against which Douglas Miller and Marion Nowak wrote in 1976. Rather than rejections of the present in favor of a simpler past, they used the Fifties as a space in which to consider America in the 1970s and the rapid changes that had taken place in American life in between the two eras. And the Fifties proved to be a resource for Americans very much outside the cultural mainstream as well. While the image of the greaser could have quite conservative cultural potential, in subcultures like the gay leather scene or the world of New York punk rock the same iconography could be reappropriated for more subversive ends.

## Looking Back on the Fifties in *Grease*

The musical *Grease* bookended nostalgia for the Fifties in the 1970s. The stage version of *Grease* premiered in Chicago in 1971, before starting its long New York run the following year. The movie version of *Grease* would appear in 1978 and was as much a vehicle for Seventies stars John Travolta and Olivia Newton-John as it was a trip to the past. Though *Grease* was often seen as a frothy piece of nostalgia, its depiction of its Fifties setting was actually more complicated and critical, as many later Seventies representations of the Fifties would also be.

When *Grease* became a Broadway hit in the middle of 1972, the media understood its success as part of the general revival of interest in the Fifties. On June 16, 1972, *LIFE* magazine featured a cover story on the "practically instant revival" of the "nifty Fifties." A few months later, on October 16, 1972, *Newsweek* put Marilyn Monroe on its cover and devoted an article to a new "yearning for the Fifties."[14] Both *LIFE* and *Newsweek* prominently featured *Grease* in their reporting on the Fifties revival. And both pieces argued that nostalgia for the Fifties and a renewed interest in Fifties fashion and, especially, music was largely a form of lighthearted escapism from a Seventies America that bore the scars of the Sixties. "Pop psychologists—and many of the kids—see the flight to the '50s as a search for a happier time, before drugs, Vietnam, and assassination," wrote *LIFE*. "To fans of the current revival," the journalist Johnathan Rodgers noted in *Newsweek*, "the point of it all is that the '50s seem to be more fun than anything going on now—or probably then."

But to understand *Grease*, especially in its stage version, as nothing but nostalgic fun is to miss the ambivalence of that show's depiction of the Fifties. The plot of *Grease* is both simple and classically comedic. High school students Danny Zuko and Sandy Dumbrowski have a summer fling. Both are surprised to find themselves at the same school the following fall. Various circumstances keep them apart for most of the musical, but at the end they are united. No doubt audiences left the theater humming the upbeat ensemble number "We Go Together," which ends both of the show's two acts. Musically "We Go Together" emphasizes the rock 'n' roll–inflected joy that was certainly one of *Grease*'s chief attractions. Lyrically, as the song's title suggests, it stresses the characters' togetherness. But, as in many comedies, most of the show explores the reasons that the two protagonists—as well as a host of more minor characters—stay apart. And the causes of conflict in *Grease* are all connected to some of the darker sides of the decade in which it is set.

The male and female characters in *Grease* live parallel, but largely separate lives, a fact perfectly captured early in the show in the song "Summer Nights," in which Sandy and Danny each tell their separate groups of friends about their recently concluded romance. The song is an exuberant duet in which neither Danny nor Sandy understands that he or she is singing a duet. Danny tells his male friends, the Burger Palace

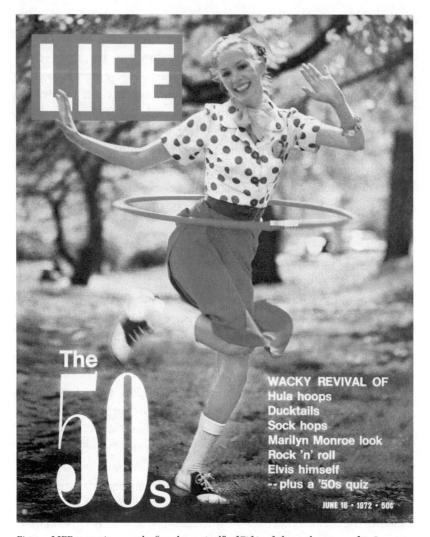

Fig. 1.1. *LIFE* magazine put the "wacky revival" of Fifties fads on the cover of its June 16, 1972, issue. (Credit: Bill Ray / LIFE Picture Collection / Shutterstock.com.)

Boys, his version of events; Sandy tells her female friends, the Pink Ladies, hers. Though Sandy and Danny are in tune with each other musically, each describes their summer fling somewhat differently:

DANNY  She swam by me, she got a cramp
SANDY  He ran by me, got my suit damp

DANNY  Saved her life, she nearly drowned
SANDY  He showed off, splashing around . . .
SANDY  He got friendly, holding my hand
DANNY  She got friendly, down in the sand
SANDY  He was sweet, just turned eighteen
DANNY  She was good, ya know what I mean?

Some of the differences between Danny's and Sandy's narrations reflect the different promptings of their friends. The Burger Palace Boys are basically interested in sexual details ("Tell me more, tell me more / Didja get very far?") while the Pink Ladies are more interested in materialistic ones ("Tell me more, tell me more / How much dough did he spend?"). Not only does the song suggest gender differences, it also underscores the different relations of the protagonists to their peer groups. While Danny is interested in the same things as his male friends, Sandy is more out of step with her female friends. Unlike Danny, she is new to Rydell High. And while Danny is, in most ways, a typical Burger Shop Boy, Sandy is different from the Pink Ladies. We soon find out that the other Pink Ladies drink, smoke, and sleep with their boyfriends. Sandy does none of these things.

Sandy's sense of self and her social desires are entirely undone by the double standard of Fifties culture. By the end of the first act, Sandy's personal moral code has caused her to lose not only Danny, but her Pink Lady friends as well. Sandy overhears Rizzo, the leader of the Pink Ladies, making fun of her moral purity (in the song "Look at Me, I'm Sandra Dee") and also comes to realize that Danny has suggested to his friends that she was "just another tramp." She tries to reconcile with Danny in the second act, agreeing to go to a drive-in movie with him, but she runs out on the date when Danny sexually pressures her after she agrees to "go steady" with him.

We later learn that Rizzo, who seems to be a figure of strength and sexual self-assurance, is herself a victim of the constrained gender roles and sexual politics of her era. Her period is late in coming and she thinks that she is pregnant. Rizzo puts on a tough facade. When Kenickie, the Burger Shop Boy who she believes is responsible, tries to talk to her about it, she tells him that it was some other boy, and refuses help from him or her other friends. When Sandy tries to express sympathy, Rizzo at first lashes out at her as well. But then Rizzo sings to Sandy of the pain she feels about the way she is perceived in the song "There Are Worse Things I Could Do." Though the neighborhood unfairly thinks of Rizzo as "trashy and no good" for "go[ing] with a boy or two," Rizzo feels that "the worst thing I could do" would be to cry in front of Sandy. The plaintive music of "There Are Worse Things I Could Do" underscores the thinness of Rizzo's tough and independent appearance.

And yet the ultimate reconciliation of Sandy and Danny, with which the show concludes, is only made possible by Sandy's decision to conform to the social style of the Pink Ladies and to the desires of the Burger Shop Boys. Sandy, alone, reprises Rizzo's taunting song about her and then telephones Rizzo and asks her to come over with her makeup case. When Sandy next appears she is (in the play's stage directions) "a Greaser's dream girl," chewing gum and smoking a cigarette. The Burger Shop Boys are bowled over ("All Choked Up"), Danny and Sandy are reconciled, and the musical comes to a close with the reprise of "We Go Together."

Much of *Grease*'s appeal was its music, which cleverly reproduced and parodied the styles of Fifties rock. Like the era in which it flourished, the music that is the basis for *Grease*'s score was both close and distant. Fifties rock 'n' roll was a direct ancestor of many of the popular styles of music in the Seventies and a close cousin of many others. But so much musical change had occurred so rapidly in the Sixties that the songs of little more than a decade earlier were already distinctly "oldies." Journalistic reports on the Fifties nostalgia wave in the early 1970s almost always placed rock 'n' roll music at its heart. As noted above, a few years before *Grease* premiered the band Sha Na Na had begun dressing like greasers and covering the hits of the Fifties.

But *Grease* not only featured music that recalled the Fifties, it also concerned itself with the place of that music in the lives of its characters. The show's first number after "Summer Nights" sets up the main plot is "Those Magic Changes." Sung by Doody, the youngest of the Burger Shop Boys, the song is prompted by the other characters' desire to hear what he has learned to play on the guitar. The song is built around the so-called Fifties progression, the set of chords that was the basis of many doo-wop songs. First Doody and then the chorus sing out the names of the chords as they appear in the song:

C-C-C-C-C-C
A-A-A-A minor
F-F-F-F-F-F
G-G-G-G seventh

But in addition to calling attention to its own musical structure, "Those Magic Changes" concerns the impact that hearing music like it on the radio has had on Doody and presumably the other characters who form the chorus. The music "sends a thrill" through Doody "'Cause those chords remind me of / The night that I first fell in love to / Those magic changes." The music evokes a love apparently lost. But unlike the chords that are named, Doody's lost love remains unnamed. What is left to name, celebrate, and experience is the music itself.

While love and sex themselves in *Grease* are fraught, frustrating, and even dangerous, music serves as a ubiquitous, safe, but not entirely satisfying surrogate. And rock 'n' roll, though once the music of rebellion, has already been commodified within the story world of *Grease*. Doody plays "Those Magic Changes" out of an instructional book. Though he's clearly moved by its heartfelt lyrics, they may not even represent his own experience. And they largely concern music coming from the radio, which moves Doody (or at any rate the lyricist) more than the love it evokes.

Later in the show, Sandy similarly melds her feelings with those emerging from the radio. She sings—or rather sings along with—"It's Raining on Prom Night," which plays on the radio as she sits alone in her room. The song captures her sadness at being home alone rather than attending the high school dance with Danny. But while the sentiment of the song reflects and enhances her own feelings, Sandy does not experience the actual action of the song—a story of rain destroying the singer's makeup, hairdo, and taffeta dress.

At the dance itself, entertainment is provided by Johnny Casino, a fellow Rydell High greaser who leads a band and wants to be a rock 'n' roll star, and Vince Fontaine, who the stage directions describes as "a typical 'teen-audience' radio disc jockey. Slick, egotistical, fast-talking. A veteran 'greaser.'" Fontaine supervises the dance competition, during which he promotes his radio station in relentlessly upbeat tones while casually groping the girls among the high school dancers. Though rock 'n' roll is the language in which the slightly rebellious Burger Shop Boys and Pink Ladies express their hopes and fears, *Grease* presents the music as already crassly commercialized at the time its action takes place.

Entirely absent from *Grease* are many of the more serious concerns that people in the 1970s associated with the Fifties: racial discrimination and the early stirrings of the modern civil rights movement in response to it; Cold War fears, both domestic and international; and what was seen, at least in the Seventies, as the stifling political conservatism of that decade. At first glance, politics seems entirely absent from *Grease*'s script. However, especially as the product of a decade in which "the personal is political" became a feminist rallying cry, *Grease*'s absence of formal politics should not be seen as an avoidance of politics in a broader sense.

General accounts from the early Seventies of the Fifties nostalgia craze treated *Grease* as a lighthearted celebration of the relatively recent past. *LIFE* magazine, in its June 1972 cover story on the Fifties craze, described the musical as an object of "misplaced nostalgia" and suggested that it was partly responsible for the revival of the "Marilyn" and "Greaser" looks.[15] *Newsweek* suggested that *Grease* was a simple effort to recapture the youth culture of the Fifties.[16]

But some of those who reviewed the musical in depth understood that it was more critical of the time it depicted. In a long, admiring article in the *New York Times* about the show on the occasion of its transfer from the Off-Broadway Eden Theater to the Broadway Broadhurst in the late spring of 1972, Harris Green defended the show as having the "old virtues" of classic Broadway theater, despite its use of rock 'n' roll and obscenities, both still controversial among reviewers. Green liked the musical precisely because it was not a simple exercise in nostalgia. According to Green, Jim Jacobs and Warren Casey, the show's creators, "view the period with [a] rare blend of affection and consternation." They are "unsentimental about the brutishness of Elvis and the inanities of Annette." "Nowhere in 'Grease,'" Green wrote, "is there that mad delight in the insipid past that has permitted nostalgia to rage like a plague on Broadway."[17] The *New York Times* head theater critic Clive Barnes had much more mixed feelings about the show, but he, too, did not see it as a mere celebration of the Fifties. According to Barnes, *Grease* was "a parody of one of those old Elvis Presley campus movies." However, Barnes

felt that "the show is a thin joke," in part because of "the nearness to contemporary pop music" of the music that it satirizes.[18]

Introducing the published version of the play, which appeared in 1972,
*Village Voice* theater critic Michael Feingold praised *Grease* for its critical
attitude toward the period that it depicted. "Nostalgia," writes Feingold, "is a pretty unhealthy emotion. In the theater, it evades, more often
than not, the reality of both past and present. . . . *Grease*, however, does
not evade, in that sense it is not a nostalgia show." To Feingold, the Fifties were an era of false calm and stability. Though it seemed as if "nothing happened" during that decade, while America debated Elvis
Presley's appearance on the *Ed Sullivan Show*, "the U.S. successfully pre-
vented free elections . . . in a small Asian country, of which very few
Americans had heard" and "committed itself to the war in Vietnam."
Armed with knowledge of what occurred *after* the Fifties, Feingold suggests, the makers of *Grease* and its audience can see the low-stakes social
conflicts of the show, conflicts that the show itself refuses to take seriously, as silently acknowledging all the forces behind the scenes that
would soon reveal the emptiness of the form of life at the play's heart:

> *Grease* does not discourse about our presence in Saigon. Nor does
> it contain in-depth study of such other 50's developments as the
> growth of mega-corporations and conglomerates, the suburban
> building boom that broke the backs of our cities, the separation of
> labor's political power from the workers by union leaders and
> organization men. Although set in and around an urban high
> school, it does not even discuss one of the decade's dominant news
> stories, the massive expansion of the university system, and the
> directing of a whole generation of war babies toward the pursuit
> of college degrees. *Grease* is an escape, a musical designed to enter-
> tain, not to concern itself with serious political and social matters.
> But because it is truthful, because it spares neither the details nor
> the larger shapes of the narrow experience on which it focuses so
> tightly, *Grease* implies the topics I have raised, and many others.
> So I think it is a work of art, a firm image that projects, by means
> of what it does contain, everything it has chosen to leave out. And
> between the throbs of its ebullience, charm, and comedy, it

conveys a feeling, about where we have been and how we got to where we are, that is quite near despair, if one wants to dwell on it.

In Feingold's view, the apparent escapism of *Grease* is a powerful, implied criticism of the Fifties as presented by the show. It is fascinating that this view of the show as a secretly despairing work of social criticism is what was chosen by the play's authors and publisher to accompany its appearance in print.[19]

The very beginning of *Grease* is the moment when the show most directly addresses the question of nostalgia for the Fifties itself. The show opens with a brief prologue set at a reunion of the Rydell High Class of '59. As the curtain opens, the assembled alums sing the Rydell High alma mater. Those gathered are the successful, well-behaved students, rather than the greasers on whom the rest of the show will focus. They have become boring, middle-class Americans: valedictorian Eugene Florczyk is now vice president for research and marketing of "Straight-Shooters Unlimited." The scene ends with Eugene giving a speech in which he proclaims that "the small portion of the alumni that I notice missing tonight are certainly not missing from our fond memories of them . . . and I'm sure they'd want us to know that they're fully present and accounted for in spirit, just the way we always remember them." At that moment, a school bell rings, rock 'n' roll music is heard, and the play leaps back in time to 1959, as a group of greasers sing a rock 'n' roll parody of the Rydell alma mater, a scene that is immediately followed by "Summer Nights" and the proper beginning of the play's action.

The prologue is so short that it is worth pondering why the show even bothers to begin in the relative present (one imagines that it is probably 1969 when the show opens, though the date at which the opening scene takes place is never specified), especially as *Grease* does not return to the reunion or the present at its conclusion. In addition to providing an excuse to hear the Rydell High alma mater, which we will soon hear parodied, the prologue establishes a number of important things. First, the show's greasers are the rebels of their era. Despite the many ways in which their cultural rebellions seem limited and even commodified within the action of the play, the play's main characters do not treat their school with reverence, will not show up at reunions, and, at least implicitly, will not become vice presidents for research and marketing.

The show also seems to suggest that it is precisely the straightlaced students who do show up at reunions who will treat the Fifties and the greasers as objects of nostalgia. The show introduces its main action as a nostalgic memory of the entirely dull valedictorian Eugene Florczyk, who disappears from the play after the prologue. We never see him in 1959. The prologue of *Grease* does not go so far as to criticize the very idea of finding pleasure in thoughts of the recent, pre-Sixties past. Eugene's nostalgic attachment does not come across as a kind of criticism of the audience's pleasure in what follows. But Eugene's wistful invocation of those absent from the reunion does serve to criticize a certain kind of straightlaced nostalgia for the Fifties, one that attempts to include even that decade's rebels in a comforting image of a safe, stable, and conservative era. That there is something fundamentally false about doing so is suggested by the greasers' absence from their class reunion, despite Eugene's declaration that they are there in spirit. That the greasers first appear making fun of the alma mater that is the very symbol of the kind of school spirit to which the reunion attendees are attached suggests that the memory of the greasers does not properly belong to the Eugene Florczyks of America. *Grease*'s prologue underscores the fact that the show is aware of the pervasiveness of nostalgia for the Fifties and those critics like Harris Green and Michael Feingold were right to see the show as raising questions about simple nostalgia for the period.

## Nostalgia for the Very Recent Past in *American Graffiti*

Given all the media attention to Fifties nostalgia in the opening years of the 1970s, as well as the success of *Grease* on Broadway in 1972, *American Graffiti*'s becoming a cinematic hit in 1973 seems almost unremarkable in retrospect.[20] But its enormous success was a surprise at the time, not least because its director, George Lucas, had not previously been considered a hitmaker. In the years since the release of the first *Star Wars* movie in 1977, Lucas has been so defined by his space-operatic franchise, for which he has been justly praised for world-building and creative marketing, and just as justly criticized for often indifferent writing and terrible directing, that the well-directed, modest, and realistic *American Graffiti* sits oddly in his filmography, especially as it was a follow-up to the director's emotionally cold science fiction debut, *THX 1138*. Lucas was part of a rising generation of young directors, many of whom had studied film at the University of Southern California (USC), as Lucas had, or at the University of California, Los Angeles, as had his friend and early collaborator Francis Ford Coppola. By the late 1960s, Hollywood's old ways of doing business had begun to fail. In the wake of the enormous and surprising success of *Easy Rider*, which had become the top grossing movie of 1969, quirky, small, often even experimental films aimed at young people seemed to be one pathway out of the wilderness for the movie industry.

Coppola, who had already directed a number of feature films but had yet to enjoy much popular success, managed to convince Warner Brothers to lend him money to help start a new independent studio, American Zoetrope, which would produce inexpensive, forward-looking films. American Zoetrope's first production would be *THX 1138*, a feature-film version of George Lucas's dystopian student film from USC. By the end of 1970, relations between Warner Brothers and Coppola had broken down, though Warner Brothers would still distribute Lucas's first film. *THX 1138*, however, proved not to be a particularly audience-friendly movie. Warner Brothers, to Lucas's disgust, cut several minutes from his movie and buried it, giving it a very limited release in March 1971. *THX 1138* received mixed reviews and failed to earn back the studio's investment. But the film gained attention for Lucas as a bright, young representative of the New Hollywood. He was invited to screen *THX 1138* at Cannes. *Newsweek* wrote on article on him that May.[21]

As *THX 1138* was being rolled out, Lucas was already at work on the screenplay for *American Graffiti*, a title that studio executives joked sounded like an Italian film or a movie about feet.[22] The Italian-sounding name was not accidental. Lucas's cinematic inspiration for his second film was Federico Fellini's *I Vitelloni* (1953), which was based on the Italian director's experience growing up in a provincial Italian town.[23] Lucas set out to make a similarly autobiographical movie about growing up in the small town of Modesto, California.

Lucas set his film in Modesto at the end of the summer of 1962, a year that was, for Lucas, of great autobiographical significance. In 1962, he was, like two of the film's principal characters, a high school senior. Like another of the main characters, Lucas was obsessed with racing cars. That June, he had an accident that nearly killed him, which led him to give up cars, go to junior college, and, eventually, pursue filmmaking.

But 1962 also had a broader historical significance that paralleled its autobiographical import. As Lucas told fellow filmmaker Larry Sturhahn in a 1974 interview,

> [*American Graffiti*]'s about a period of transition in history in America where in one year you had a President that a lot of kids admired, were proud of; you had a certain kind of rock 'n' roll music; a certain kind of country where you could believe in things. You were also a teenager, 18 years old, going to school, living at home. You had a certain kind of life. But in the next two years everything changed: no longer were you a teenager, you were an adult going to college or doing whatever you were going to do. The government changed radically, and everybody's attitude toward it changed radically. Drugs came in. Although it had always been there, a war surfaced as an issue. The music changed completely.[24]

One key to *American Graffiti*'s success—and a fact that the film highlighted in its choice of music—was that the world it showed seemed very distant, on the other side of the cultural divide that was the Sixties. Yet the film took place only eleven years before the year in which it was released.

The cultural distance between America in 1973 and the film's version of Modesto in 1962 was even vaster than Lucas suggested to Sturhahn. Racial conflict—and, indeed, racial diversity—is notably absent from the world of *American Graffiti*. Other than a couple of Asian and African American faces briefly glimpsed in a high school sock hop scene and a couple of (probably) Latino members of the Pharaohs gang (neither of whom has many lines), *American Graffiti*'s large ensemble cast is entirely white. The only mention of race in the film comes when one character says that her parents will not let her listen to the ubiquitous, but mysterious, disc jockey Wolfman Jack "because he's a Negro" (in fact, he was not).

The film also took place on the other side of the sexual revolution and of Second Wave feminism. Although *American Graffiti*'s large ensemble class includes a number of women, the film's story is built entirely around its male characters, for whom the female characters essentially serve as ethical tokens of a sort. This probably had less to do with Modesto in 1962 (real or imagined) and more to do with Hollywood (even the New Hollywood) in 1973. As Pauline Kael argued in the *New Yorker* that year,

> Using women (and not only women) as plot functions may be a clue to the shallowness of many movies, even of much better movies—*American Graffiti*, for example. The audience at *American Graffiti* appears to be ecstatically happy condescending toward its own past—how cute we were at seventeen, how funny, how lost—but for women the end of the picture is a cold slap. . . . At the close, it jumps to the present and wraps up the fates of the four principal male characters—as if lives were set ten years after high school!—and it ignores the women characters. This is one of those bizarre omissions that tell you what really goes on in men filmmakers' heads.[25]

That the film was set at the very end of the long Fifties highlighted the more-or-less instant nature of its nostalgia for a past that was so close in time yet so distant culturally from the world of the Seventies. Though *American Graffiti* was a deeply autobiographical project for Lucas, it was sold as much more generalized nostalgia. "Where were you in '62?" read the principal tagline of the film's marketing.

*American Graffiti* focuses on four young men in Modesto at the end of the summer of 1962. Steve Bolander (Ron Howard) and Curt Henderson (Richard Dreyfuss) have just graduated from high school and are enjoying their last night in town before flying off the next morning to go to college somewhere in the East. As the film begins, Curt is getting cold feet. Terry "Toad" Fields (Charles Martin Smith) is staying in town, but is delighted to be given Steve's beautiful car to look after in the latter's absence. Finally, twenty-two-year-old John Milner (Paul Le Mat) is living a kind of extended teenage life as the town's most famous hot-rod racer.

The film follows the characters over the course of a single night, which they largely spend cruising around the town in cars. Though Steve begins the night telling his girlfriend (and Curt's sister) Laurie (Cindy Williams) that they should see other people in his absence, by the end of the film, he has decided to stay in town and cultivate this relationship. He can go to college in a year, he says. After a series of adventures that include trying to locate a mysterious blonde (Suzanne Somers) in a

Fig. 1.2. Asking "Where Were You in '62?," the 1973 poster for *American Graffiti* sold nostalgia for the very recent past. (Credit: SilverScreen / Alamy Stock Photo.)

white T-Bird (who might have said "I love you" to Curt through its closed window) and proving his manhood with the local Pharaohs gang, Curt eventually finds the inner strength to leave town and attend the unnamed college in the East. Blessed with Steve's Chevy Impala, Toad picks up Debbie Dunham (Candy Clark), whom he more or less successfully woos, despite lying to her, losing the car, getting sick on whiskey, and having his lies exposed. And following an evening driving around and essentially playing older brother to the much younger Carol Morrison (Mackenzie Phillips), John races Bob Falfa (Harrison Ford), who has spent most of the evening looking for John in order to beat him at his game. Eventually Bob crashes his car, allowing John to win a race that he would otherwise have lost. Though Bob and Laurie (who was riding with him) escape apparently unharmed, Bob's car goes up in flames as dawn breaks. The film ends with Steve, Curt, Laurie, and the latter two's parents bidding Curt farewell as he flies off in a Magic Carpet Airlines plane to somewhere in the East. Curt looks out the window of the plane and, on the highway below, a white T-Bird seems to be driving in the same direction as the plane. The film ends with titles informing the audience what would later happen to its four male main characters.

The entire film is scored to rock 'n' roll, nearly all of which appears diegetically, both at the high school dance that Steve, Curt, and Laurie attend toward the film's beginning, and booming from the various car radios throughout the rest of the movie, which all seem to be tuned to Wolfman Jack's overnight show. Interestingly, the music is not particularly focused on 1962 or even the early 1960s. Instead it includes songs from the entire early rock 'n' roll era. "The film," Lucas noted, "is about the end of an era, not the end of one particular year."[26]

The film opens with Bill Haley & His Comets' iconic "Rock around the Clock," a 1954 hit (which would later come to serve as the theme song for the early seasons of *Happy Days*). The music thus evokes not a year, but an era, and one about to come to an end. Lucas listened to rock 'n' roll while writing the film and thought of each scene as being set to a rock 'n' roll song. *American Graffiti*'s soundscape was largely created by the brilliant sound designer Walter Murch, whom Lucas had met when they were both students at USC.[27] Throughout the film, the music is not only formally diegetic, it also sounds as if it is inhabiting the same space

WHERE WERE YOU IN '62?"

as the characters. Even before we hear "Rock around the Clock," *American Graffiti* opens with the sound of a car radio being tuned. The music defines the world of the characters in the film, but it is a world that is disappearing. One of the few conversations about music takes place between John and Carol, who represent the closest thing to an on-screen generation gap. Carol, who's wearing a surfing-related shirt, praises the Beach Boys, for whom Wolfman Jack predicts great things before playing their 1962 hit "Surfin' Safari." "I don't like that surfing shit," says John. Echoing a sentiment most famously expressed in Don McLean's hit song "American Pie" (1971), John declares that "rock 'n' roll's been going down-hill ever since Buddy Holly died."

The lack of conflict around the youth culture on display in *American Graffiti* is one of the most notable things about the film. Parents are almost entirely absent (only Laurie and Curt's parents appear, and then only at the very end of the movie to see their son off at the airport). Other authority figures from the characters' parents' generation are few and far between. And when they appear on screen, they seem hypocritical or weak, like the teachers chaperoning the sock hop and the Moose Lodge members whom Curt encounters at a mini-golf establishment while the Pharaohs gang members, with whom he's riding, steal money from pinball machines. Cops are more serious authority figures, but they are relatively young and easily foiled. That the main generation gap on-screen is between the twenty-two-year-old John and the sixteen-year-old Carol (and that it involves the Beach Boys) suggests how established and stable is the movie's version of Modesto youth culture in 1962. Carol's parents think she ought to avoid listening to Wolfman Jack, but they obviously represent no real bar to her doing so.

For a movie about rock 'n' roll and youth culture, *American Graffiti* features remarkably little rebellion or anti-establishment sentiment. Even the film's most apparently anti-establishment acts, which are initiated by the Pharaohs and culminate with Curt helping to rip the rear axle off a cop car, are played to emphasize Curt's dealing with his coming of age rather than as serious challenges to authority. Playing pranks on law enforcement is just what kids in Modesto in 1962 do.

Framing the innocence of Modesto youth culture are all the unstated changes that are to come. And part of the effectiveness of *American Graffiti* involves Lucas's decision not to foreshadow those changes until its final title cards. Lucas understood that his audience all knew what changes were coming. That Modesto in 1962 is almost entirely unmarked by what we think of—and American audiences in the 1970s would have thought of—as the Sixties makes its so-near-and-yet-so-distant world all the more poignant.

In case film's viewers had somehow missed seeing the temporal divide that is, in a sense, the real subject of the film, Lucas provided that final set of title cards. Alongside pictures of the characters as they were in 1962 (though now dressed in jackets and ties), we are told that

> John Milner was killed by a drunk driver in December 1964.
> Terry Fields was reported missing in action near An Loc in December 1965.
> Steve Bolander is an insurance agent in Modesto, California.
> Curt Henderson is a writer living in Canada.

Though all four appear to triumph over the personal challenges they face within the plot of *American Graffiti*, their fates prove to be tragic or ambivalent. John, apparently through no fault of his own, ends up killed by an automobile, the fate he vaguely feared in the movie (and the fear of which led George Lucas himself away from hot rods and toward movies). Toad is killed in Vietnam. Steve never escapes the world of Modesto, which seems much less exciting from the point of view of an adult (what could be more dull than being an insurance agent?). And while Curt is a writer, his "living in Canada" would suggest, to audiences in 1973, that he was a draft dodger, whose life would have been fundamentally altered by the Vietnam War, if in a less tragic way than Toad's.

Not surprisingly, given the great cultural conversation about nostalgia in the Seventies that had already taken place by 1973, critics linked *American Graffiti*'s nostalgia to larger trends in American culture and filmmaking. Despite its marketing as such, Lucas was ambivalent about his film's status as a work of nostalgia. When asked in, a 1974 interview, if *American Graffiti* was a "nostalgia genre" film, Lucas was quick to point out that there was nothing new about nostalgia in American cinema; it simply had not been identified as a genre in the past. When John Ford did nostalgia, Lucas argued, they called it a Western. *Citizen Kane*, he suggested, was also deeply nostalgic. "It's just that now they've made it a classification, so any time you do a film that's set five years in the past, it's a nostalgia film."[28]

But having said that, Lucas admitted that *American Graffiti* was about nostalgia, and defended it as such:

> Originally I didn't think about it as nostalgia, even though it took place in 1962. The film is about teenagers; about teenagers moving forward and making decisions about what they want to do in life. But it's also about the fact that you can't live in the past, which is part of that same idea. You have to move forward, things can't stay the same; essentially that's the point of the film. No matter how much you want things to be the same, they won't and can't; everything is always changing, and you have to accept change. So a movie about accepting change is called a nostalgia film, even though you're dealing with change and the past, present, and future. *Graffiti* is partially a nostalgia film, partly a film about teenagers, and partly a film about the future.[29]

Lucas went out of his way, however, to distinguish *American Graffiti* from *Grease*. Unlike the hit Broadway musical, he insisted, his film took its characters and their culture seriously: "My high school years had a big impact on my life. When I made the film I knew I wasn't going to make fun of it. Like the music—I liked and still like that kind of rock 'n' roll. As a result I didn't treat it like they do in *Grease*. They make fun of it! Well, it was kind of crazy, but it had charm; something about it was really quite nice. And there was respect for it, which I still have. Just like I still have respect for cruising, for being a teenager."[30] While the film was about a period of American history that, whatever its attractions, Lucas believed had passed and to which Americans could not return, *American Graffiti* was also about a stage of life that everyone still had to go through and that Lucas felt his generation had experienced in a more satisfying way than teenagers in the Seventies did:

> Part of that stuff about innocence and a different time has to do with being a teenager; things are much more innocent. Even

now—today [in 1974]—we are more aware of the pressures than a teenager is. I talked to a lot of them in the process of doing *Graffiti*—in the interviews, in the making, in the screening of the finished film. A lot of teenagers today are just like we were when we were teenagers, but when you grow up you forget. You become aware of the world around you. You realize all these things about life. You forget when you were a teenager how you sort of knew about it but you didn't really care as much. What you cared about were a lot of things that you would now call petty—like kissing a girl and all the other stuff in the movie. But that's the time when those things should be important and you shouldn't have to be burdened with all the problems of the world; when you should worry just about girls, and cars, and homework—all that kind of stuff. When you hit college is time enough to confront the other aspects of life.[31]

In *American Graffiti*, Modesto in 1962 is presented as a place and time in which conflicts were local and manageable and challenges could be met and conquered. What was to come, the film reminds its audience, would not be so simple. To the extent that this was a story about permanent changes in American life, the film could not be a call to return to that world. Taken in this way, the film presents a world that evoked for its audience not "so much nostalgia, as culture shock," as Roger Ebert had put it in his admiring review of *American Graffiti*:

When I went to see George Lucas's "American Graffiti" that whole world—a world that now seems incomparably distant and innocent—was brought back with a rush of feeling that wasn't so much nostalgia as culture shock. Remembering my high school generation, I can only wonder at how unprepared we were for the loss of innocence that took place in America with the series of hammer blows beginning with the assassination of President Kennedy.

The great divide was November 22, 1963, and nothing was ever the same again. The teenagers in "American Graffiti" are, in a sense, like that cartoon character in the magazine ads: the one who gives the name of his insurance company, unaware that an avalanche is about to land on him. The options seemed so simple then: to go to college, or to stay home and look for a job and cruise Main Street and make the scene.[32]

But to the extent that *American Graffiti* was a film about teenage life, it might alternately suggest—and its director thought that it did suggest—that Modesto in 1962 had simply been a better world for teenagers than America in the Seventies was. And to the extent that the innocence of that world was the innocence of youth, it might be recaptured.

Though *American Graffiti* took the youth culture of the long Fifties more seriously than had *Grease*, it shared an important quality of that earlier musical: Fifties-style youth rebellion is presented as entirely unthreatening. Though the film depicts numerous things that, at the time, were serious acts of rebellion—most obviously drag racing and vandalizing a police car, but also purchasing liquor underage, cruising, and even listening to rock 'n' roll—none of these acts is remotely threatening to the established order in the film. While *Grease* suggests that youth culture is always already co-opted by the culture industry, *American Graffiti* largely keeps off-screen the adult characters who might feel threatened by its protagonists' actions. Of course, some of these very actions—listening to particular kinds of music, consuming certain illegal substances, challenging the authority of the police—would all recur in more obviously threatening forms in the Sixties and the Seventies. However, shorn of any revolutionary intent and performed by middle-class white kids in a mythicized pre-Sixties world, they seemed charming and safe. But neither *Grease* nor *American Graffiti* had domesticated Fifties rebellion as much as *Happy Days* would.

## *Happy Days*, the Fonz, and the "Domesticated Greaser"

*Happy Days* premiered in early 1974 but took a few seasons to establish itself as one of the nation's most popular television shows. A number of things changed *Happy Days* from an unpopular show during its first two seasons (1974–1975) to one of the most popular shows in the United States during and after its third season (1975–1976). In the first two seasons, the show was shot with a single-camera setup, the movie-like style that had become dominant during the 1960s. At the start of its third season, the show permanently switched to a multicamera setup and began being filmed before a live audience. Though in certain ways more old-fashioned—most situation comedies in the Fifties had been produced with multiple cameras—multicamera setups were repopularized in the Seventies by shows such as *All in the Family* (1971–1979), which was the top-rated television series in America from the 1971–1972 television season through 1975–1976, until *Happy Days* grabbed the top position. The arrival of its spin-off show, *Laverne & Shirley*, also boosted *Happy Days'* fortunes. *Laverne & Shirley* began in early 1976, running immediately after *Happy Days*. The spin-off was an immediate success. It quickly boosted the ratings of *Happy Days* and by its third season had surpassed *Happy Days* in popularity.

But the other crucial factor in *Happy Days'* growing success was the ever-increasing importance of the character of Arthur "Fonzie" Fonzarelli (Henry Winkler). Fonzie began the series as a fairly minor character, the show's one embodiment of the greaser stereotype that was so important in the larger wave of Fifties nostalgia. By the second season, he had become one of the show's major characters. At the start of the third season, he became a tenant of the Cunningham family, on whom the show centered.

Fonzie not only emerged as the central figure in the cast of *Happy Days* as that show reached the height of its popularity, but he also became a cultural icon, perhaps the single most beloved and influential character from any of the Seventies' works that took place in the Fifties. Fonzie was, in a sense, both an imagined Fifties figure and an actual Seventies one. Coming to a greater understanding of his appeal can help clarify some of the positive things that Seventies audiences and cultural producers associated with the Fifties. But Fonzie was not only a version of a Fifties type, but also a model of Seventies masculinity. And it is as a kind of post-Sixties cultural synthesis that Arthur Fonzarelli can best be understood. To explore that synthesis, we should take a closer look at the image of the Fifties greaser in Seventies culture.

Greasers, young men who wore ducktail haircuts, leather jackets, and blue jeans, were central figures in Seventies representations of the Fifties. The Fifties revival band Sha Na Na dressed like greasers. The musical *Grease* concerned greasers. The soft drink 7 Up featured a greaser in one of its most famous ad campaigns of the early Seventies: the "Teen Angel," a greaser ghost complete with leather jacket and ducktail, re-

Fig. 1.3. Though initially a side character, The Fonz (Henry Winkler) emerged as the breakout star of ABC's hit sitcom *Happy Days*, creating an image of Seventies cool in the form of a reimagined Fifties greaser. (Credit: ABC / Photofest.)

counts how kids in his day all drank cola, but—observing a hippie chick in a contemporary diner—kids these days are drinking the "Uncola." Sounding suddenly more like a beatnik than a greaser, the Teen Angel concludes that 7 Up is "Nowsville, man!" A young Mandy Patinkin, who played the Teen Angel, told *Newsweek* that when he got the role he knew little about the Fifties. "As soon as I put on the black leather jacket, the jeans and boots, and combed my hair into a greasy ducktail," Patinkin told the magazine, "something happened to me. My shoulders dropped, my head cocked at an angle and I felt tough and sexy. I felt on top of the world. And then I knew what the '50s were about."[33] For many Seventies Americans, greasers were figures of youthful rebellion and cool. "Those greasers were the first freaks," a fifteen-year-old girl enthusiastically told *LIFE* magazine in 1972.[34]

The first Seventies film focused on greasers was *The Lords of Flatbush* (1974), a low-budget independent movie from first-time writers and directors Stephen F. Verona and Martin Davidson. Filmed in 1972, as the American news media was beginning to comment on a growing interest in the Fifties, it was not released until two years later. The film concerns four leather-clad, ducktail-wearing, gum-chewing, and cigarette-smoking high school boys in Brooklyn in 1958: Chico Tyrell (Perry King), Stanley Rosiello (Sylvester Stallone), Butchey Weinstein (Henry Winkler), and Wimpy Murgalo (Paul Mace), who together form a gang (they call it a "social and athletic club") called the Lords. *The Lords of Flatbush* is now most interesting as an artifact of the Seventies. Its loose episodic structure and occasional cinema verité techniques mark it as the product of a moment when such once avant-garde approaches were entering the Hollywood mainstream. The film drew lukewarm reviews and little audience interest at the time of its release, but it enjoyed a more successful afterlife later in the decade as both Stallone and Winkler became major stars, the former as the writer and star of *Rocky* (1976), the latter for his role in *Happy Days*.

However, precisely because reviewers saw the film as so run-of-the-mill, *The Lords of Flatbush* might be seen as a representative portrait of the greaser stereotype in the Seventies. Throughout the film, at least until its concluding sequence, the Lords are humorously contemptuous of the largely weak and sometimes oblivious authority figures with whom they interact. Early in the film, in the one sequence that takes place at school, they lead a classroom effort to play a series of practical jokes on their flustered homeroom teacher. Chico successfully sweet-talks his mother out of ten dollars and convinces the army officer father of a girl in his school to let him and the girl babysit her younger sister. Later, Stan threatens a jewelry store owner whom he believes has convinced his fiancée to demand an expensive engagement ring. The Lords frequently harass passing high school girls; indeed, the film opens with them doing this outside school as students are arriving in the morning. They threaten and attempt to beat up rival boys. They steal a car. Though the film treats none of these activities as very significant or even blameworthy, they establish the Lords as teenage delinquents.

Like the Burger Palace Boys and the Pink Ladies in *Grease*, boys and girls in *The Lords of Flatbush* exist in separate, parallel worlds. As in *Grease*, as well, much of the action of the film revolves around the mutual, but somewhat misaligned, desires of the boys and girls for each other. The Lords are principally interested in sex without consequences; the girls in the film, on whom the film spends less time, want to land husbands and are much more ambivalent about sex. Like the Burger Palace Boys, the Lords are a gang, though also a relatively harmless one. Indeed, gangs form much of the distinctive culture of stereotypical Seventies representations of greasers. The Lords even sing a doo-wop number in one scene.

Most of all, the Lords are boys in the midst of the transition to manhood. While they drive and have sex, they still grudgingly attend school, live at home, and seem to have little sense of what they want to do with their lives. The fact that the four actors who played the Lords were all in their twenties and look much older than high school age underscores the sense that these are men though they are still largely living as boys. Indeed, the transition to adulthood is the main theme of the film. The two clearest plot strands in this very episodic movie involve Chico's attempts to woo Jane Bradshaw (Susan Blakely), the WASPy, straight-laced new girl in school whose father is an army officer, and Stanley's response to the news that his girlfriend Frannie Malincanico (Maria Smith) is pregnant. Chico seems largely interested in sex, so Jane, who is looking for a steadier and more serious relationship, dumps him. After some resistance, Stanley agrees to marry Frannie and follows through on the promise even when he discovers that she is not actually pregnant.

The film concludes with Stanley and Frannie's wedding, which is in many ways the Lords' symbolic admission to adulthood. For the only time in the film, the Lords share an experience with the older generation. And the film ends with a montage of stills from the earlier action in the movie. Like a wedding-party slideshow, these memories, many of which happened only weeks before, now belong to another phase of their lives.

Though *The Lords of Flatbush* ends in a way that emphasizes that its four main characters are on the verge of entering adulthood, the film does not draw its audience's attention to the larger social changes that are about to take place as much as does *American Graffiti*, with its portentous closing credits, or even the theatrical version of *Grease*, whose opening reunion scene underscores how near in time, yet culturally distant, its main action is from the 1970s present. This absence of intimations of the changes that the next decade would bring in certain ways blunts *The Lords of Flatbush*'s nostalgia. In this sense, the movie feels more like a period drama and less an ode to a recently vanished world.

Although two years passed between the filming of *The Lords of Flatbush* in 1972 and *Happy Days*' first season in 1974, the movie was released only a few months before *Happy Days* began production. Henry Winkler was essentially an unknown actor when he was cast as Fonzie, though he was playing a role that bore at least a superficial resemblance to Butchey Weinstein, whom he had played in *The Lords of Flatbush*. Winkler himself would later claim that when *Happy Days* began, he tried to model his performance after Sylvester Stallone's *Lords of Flatbush* character, Stanley Rosiello, a much larger role in that film than Winkler's own.[35] Like Fonzie, but unlike Butchey or Winkler himself, Stanley was an Italian American.

Marked as a greaser by his ducktail haircut and motorcycle, Fonzie differed from the stereotype in important ways, many of which seemed driven by the network's desire to tone down the standard greaser stereotype for television audiences. In the first episodes, Fonzie wore a windbreaker, only switching to his soon-to-be iconic leather jacket later in the first season. In episode six of season one, "The Deadly Dares," which initially aired on February 19, 1974, we learn that Fonzie had been in the Demons, a gang that Richie and Potsie hope to join. But Fonzie is extremely dismissive of the group ("They're a bunch of bananas") and is never actually shown as part of a gang. Indeed, Fonzie is a bit of a loner.

While the greasers of *Grease* and *The Lords of Flatbush* spend much of their time chasing after girls, they remain oddly apart from them. The greasers' world is a largely homosocial one. And boys and girls in *Grease* and *The Lords of Flatbush* seem to constantly talk past each other. Fonzie, on the other hand, has no need to chase after women, as they are always at his beck and call. By the end of the first season, the show had established what was essentially a running joke: the Fonz would always have a girl by his side. She would be silent and attentive. Though Fonzie would occasionally tell other male characters that he was doing something for the sake of his date, the date herself never speaks a word and follows Fonzie's often silent commands. The high school girls in *Happy Days* are often underwritten, and this is especially true of Fonzie's many girlfriends, who seem to be essentially without minds of their own when in his presence. While other greasers in Seventies fictional narratives constantly misunderstand girls, Fonzie is represented as understanding girls perfectly.

Fonzie is unquestionably the rebel among the core cast of *Happy Days*. But his rebellion is even less pronounced than that of the greasers in other works from the Seventies. His chief act of rebellion seems to be his having dropped out of high school. Fonzie's status as a high school dropout leads Richie Cunningham's parents, Howard and Marion, early in the series, to express concern about Richie's hanging out with him (e.g., in episode four of season two, "You Go to My Head"). But *Happy Days* presents Fonzie's status as a dropout as being largely about self-expression. In the show's first episode focused on him (episode seven of season one, "Fonzie Drops In"), Fonzie explains that he dropped out of high school because there were "too many rules." But he is not a ne'er-do-well. He has a steady job as an auto mechanic, at which he is something of a genius; indeed, another running joke about Fonzie is that he can fix any machine, often simply by hitting it. In "Fonzie Drops In," he attempts to return to high school. After trying unsuccessfully to cheat on a test, Fonzie eventually manages to pass it honestly. But at the episode's end, he has decided to drop out again. He simply prefers his life as an auto mechanic. Nevertheless, after pretending not to care much about his successful test, he holds on to it with pride.

While Fonzie dislikes rules, he seems not to harbor hostility to authority as such. His brief return to high school is motivated in part by a dream of becoming a cop. And while he is perfectly willing to defy authority in small ways, such as hitting a soda machine to get a couple bottles of soda for free, he is also willing to work with authority on occasion. In the episode "Richie's Car," which originally aired early in the second season of the show on September 17, 1974, Fonzie sells Richie a car that he won in a drag race from "some nerd." As Fonzie is completing the sale, having repainted the car to look less like a hot rod, a cop comes around his auto shop looking for a stolen car that matches the description of the original paint job. When it turns out the license plates match as well, Richie spends the rest of the episode trying to hide the car and avoid telling his father the truth about it. Eventually Richie confesses to a police officer and everyone ends up at the station, where Fonzie calmly explains what happened. Producing Rocky Baruffi, the kid from whom he won the car, Fonzie explains that Baruffi bought the car from someone else who then reported it stolen. But the report was entirely false. Everyone seems pleased by this explanation, all charges are dropped, and Richie and the Cunninghams get the car. Fonzie exclaims that he had to keep his reputation spotless. Fonzie's parents are entirely absent, which both makes him even more of a free agent and eliminates another potential set of authorities with which he might have clashed.

Indeed, Fonzie's lack of a family allowed the show to build some pathos into his character. Despite Fonzie's tough exterior and preternatural sense of coolness, in the middle of the second season the show began to give his character depth by suggesting that he was hiding significant personal pain. In "A Star Is Bored" (episode ten of season two, which originally aired on December 3, 1974), Fonzie is talked into playing Hamlet in a church theatrical production because Richie thinks his popularity will help sell tickets. Fonzie has no idea who Hamlet is and refuses to wear his costume. But on the night of the performance, Richie explains that the "To Be or Not to Be" soliloquy concerns Hamlet's contemplation of suicide. In his first really serious dramatic moment in the show, Fonzie tells Richie how his dad left him when he was a kid (at least Hamlet's dad shows up, he says). And Fonzie admits that he had contemplated whether to be or not to be in the past. Eventually Fonzie's performance of the soliloquy turns into a teaching moment, as Fonzie breaks character and explains to the audience what is really going on. The following week, that season's Christmas episode

("Guess Who's Coming to Christmas") built on this newly serious portrait of Fonzie. The Cunninghams discover that Fonzie, who is full of holiday spirit, has nowhere to go for the holidays and invite him into their home. These two episodes are carried by Henry Winkler's unusually nuanced performances, which transform potentially maudlin material into effective television.

Fonzie's sensitive side makes him resemble in some ways a different Fifties rebel icon: Jim Stark, the character played by James Dean in *Rebel without a Cause* (1955). Indeed, in at least one *Happy Days* episode ("You Go to My Head," which aired on October 1, 1974), Fonzie praises and imitates Dean. Richie is scared to ask out Carol Lipton, a girl whose intelligence intimidates him. Fonzie suggests that Richie try acting "nutsy" like Dean and proceeds to demonstrate by picking up a girl in Arnold's with this technique. Fonzie's performance as Dean highlights one of the major differences between their personae: Dean's vulnerability (as Jim Stark) was much more on the surface than Fonzie's. In his seduction lesson for Richie, Fonzie-as-Dean tells a girl in a high-pitched voice to forget about him because he's "bad news." This very Dean-like maneuver would otherwise be very out of character for Fonzie.

Jim Stark in *Rebel without a Cause* is different from Fonzie in a number of other substantial ways. First, the single most important psychological dynamic in Jim Stark's life involves conflict with his parents and especially his father Frank Stark (Jim Backus). This kind of conflict is absent from the life of the parentless Fonzie and from the larger world of *Happy Days*. Secondly, Jim is a much more socially marginal figure than Fonzie. A new kid in his school at the start of *Rebel*, Jim has trouble fitting in. He quickly becomes a target for bullies in the school. Fonzie, on the other hand, is the center of the social universe of *Happy Days*. All of his peers, male and female, seem to idolize him. The waitresses at Arnold's, who clash with other youthful characters, get along with him. While the older generation tends to initially be skeptical of him, seeing him as a dropout and even a "hood," Fonzie always manages to win them over relatively effortlessly. Finally, Jim Stark responds to the inadequacies of his actual family by attempting to create a substitute family among his peers, with himself in the paternal role, Judy (Natalie Wood) playing the wife and mother, and Plato (Sal Mineo) as a kind of child. Though this attempt ends tragically with Plato's death, it underscores Jim's felt need for a stable, nuclear family. Though Fonzie occasionally craves family, as in the "Guess Who's Coming to Christmas" episode, he is much more committed than Jim to being a loner, unencumbered by long-term commitments to people.

What all these differences between Fonzie and rebel characters in Fifties popular culture highlight is Fonzie's apparent lack of alienation. Teenage rebel characters in 1950s popular culture, like Jim Stark in *Rebel without a Cause* and Johnny Strabler (Marlon Brando) in *The Wild One* (1953), were represented as deeply alienated and, thus, as serious potential sources of social instability. Their Seventies echoes, even when also presented as alienated, were rarely so threatening. The rebellion of the characters in the musical *Grease* and films like *American Graffiti* and *The Lords of Flatbush* still proceeded from a sense of alienation from the world in which they found themselves. But these Seventies texts made both their alienation and rebellion seem quaint. The alienation of the characters in both *Grease* and *American Graffiti* was transformed by indications of the impending upheavals of the Sixties, the audience's knowledge of which make the characters' alienation and rebellion seem trivial. In *The Lords of Flatbush*, adulthood arrives before the Sixties do, thus apparently ending the rebellion and alienation of its characters. *Happy Days* goes a step farther than these other Seventies texts, which tend to retrospectively trivialize teenage alienation in the 1950s, by imagining Fonzie as utterly unalienated.

Although Fonzie can be aloof, he seems more at home in his world than any other character, young or old, in *Happy Days*. He is the center of social attention. He is a master of both human relationships and mechanical objects. Richie, Potsie, and Ralph constantly turn to Fonzie for relationship advice. Howard Cunningham and many more minor adult characters rely on Fonzie to fix their cars. The show occasionally humorously hints that Fonzie's persona will one day be out of date. "I figure that hot rods and draggin' are gonna be around a long time, like the ducktail and Buddy Holly," Fonzie muses as he decides to drop out of school again in "Fonzie Drops In." But in fact, even in the world of *Happy Days*, Fonzie outlasted both the ducktail and Buddy Holly. His character survived largely unchanged through the show's run, which by its end in 1984 had brought the characters into the mid-Sixties.

That Fonzie was a fantasy rather than an attempt to portray the lived reality of the Fifties was of course perfectly clear to critics and audiences in the Seventies. "The Fonz," wrote David Kehr in an essay on Seventies star personae in *Film Comment*, "is less a greaser, circa 1955, than the *idea* of a greaser circa 1955. He exists almost entirely on the level of his iconography.... But the T-shirt is a little too clean, the hair a little too heat-styled, to allow the iconography the full force of its traditional threat. The Fonz, significantly unlike any other movie hoodlum in history, doesn't smoke: he's a domesticated greaser, which is to say, no greaser at all."[36] Kehr goes on to argue that Fonzie is essentially a comic-book superhero with one important difference. Fonzie enters "an area that the comic books have long shied way from: he's a sexual superhero, too." But, argues Kehr, Fonzie's exaggerated sexual prowess serves only to defuse and distance the "disruptive specter of sex" in *Happy Days*. "By validating the triteness of the drama," Fonzie makes the Cunningham family, which the show's creators self-consciously modeled on television families *from* the Fifties, into an "acceptable fantasy" for the Seventies.

Kehr is right that Fonzie represents all that traditional middle-class families repress: "sex, violence, and freedom from an oppressive family structure." But, in fact, the Cunningham family is incredibly accepting of Richie's admittedly moderate involvement with these things. *Happy Days*, especially in its early seasons, largely concerns Richie and his friends' never entirely successful attempts to woo girls (whether the ultimate goal is to sleep with them is never made entirely explicit). Although these adventures involve a lot of sneaking around behind their parents' backs, the Cunninghams, at least, are remarkably accepting of Richie's antics. Fonzie does represent sexual territory beyond that approved by the elder Cunninghams. But, in part due to the moderate nature of Richie's apparent desires, remarkably little intergenerational repression takes place in *Happy Days*. Indeed, the ability of youth culture to exist more or less comfortably alongside middle-aged and middle-class people who are not themselves involved in it is one of the hallmarks of the world of *Happy Days* and one of the things that distinguishes the show not simply from the American present—shaped by the ongoing generational divisions that became clear in Sixties, as represented in other television shows like *All in the Family*—but also from such representations of the

Fifties as *Grease* and *American Graffiti*, in both of which parents seem benevolently absent from the lives of the teenage protagonists.

The popular representations of the Fifties that I've focused on so far in this chapter did not present the Fifties as a decade of simple conformity and consensus. Each features central figures who, in one way or another, see themselves as rebelling against the constraints of their society. But *Grease, American Graffiti, The Lords of Flatbush*, and, above all, *Happy Days* present these characters' rebellion as deeply unthreatening, not only to their Seventies audiences, but even in many cases to the story worlds in which they find themselves. Especially in the cases of *Grease* and *American Graffiti*, the looming upheavals of the Sixties underscore the retrospective quaintness of Fifties rebellion. But Fifties rebels were not always treated as such unthreatening characters in the Seventies.

## Countercultural Greasers in the 1970s Leather and Punk Scenes

While Fonzie in *Happy Days* represented an updated version of a greaser, shorn of any real sense of alienation or cultural rebellion, certain American subcultures in the 1970s continued to see in the greaser, and related images of young, Fifties masculine rebellion, more oppositional figures. One of the more surprising hit albums of the early 1970s was Lou Reed's second solo effort, *Transformer*. Reed was famous among musicians for his work with the Velvet Underground in the Sixties, but that group had never achieved popular success. After the critical and commercial failure of Reed's eponymous first solo album, David Bowie approached him and offered to produce his next record. Like many of his fellow musicians in the then-rising glam rock scene, Bowie was an enormous fan of the Velvets. And unlike Reed, he had already achieved some commercial success both in his native England and in the United States. Working in London with Bowie and co-producer Mick Ronson, who would later become the guitarist for Bowie's backing band the Spiders from Mars, Reed recorded an album that was largely a memory of the sexually transformative scene around Andy Warhol's Factory in which the Velvet Underground had worked. To nearly everyone's surprise, *Transformer* made Lou Reed a rock star when it was released in November 1972. The album cracked the top twenty. And Reed scored an even more surprising hit single with "Walk on the Wild Side," which, in sometimes sexually explicit terms, told the stories of a number of transgender members of Warhol's circle.

The back cover of the album featured Reed's friend Ernie Thormahlen dressed in clothes that superficially resemble the Fifties revival outfits that *LIFE* and *Newsweek* had written about earlier that year: tight white T-shirt with cigarette pack rolled into its sleeve, blue jeans cuffed at their bottoms, black leather boots, black leather motorcycle hat. Although the black leather jacket is missing, Thormahlen is dressed like a stereotypical greaser. Except to read Thormahlen's outfit this way would have been to seriously misunderstand the image. Thormahlen's outfit, like those of the greasers of the Seventies, was descended from Fifties motorcycle wear. But he is dressed as an archetype of the downtown New York gay scene about which Reed sings on *Transformer*. The famous picture of Ernie Thormahlen stands as an important reminder that the dominant 1970s image of Fifties masculinity—the young white man wearing jeans, a white T-shirt, and leather—was far from exclusively a culturally conservative image in that later decade. Thormahlen's clothing is a variation of the outfit worn by gay men in the leather scene, which would, over the course of the Seventies, become, in the words of the anthropologist Gayle Rubin, "a kind of uniform for urban gay men—most of whom would never experience the business end of a whip."[37] The modern leather subculture was itself largely a product of the 1950s, a fact reflected in the clothing worn by men in the leather scene, as well as the growing ranks of leather "clones" (gay men not part of the scene who adopted its iconic clothing) in the Seventies.[38]

Just over three years after *Transformer* arrived in record stores, a cartoon of Lou Reed's glowering face would be featured on the cover of the first issue of *Punk* magazine. *Punk*'s Lou Reed cover story was the product of two of the magazine's founders—nineteen-year-old Legs McNeil and his twenty-one-year-old cartoonist friend John Holmstrom. Along with the aspiring writer Mary Harron, McNeil and Holmstrom had attended a 1975 Ramones show at the East Village club CBGB. Not only did the trio get to speak to the Ramones, who at that point were emerging as the leading figures in what would soon be known as punk rock—"I really thought I was at the Cavern Club in 1963 and we had just met the

Beatles," McNeil would later say—but McNeil had also noticed Lou Reed sitting in the audience. McNeil, Holmstrom, and Harron wheedled their way into an instant interview with Reed who, under the best of circumstances, treated the press with hostility. Though things with Reed went predictably badly, the evening produced both the cover story on Reed and a second story on the Ramones.[39]

Published in New York City by three young friends—the publisher Ged Dunn was its third founder—*Punk* helped name a musical genre and achieved almost instant fame and significance before almost as quickly fading away.[40] Only fifteen issues were published before *Punk* essentially went out of existence in 1979, though a final special issue appeared two years later. Nevertheless, the journalist Glenn O'Brien is said to have called it the most important magazine in the world for a year.[41] The music that came to be known as punk had been percolating for a while. Hilly Kristal had opened CBGB, which would become the center of the early New York punk scene, in 1973. By 1974, bands like the Ramones had started playing there. *Punk* arrived at a nearly perfect moment to chronicle—and help shape—punk rock and the culture around it.

As the scholar Nicholas Rombes has noted, punk in the Seventies "took its initial codes and signals from the fifties."[42] Indeed, the very first item in that first issue of *Punk* was an article by Joe Koch entitled "Marlon Brando—the Original Punk." Though Koch begins by evoking Brando's role in Bernardo Bertolucci's *Last Tango in Paris* (1972), his focus is on Brando's roles from the Fifties. *Last Tango* was, according to Koch, "Bertolucci's funeral oration for Marlon Brando, the punk." That Marlon Brando was the figure from such films as *A Streetcar Named Desire* (1951), *On the Waterfront* (1954), and, above all, *The Wild One* (1953), the film in which Brando plays a rebellious, leather-clad biker. Koch continues:

> The audience [in the 1950s] had found a better fantasy: Brando was cool without oppressing the audience with too much sharpness. He was powerful without having to be invulnerable. A whole generation feeling that perhaps it was riding the train without a ticket saw Brando's "Wild One" being told (by the sheriff's daughter, no less) that he was a fake: yet still, she stands up for him in the end. He

provided new, vicarious life for a public starting to feel intimidated by the always-competent film heroes of the thirties and forties. Vulnerability in a leather jacket. Brando prowled, not as a predator, but as a formidable victim.

This character was clearly a rebel in the Fifties. And though any number of less rebellious variations of the leather-clad greaser had entered American culture since the Fifties—from comeback Elvis to the characters of *Grease* to Fonzie—*Punk's* featuring the rebellious Brando of the Fifties as the subject of its very first article suggests that, even in the middle of the Seventies, this image retained some of its rebellious power and was attractive to some Americans for just this reason.

One punk group that made the connection between the iconography of the Fifties and punk rock clear was the above-mentioned Ramones. From their beginnings in 1974, their basic uniform was T-shirts, jeans, and black leather biker jackets. Their look was not entirely nostalgic. Their shoulder-length haircuts were completely contemporary and their T-shirts featured logos, rather than being the classic white tees of the Fifties. But the somewhat severe and, by the Seventies, almost classic, T-shirt, jeans, and leather jacket combination fit the stripped-down quality of the Ramones' music.

The Fifties recommended themselves as an important source of the punk aesthetic because the punk scene explicitly defined itself in opposition to the Sixties counterculture. In one of the seminal songs that punk forerunner Jonathan Richman wrote for his band the Modern Lovers, "I'm Straight" (recorded in 1973), the singer is trying to woo a girl by contrasting himself to her current boyfriend, "hippie Johnny," who is "always stoned, he's never straight":

> See he's stoned, hippie Johnny
> Now get this, I'm straight
> And I wanna take his place

For many, punk was the antithesis of hippie, and what could be less hippie than the Fifties? "In their rejection of the hippies," writes Nicholas Rombes, "the punks—in the United States especially—had turned to the detached cool of the fifties."[43]

Fig. 1.4. The Ramones' look combined clothing that harkened back to Fifties greasers—black leather jackets, T-shirts, and blue jeans—with long haircuts that would have been entirely out of place in that era. (Credit: Photofest.)

Not surprisingly, punk rockers were at pains to emphasize that their relationship to the Fifties was not mere nostalgia. The cover of the twelfth issue of *Punk*, which appeared in January 1978, featured the singer Robert Gordon. Gordon had first become known in New York as a member of the punk band Tuff Darts, who became popular at CBGB and other downtown clubs in the early 1970s. But Gordon left the band before they ever recorded a studio album and remade himself as a rockabilly revivalist. In 1977, he began to record and tour with the guitarist Link Wray, whose recording career went back to the late 1950s. Performing in Fifties garb, Gordon and Wray scored a minor U.S. hit in 1977 with "Red Hot" ("My gal is red hot / Your gal ain't doodley squat!"), a pretty straight rockabilly number. It was in this guise that Gordon was drawn for the cover of *Punk*: snapping his fingers and sporting a fifties haircut, Gordon is wearing a white sleeveless T-shirt, jeans, and black boots and is identified as the "Bop King." But *Punk*'s article on Gordon opens by denying what might otherwise have seemed obvious to his audience: "Robert Gordon is not into camp or nostalgia. He plays modern rock and roll music just like the Ramones, Heartbreakers, or Blondie. Robert just stays closer to the roots of the original sound of the Fifties: his premiere album—*Robert Gordon with Link Wray*—is a real punk-rock record."[44]

The opening sentence of *Punk*'s piece on Robert Gordon captured another of the attractions of the Fifties to the punk scene: the Fifties represented the raw, presumably authentic origins of rock 'n' roll. While punk musicians and publicists insisted that their music was modern, like the folk scene that had dominated some of the same neighborhoods of New York a decade earlier, they also hoped to achieve an authenticity grounded in what they saw as their music's roots. Like so many other cultural producers in Seventies America, punks involved themselves in a quite self-conscious rejection of the immediate past of the Sixties and, with it, much of the present. And this, in turn, meant reaching back into the slightly more distant past.

Those outside the punk scene often appreciated—and occasionally deprecated—punk music precisely for its throwback qualities. "If today's *Rolling Stone* were the *Cahiers du Cinema* of the late Fifties," Paul Nelson's *Rolling Stone* magazine review of the Ramones' eponymous 1976 debut album began, "a band of outsiders as deliberately crude and basic as the Ramones would be granted instant auteur status as fast as one could say 'Edgar G. Ulmer.'" Nelson went on to praise the band as "authentic American primitives" whose work was "of an exhilarating intensity rock & roll has not experienced since its earliest days." Nelson admitted to his readers that this paragraph of praise was a self-conscious reworking of a paragraph of movie critic Andrew Sarris's praise for underground film auteur Sam Fuller.[45] Nelson's admiration for the Ramones is almost recursively caught in the Fifties. The music itself is valuable precisely because it is of the Fifties; it belongs to "rock & roll and not to rock and avant-garde musical trends." But Nelson also imagines himself as a cultural critic in the Fifties, appreciating the Ramones as French film critics of that decade appreciated the great directors of B movies. And Nelson authenticates this image by suggesting that what Andrew Sarris says of Sam Fuller's films of the 1940s and 1950s is also true of the Ramones.

While *Rolling Stone* saw the Ramones as glorious primitives, they were less enthusiastic about other downtown New York bands. Reviewing the 1977 debut albums of Blondie and Television, along with the Ramones' second album, for *Rolling Stone* about a year later, Ken Tucker was largely dismissive: "These bands achieved their initial notoriety while playing in the same place (an esophagus of a bar called CBGB, in lower Manhattan) and have been lumped together with other habitués of this joint as purveyors of 'punk rock.' In their self-consciousness and liberal open-mindedness, these bands are as punky as Fonzie: that is, not at all."[46] Like Nelson writing on the Ramones' debut, Tucker links punk rock to the music of the past. But rather than an authentic, primitive past, Tucker sees only the figure who had already established himself as a symbol of empty Fifties nostalgia: *Happy Days*' Fonzie. Tucker particularly disliked Blondie, whose music he called "a playful exploration of Sixties pop interlarded with trendy nihilism."

But the American punk subculture of the 1970s frequently transcended the dichotomy between authenticity and camp invoked by both Tucker's partial dismissal of the CBGB scene and *Punk*'s praise for Robert Gordon. Groups like the Ramones and Blondie and magazines like *Punk* created an aesthetic that self-consciously mocked what they saw as the seriousness and niceness of the Sixties counterculture. "Punk humor," Nicholas Rombes notes, "was directly rooted in the rejection of what was perceived as hippie sincerity."[47] *Punk*'s Mary Harron later noted that "punk . . . embraced everything that cultured people, and hippies, detested: plastic, junk-food, B-movies, advertising, making money—although no one ever did. You got so sick of people being so nice, mouthing an enforced attitude of goodness and health."[48] Unlike the British punk scene, which emerged later in the decade, and at least some aspects of American hardcore punk culture in later decades, the 1970s New York punk subculture studiously avoided serious political statements.[49]

The dominant Seventies vision of the Fifties as a youth-culture-dominated, simpler, largely apolitical era defined by a commercialized culture of consumption and a socially detached vision of coolness, formed a perfect touchstone for the punk subculture, even as that subculture spun this vision of the Fifties in a more rebellious direction. That this Seventies vision of the Fifties was already deeply commodified by the middle of the decade if anything made it even more attractive to punk musicians, artists, and journalists. Though *Rolling Stone*'s Ken Tucker was critical of Blondie's pastiche approach to exploring the cultural past, the musicians in Blondie understood what they were doing. "Blondie always thought pop—i.e. dance music, movie themes, and the strict attitudes of modernist Fifties design. We were definitely combining these ideas in rock & roll," the band's lead singer Debbie Harry later said.[50]

While Ken Tucker invoked Fonzie—the ultimate example of a defanged Seventies version of Brando's leather-clad motorcycle-riding Fifties outlaw—to attempt to discredit the CBGB bands, in 1976, another important critic from outside the punk scene itself, the *Village Voice*'s James Wolcott, compared punk to the iconic *Happy Days* character in a very different way:

> Punk humor, a healthy parody of rock machismo, can be found in the music of the Dictators (who sing: "The best part of growing up / Is when I'm sick and throwing up / It's the dues you got to pay / For eating burgers every day. . . .") and the leather-jacketed Ramones, in the Daffy Duckery of Patti Smith, in magazines like *Punk* and *Cream*, and in television heroes like Fonzie and Eddie Haskell [of *Leave It to Beaver* (1957–1963)]. It's a style of humor which reverses banality, thrives upon it, and enjoys juxtaposing it with high culture references in order to create a comically surreal effect.[51]

Whether or not *Happy Days*, let alone *Leave It to Beaver*, knowingly engaged in such surreal humor, both shows could be—and sometimes were—consumed in this spirit. In a sense, the comic strategy that Wolcott described was akin to the attitude toward the Fifties that his fellow *Voice* critic Michael Feingold had attributed to the Broadway show *Grease*, which he argued had presented the banality of white Fifties suburban youth culture in order to draw attention to the unmentioned social and political problems that swirled around it.

But while Feingold had suggested that *Grease* harbored a progressive political message behind its feel-good score and book, the political valence, if any, of the punk scene's ironized and studiedly apolitical invocations of Fifties culture was less clear to critics in the mid-decade. In a generally admiring *Village Voice* review of a three-day festival of then-unsigned bands including the Ramones, Blondie, Television, Talking Heads, and many others, which CBGB hosted in August 1975, Wolcott himself had detected a culturally conservative strain in punk music: "No longer is the rock impulse revolutionary—i.e., the transformation of oneself and society—but conservative: to carry on the rock tradition."[52]

Fellow rock critic Ellen Willis took longer to appreciate punk rock. In a December 1972 essay, she had associated the term "punk-rock" (not yet firmly attached to the music that it would later describe) with the revival of Fifties rock 'n' roll, about which she had "mixed feelings": "For one thing, the blood-'n'-raunch approach to rock tends to degenerate into a virility cult. Besides, having lived through the fifties, I find it impossible to romanticize them. In spite of rock and roll, they were dull, mean years—at least for middle-class high-school girls. For all the absurdities of the counterculture, it was better than what we had before; there's something to be said for a little cosmic awareness, provided it doesn't get out of hand."[53] Though seven years younger than Joan Didion was, Willis, who was born in 1941, had, like Didion, lived through the Fifties and looked back on them with no nostalgia. But Willis, unlike Didion, was a cultural and political radical and this would ultimately make her more receptive to punk rock.

Later in the decade, Willis was initially bored by the Ramones ("I felt they were not only distanced but distant, apologists for coldness as a worldview"). And, like a number of other critics (including, most famously, Lester Bangs), she had been concerned about a kind of incipient fascism in punk, not so much, in her case, because of punk's willingness to play with the symbols of Nazism, but rather because "sexism combined with anger was always potentially fascistic." Willis, whose commitment to a radical and liberating vision of feminism was even stronger than her love of rock music, felt that the latter half of the Seventies was a time of severe gender backlash, seen even among some rising stars in the Democratic Party, such as the new president Jimmy Carter and then New York mayoral candidate Mario Cuomo, both of whom Willis saw as deeply antifeminist. Willis only came to appreciate punk in 1977 when she began listening to the Sex Pistols' British version of it. The more overtly political stance of the British punk bands awakened Willis to the virtues of the Ramones, whose first album she now found "moved [her] more than before."

Tellingly, Willis's grappling with punk in both its British and American versions led her to think about the legacy of the Sixties, both as lived reality and as Seventies myth. Writing in 1977, Willis described her editor telling her that all the CBGB bands were "still caught up in the past, in the myth of the sixties":

> Talk about irony: the worst insult you could throw at those of us who had been formed by the sixties was to imply that we were living in the past; not to be totally wired into the immediate moment meant getting old, which we hoped we would die before. The thing was, I really felt not guilty. In the past couple of years, especially, the sixties had seemed very distant to me. When I thought of the person I had been in 1967, or even 1970, she was almost as much of a stranger as my college-student self. I rarely played music that had been popular in the sixties; most of it lacked a certain dour edge that felt necessary in this crabbed decade. It was nevertheless true that many of my favorite records had been made by veterans of the sixties, just as it was true that I was still interested in my past, felt a continuing need to understand and absorb it. Was this need regressive?

Part of the problem, in Willis's view, was the nature of the Seventies, which "had been at best dull, at worst grim."

Eventually, Willis unasked her own question about whether or not being caught up in the Sixties past was somehow regressive by asking what it meant to "relegate Patti Smith or the Ramones to the sixties" as her editor had done. "The Sixties" in this sense, Willis thought, was nothing more than "a dismissive label with which to quarantine certain ideas and attitudes. . . . I couldn't help suspecting that 'You're still living in the sixties' was often nothing more than code for 'You refuse to admit that what really matters to you is to stake out a comfortable position in the upper middle class.' Well, not only did I refuse to admit that: I didn't even think it was true."

Ellen Willis did not abandon her sense that one ought to live in the present, not the past. But in the seemingly dull and grim Seventies, living in the present meant dealing with the past, or at least a mythic version of it. As skeptical as Willis could be about many aspects of the punk scene, this was something she shared with it. Willis's understanding of the relationship between the Sixties and the Fifties was, however, interestingly different from the punk scene's. The magazine *Punk*, and many of the artists it promoted, embraced what it saw as a Fifties model of cultural rebellion as a kind of antidote to a Sixties counterculture it viewed as too nice and naïvely political. Despite her skepticism earlier in the decade, Willis eventually came to view the punk scene's self-conscious reworking of cultural materials from the Fifties as a potential continuation of the Sixties challenges to an American establishment that had managed, by the Seventies, to cynically "quarantine certain ideas and attitudes" by associating them with the past.

Neither *Punk*'s nor Willis's attitudes toward the past can be dismissed as simply nostalgic (though there certainly was some nostalgia in *Punk*'s portrait of Marlon Brando and in artists like Robert Gordon, despite the magazine's insistence otherwise). Far from viewing the past as an escapist fantasy and a means of avoiding the present, both Willis and the punk scene saw, in different ways, aspects of Fifties teen culture that could be of active, contemporary use in confronting the challenges of life in the Seventies.

## Conclusion: How Nostalgic Were the Seventies?

While many cultural critics had begun the Seventies complaining about the rising tide of nostalgia, that decade's intellectual discourse about nostalgia led to ever more sophisticated understandings of the issue. Two of the most prominent authors to address the topic as the decade came to a close were the sociologist Fred Davis and the historian Christopher Lasch.

In 1979, University of California, San Diego, sociologist Fred Davis published *Yearning for Yesterday*, the first book-length sociology of nostalgia.[54] Though clearly inspired by the much-noted phenomenon of nostalgia in the Seventies, Davis's focus was not on contemporary American nostalgia but on the phenomenon of nostalgia in general, which he saw as driven much more by present than by past concerns. For example, Davis argued that nostalgia often played a key role in individuals' identity formation. At the end of his book, however, he turned to the particular phenomenon of nostalgia in Seventies America. What was new and unusual about Seventies nostalgia, Davis suggested, was the central role that the media played in it, both in the fact that media objects had become the central focus of nostalgia and in the mass media's direct creation of nostalgic productions. The result, Davis suggested, was a media-driven "collective nostalgia" that had come to be more important than the "private nostalgia" that individuals had for the particular details of their own pasts, though these two nostalgic realms were connected by a "seamless symbolic web."[55] The mass media had, according to Davis, made American collective nostalgia ever more unified and nationalized. This collective nostalgia had not drowned out private nostalgias, but it created "umbrellas" under which private nostalgias existed and by which ever-more-similar private nostalgias were shaped.[56] In the future, predicted Davis, media companies would hire "nostalgia specialists" who would build future "nostalgia exploitation potential" into media products.[57]

Though he is at pains to present himself as a moderate when it comes to assessing the potential for the mass media to control individual minds ("visions of absolute control . . . must for now, however, be relegated to the rantings of some megalomaniacal minister of propaganda"), Davis nevertheless still presents a social-control model of the media that was already rather old-fashioned by the late Seventies.[58] Davis's media seem to function as an entirely independent social actor that presents a uniform product to their mass audience. Though people retain their individuality and a certain level of cultural freedom, that independence from the media is largely found in their unique lives and experiences. Davis does not present their relationship to the media as itself a realm of potential play or individuality. According to Davis, the instant nostalgia for the Fifties that blossomed in the Seventies tells us less about the enormous changes that took place in between these two periods than it does about the media's relatively new and apparently insatiable desire for, and ability to make money from, nostalgia. Thus, Davis sees the nostalgia of 1973's *American Graffiti* for the world of eleven years earlier as simply absurd on its face: "Perhaps by now we can nostalgically remember doubting in 1973 whether one could feel nostalgic for what happened as recently as 1962, as the advertisements for the film *American Graffiti* were inviting us to do."[59]

Five years after Davis published his book, *Yearning for Yesterday* would be one of eight books discussed by the intellectual historian and social critic Christopher Lasch in an article on "The Politics of Nostalgia" in *Harper's* magazine.[60] From the vantage point of the mid-1980s, Lasch looked back at the Seventies and questioned the very existence of the wave of nostalgia in which America had supposedly been awash since the start of that decade. Toward the end of his piece, Lasch even quoted approvingly Gore Vidal's dismissive comment from Gerald Clarke's 1971 *Time* magazine piece on "The Meaning of Nostalgia": "It's all made up by the media," Vidal had said, "it's this year's thing to write about."

For Lasch, nostalgia was not a mass phenomenon at all, but rather almost exclusively a concern of intellectuals, who, Lasch pointed out, had been accusing Americans of excessive nostalgia since at least the late 1940s. Concerns about nostalgia, argued Lasch, were the product of progressive intellectuals who no longer believed in progress. In the absence of the "dogma of progress," these intellectuals came to believe that the best we could do was to "muddle through" the present, "if only [Americans] can cure themselves of the habit of looking backwards." "By the early sixties," wrote Lasch, "the denunciation of nostalgia had become a liberal ritual, performed, like all rituals, with a minimum of critical reflection." The great rash of commentary on nostalgia in the Seventies, according to Lasch, reflected not a growing yearning for yesterday among the great mass of Americans, but rather the ever-growing anxieties of intellectuals about the present.

The supposed "nostalgia boom" of the Seventies, was, Lasch suggested, echoing Vidal, "a media promotion, a non-event that proclaimed the demise of the sixties—of protest marches, riots, and countercultures." The media was much more interested in nostalgia than "ordinary men and women" were because "ordinary men and women live in a world in which the burden of the past cannot easily be shrugged off by creating new identities or inventing usable pasts. Ordinary men and women are much more obviously and inescapably prisoners of circumstance than those who set cultural fashions. . . . Trapped in a past not of their making, most people cannot afford the illusion that tradition counts for nothing, even if much of their energy goes into a struggle against it." In contrast, Lasch argued, "the educated classes in general," freed of ordinary people's necessary, concrete, and binding relationships to the actual past, "swing between nostalgia and a violent condemnation of nostalgia."

While Davis and Lasch were right to remind readers of the important ways in which the mass media and cultural elites shaped the public discourse about nostalgia in the Seventies, both were too quick to overlook the ways in which mass audiences embraced and, in certain cases, creatively appropriated the mythical pasts that played an important role in Seventies popular culture. This was, perhaps, especially true of representations of the Fifties, an era of which the 47 percent of the American population who were thirty or older in 1970 would have had personal memories.[61] Indeed, the creators of many of the major mass-mediated works of Fifties nostalgia from the Seventies, including *Grease*, *American Graffiti*, and *Happy Days*, based their works of collective nostalgia, to borrow Fred Davis's terminology, on quite personal forms of nostalgia. *American Graffiti*'s tagline—"Where were you in '62?"—was not an absurd media creation, but an effective way to market a movie that connected with many in its audience in just this way. And the film's plot and characters reflected its writer and director George Lucas's very personal relationship to his own past. Neither Davis's hard line between the products of a culture industry and the experience of individuals nor Lasch's equally hard one between "intellectuals" (who would, in Lasch's sense, likely include the creators of works like *Grease*, *American Graffiti*, and *Happy Days*) and "ordinary men and women" hold up under closer inspection.

Far from being a calculated product of a faceless culture industry, *American Graffiti* was a huge, *surprise* hit. Universal, the studio that produced it, hated the film and considered it "unreleasable" despite repeated positive responses from test audiences. George Lucas and his friend Francis Ford Coppola had to exert enormous pressure on the studio to even give the film a theatrical release; top studio executives felt that they ought to cut their losses and sell it directly to television.[62]

Though they disagreed about many things, both Fred Davis and Christopher Lasch presented mass culture as profoundly disconnected from the lives of ordinary Americans, though Davis seemed more convinced that that culture could shape those ordinary men and women than Lasch did. This image of American mass culture in the Seventies as structurally alienated and necessarily inauthentic did capture an important aspect of the felt experience of American life in that era (among both elites and "ordinary men and women"). In fact, as we've seen in this chapter, Seventies images of the Fifties that were, even at the time, frequently dismissed by critics as mere escapism and nostalgia, were often actively engaged with just such issues of authenticity, from *Grease*'s concerns about the commodification of youth culture in the Fifties—and about the commodification of the memory of that culture in the Seventies—to the punk scene's hoping to find in the iconography of Fifties youth culture a more authentic kind of rock 'n' roll.

Two very important aspects of Davis's and Lasch's assessments of nostalgia in the Seventies seem absolutely on the mark. In different ways, both Davis and Lasch tried to argue against the notion that the apparent prominence of nostalgia in Seventies popular culture suggested that ordinary American men and women were finding in cartoonish images of the past a simple escape from the present. And both wanted to push back against the idea that individuals' relationships to the past were largely matters of (trivial) cultural taste. Davis emphasized lived experience in his account of "private nostalgia," while Lasch saw a *necessary* connection with the past as one of the distinguishing features of the lives of "ordinary men and women," as opposed to those of intellectuals.

As we've seen in this chapter, however, even the Seventies texts most often dismissed as mere nostalgia for the Fifties frequently grappled with serious, contemporary issues. Many were grounded in the knowledge that much of their audience had personal memories of the era, experiences that made confronting the legacy of the Fifties quite necessary, as even Davis and Lasch would admit. Though, from the start of the Seventies, other cultural critics frequently associated images of the Fifties with the emptiness of nostalgia, Seventies culture produced works that were more than merely nostalgic.

# 2

## Rip Van Marlowe

### Seventies Noir and the Pre-Sixties Past

Film noir was one of the most distinctive products of Hollywood during the two decades before the Sixties.[1] Films such as *Double Indemnity, Out of the Past, The Big Heat,* and *Kiss Me Deadly* painted a dark portrait of America in the middle of the twentieth century, a counterpoint to the images of Fifties innocence that formed the basis for many of the Seventies portraits of that decade we discussed in chapter 1. In the early twenty-first century, film noir remains extraordinarily popular. The classic noir films of the Forties and Fifties are now widely available in digital formats. They are extensively discussed on websites, podcasts, and social media. The vast scholarly literature on film noir continues to grow. Film festivals are devoted to noir. The Film Noir Foundation, which grew out of one of those festivals, has been preserving and restoring classic film noirs since 2005. And contemporary filmmakers from Paul Thomas Anderson to Tom Ford continue to make neo-noirs like *Inherent Vice* and *Nocturnal Animals.*

The peculiar origin of the term "film noir" is by now well known. Though most often used to describe American movies, the term itself is of course French, coined in the summer of 1946 by a number of movie critics in France who believed that Hollywood had begun to produce a new strain of darker cinema during the war years. The origins of the term are interesting in part because the American filmmakers who made the classic film noirs of the 1940s and 1950s were, by and large, utterly unaware of it. The French critics continued to write about film noir, eventually declaring that it had come to an end sometime in the 1950s. But it was only later that the term made its way to the United States.[2]

Accounts of the arrival of the idea of film noir in the United States often highlight Paul Schrader's "Notes on Film Noir," the groundbreaking essay by the young critic and future screenwriter (*Taxi Driver*) and director (*American Gigolo*). Written as screening notes for a film festival in 1971 and published in *Film Comment* in 1972, Schrader's "Notes on Film Noir" was the first American essay devoted to film noir and quickly became a foundation for critics and filmmakers grappling with the legacy of noir.

What is less remarked upon, however, is the particular importance of the Seventies to the rise of American interest in classic film noir and the development of neo-noir. Schrader's domestication of the idea of film noir had a special importance to Seventies culture. In that decade, film noir became another site for American audiences and cultural producers to grapple with the changes wrought by the Sixties through an understanding of the pre-Sixties past, though one considerably darker than the image of the Fifties in *American Graffiti*, *Happy Days*, and *Grease*. Indeed, in "Notes on Film Noir," Schrader predicted that the new decade would bring about renewed interest in these old films: "As the current political mood hardens, filmgoers and filmmakers will find the film noir of the late Forties increasingly attractive. The Forties may be to the Seventies what the Thirties were to the Sixties."[3]

This chapter will explore the emerging interest in film noir in the 1970s through some of the New Hollywood films that drew on the legacy of film noir, films that were early examples of a genre that eventually, in the 1980s, became known as neo-noir. The popularity of early neo-noir among filmmakers, audiences, and critics in the 1970s reflected the rich and complicated potential of the genre. We will focus on one important aspect of these films. Film noir, from its beginnings in the 1940s, had dealt with issues of contemporary social and cultural decay and the possibility—or impossibility—of finding a moral, or even simply meaningful, path through a fallen world. Neo-noir was thus, among other things, a way of exploring the problems of Seventies America. And, given the connection between classic noir and the world of pre-Sixties America, it could often be a way of contrasting the values of the world before the Sixties with the world that had emerged out of them.

This chapter will focus on a diverse series of films that, in one way or another, place protagonists associated with pre-Sixties values in contemporary, Seventies settings. Perhaps the most famous example of this storytelling strategy is Robert Altman's 1973 film of Raymond Chandler's final Philip Marlowe novel, *The Long Goodbye* (1953). Chandler's novel took place in early 1950s Los Angeles, when and where it was written. Altman's movie takes place in early 1970s Los Angeles, when and where it was filmed. But Altman self-consciously made the decision to make his Philip Marlowe a character from an earlier era. In nicknaming him "Rip Van Marlowe," Altman's idea to was to imagine Chandler's mid-century Marlowe waking up a generation later in Seventies Los Angeles. While few Seventies films are quite as explicit in presenting their protagonists as men from the world before the Sixties, as we will see, this basic setup repeats itself in a number of Seventies neo-noirs, including *Joe* (1971) and two films scripted by Paul Schrader himself, *The Yakuza* (1975) and *Rolling Thunder* (1977). Each of these films has a slightly different take on the contrast between the pre-Sixties morality of its protagonist and the world of the Seventies.

## The Idea of Film Noir in Seventies America

As the Seventies began, American film critics, let alone the American public, had done remarkably little thinking about film noir. Indeed, the very expression "film noir" was little known in the United States. While the movies that we now know as "film noir" had attracted much American critical attention in the 1940s and 1950s, they did so under a variety of other generic names. And while, by the late Sixties, many Hollywood films of that period had begun to become objects of critical interest and popular nostalgia, relatively little attention had been given to film noir. All of this would change in the 1970s, as critical conversations about film noir as such blossomed in America, audience interest in classic film noir grew, and filmmakers began to make new films that drew on the legacy of noir.

While French discussions of film noir that had begun in the mid-1940s continued through the 1950s and into the 1960s, the idea of film noir slowly made its way across the Atlantic to the country that had produced the films themselves. Over the course of the 1950s and 1960s, French film criticism became both an ever more important part of the academic film curriculum in the United States and a great influence on American film commentary. But while the essays of André Bazin on the nature of cinema or the auteur theory popularized in this country by Andrew Sarris became part of serious film writing during the 1960s, French work on film noir remained relatively little noticed.

At least some of the films that the French had labeled "noir," however, were kept alive in the United States through the 1950s and 1960s by film clubs, repertory cinemas, and late-night television. And there was certainly some critical interest in them, including in some of the surreal and existential aspects of these movies that had particularly attracted the French. But the term "film noir" did not enter the English-language critical vocabulary until the very end of the 1960s. In 1968, Australian film critics Charles Higham and Joel Greenberg included a discussion of film noir, which they described as a genre, in their book *Hollywood in the Forties*. Then, in 1970, the British film critic Raymond Durgnat published what is generally said to be the first English-language article devoted to film noir.[4]

The first American article on film noir was written in 1971, the year after Durgnat published his piece. It was authored by a young film school graduate and film critic, Paul Schrader. Born in 1946 into a conservative Calvinist family in Grand Rapids, Michigan, Schrader had been prohibited from even seeing movies during his childhood. He only began to experience film as an undergraduate at Calvin College. Originally planning to enter the ministry, Schrader studied literature, became the president of the college's film society, and began to write film reviews for the college newspaper. By the middle of college, Schrader had begun to think about becoming a writer rather than a minister. Still in college and hoping to broaden his understanding of film, Schrader spent the summer of 1967 in New York, watching movies and taking a number of courses at Columbia University. A fellow Columbia student took Schrader to meet Pauline Kael, who was at the time writing for *The New Republic* and was already a major figure in film criticism whom Schrader greatly

admired. After a long night spent talking about movies at Kael's apartment, Schrader fell asleep on her couch. The next morning, Kael told
Schrader that he should become a film critic, not a minister. During his
remaining year at Calvin, Schrader sent Kael his newspaper articles. By
the end of the year, he had decided to attend the University of California, Los Angeles (UCLA), film school. On the strength of a personal letter of recommendation from Kael, he gained admission to and enrolled
at UCLA in the fall of 1968.[5] Schrader graduated from UCLA in 1970
intending to become a film critic. He was, at the time, seen as one of the
"Paulettes," a group of young critics connected to Pauline Kael that also
included, among others, David Denby and Roger Ebert. His friendship
with Kael came to a conclusion when, in late 1971, he turned down a job
that Kael had found for him as a film critic in Seattle.[6] By this time,
Schrader had already begun to toy with the idea of making movies rather
than writing about them.

Fig. 2.1. Screenwriter Paul Schrader (*left*), with director Martin Scorsese (*center*) and
actor Robert DeNiro (*right*) in 1975 during the production of *Taxi Driver*. Over the
course of the 1970s, Schrader went from working as a film critic to screenwriting and
directing. His first four produced screenplays, including *Taxi Driver*, were all neo-noirs.
(Credit: TCD / Prod.DB / Alamy Stock Photo).

In November 1971, around the time of his falling out with Kael, Schrader curated a film noir series for the first Los Angeles International Film Exposition. His screening notes for that series were published the following spring in *Film Comment* as "Notes on Film Noir," kicking off a vigorous American critical discussion of film noir that continues to this day.[7] As it was for Durgnat, Schrader's starting point is the invention of the idea of film noir by French critics in 1946. Schrader rejects the notion that noir constituted a genre. Rather than being defined by "conventions of setting and conflict," it was defined by "the more subtle qualities of tone and mood." And, echoing the French film critics who had declared that noir ended sometime in the Fifties, Schrader also notes that noir was "a specific period in film history." Most of "Notes on Film Noir" consists of Schrader's attempt to identify the essence of noir while denying that he is offering a definition as "it is almost impossible to argue one critic's descriptive definition against another." Rather than produce a list of subcategories of noir, like Durgnat, who had mapped what he called its "family tree," Schrader attempts to identify what factors brought about film noir, to describe its distinguishing stylistic and thematic features, and to identify how noir changed from its start in 1941 to its conclusion in 1953.

Two aspects of Schrader's understanding of film noir in "Notes" were particularly important in making the new noir cinema of the Seventies a site for reflections on the pre-Sixties past. First, Schrader emphasizes the importance of the relationship between the past, the present, and the future in film noir. He writes that "a passion for the past and present, but also a fear of the future" is "perhaps the over-riding *noir* theme." A particular kind of focus on the past was important in many film noirs: "The narration creates a mood of *temps perdu*: an irretrievable past, a predetermined fate and an all-enveloping hopelessness. In *Out of the Past* Robert Mitchum relates his history with such pathetic relish that it is obvious there is no hope for any future: one can only take pleasure in reliving a doomed past."[8]

Secondly, Schrader especially praised what he saw as classic noir's final phase, which ran from 1949 to 1953. "The *noir* hero," wrote Schrader of this period, "seemingly under the weight of ten years of despair, started to go bananas." The films of this phase, wrote Schrader, were "the most aesthetically and sociologically piercing," as they "finally got down to the root causes of the period: the loss of public honor, heroic conventions, personal integrity, and, finally, psychic stability."[9] These very concerns would become central to the way many neo-noirs viewed America in the Seventies. Though film noir had stretched what was allowed under the Production Code, the rules of classic Hollywood still restrained the depiction of heroes "going bananas." Many fewer restrictions would limit the neo-noirs of the Seventies. In New Hollywood cinema, protagonists could engage in brutal acts of violence without even the formal retribution demanded of them under the Production Code.

Early in "Notes," Schrader pauses to address the status of film noir in America at the beginning of the Seventies and makes a bold prediction about the place of noir in that then-young decade:

> Hollywood's *film noir* has recently become the subject of renewed interest among moviegoers and critics. The fascination *film noir* holds for today's young filmgoers and film students reflects recent trends in American cinema: American movies are again taking a look at the underside of the American character, but compared to such relentlessly cynical *films noir* as *Kiss Me Deadly* or *Kiss Tomorrow Goodbye*, the new self-hate cinema of *Easy Rider* and *Medium Cool* seems naive and romantic. As the current political mood hardens, filmgoers and filmmakers will find the *film noir* of the late Forties increasingly attractive. The Forties may be to the Seventies what the Thirties were to the Sixties.[10]

Not only was the particular past, the 1940s, that produced the films that we call "noir" important to Schrader, but so was its relationship to his 1970s present. Like so many of his fellow cultural producers at the start of the Seventies, Schrader saw the Sixties as a distinctive and transformative era, but one that had in many ways come to an end. Classic film noir had reflected, perhaps had even helped constitute, a Forties that was more cynical, curdled, harder than the sometimes hopeful radicalism of Thirties American culture in the face of the Great Depression. The renewed interest in noir, which Schrader both observed and actively helped bring about, similarly reflected and constituted the new, more cynical decade in which Schrader wrote and its relationship to the apparently transformative decade that preceded it.

World War II plays a central role in Schrader's analysis of film noir. The first two "conditions in Hollywood" that Schrader identifies as leading to film noir were both related to World War II: "war and post-war disillusionment" and "post-war realism."[11] And war remained subtly important to the plots of many film noirs, especially in what Schrader sees as the middle period of the cycle. In the second half of the Forties, classic film noir frequently featured protagonists who were World War II veterans and their military service often played a role in the films' plots.[12]

Although Schrader does not say so explicitly, the experience of war was one of the factors that linked the Seventies and the Forties. As the film scholar James Naremore has argued, the Vietnam War functions as a "structuring absence" in Schrader's essay.[13] If the United States went through a period of disillusionment as a result of its experience during and after World War II, the disillusionment brought about by Vietnam was even more powerful. Films that showed the seamier and more ambivalent aspects of the post–World War II world might hold a particular attraction in the Seventies.

At the dawn of that decade, Schrader was not alone in his sense that noir had begun to interest not only filmmakers and critics but also audiences, perhaps especially those who felt the hardening political atmosphere most intensely. Looking back on this period, film noir scholar Paul Arthur recalls "quite clearly how initial retrospectives and underground screenings of noir in the early 1970s struck a responsive chord with an increasingly besieged segment of the radical protest movement via romanticized identification with the plight of noir protagonists. Indeed, I trace my impassioned interest in this work from the period in which the rebellious social energies of the 1960s began to splinter and ebb."[14] Schrader's analysis of film noir at the start of the decade played a key role in both identifying and encouraging this growing interest in noir. "Notes on Film Noir" formed the foundation of, and helped to shape, an American critical conversation about classic film noir that would gain momentum during the Seventies and over the next several decades.

By 1974, only two years after Schrader had published "Notes on Film Noir" in *Film Comment*, the critic Richard T. Jameson published, in that same journal, "Son of Noir," an essay surveying the recent Hollywood revival of noir. Jameson felt the need to remind his readers at the start of his piece that "film noir" was not a term that anybody in Hollywood in the Forties would have used. But, Jameson argued, "film noir has finally been discovered at home. Not every workaday reviewer employs the term, but many of them have a vague idea what it's about, and whenever a new movie comes along in which the atmosphere is wishfully sinister and oddball characters proliferate to the confounding of any hope of lucid plot explication, they've learned to dive for prototypes in *The Big Sleep* the way a seal dives for a fish." Jameson noted that Seventies filmmakers were also drawn to noir, though he dismisses most of their efforts as mere "nostalgia trips."[15]

Jameson was being unfairly harsh about the efforts of Seventies Hollywood filmmakers to reimagine noir on the screen. The Seventies would see the birth of what would eventually be called neo-noir, a self-conscious Hollywood genre, unlike the film noir of the Forties and Fifties, which had been a category of American film that only the French initially perceived from afar. At the time that he was writing and publishing "Notes on Film Noir," Schrader was also just beginning a screenwriting career; by the decade's end, he would be directing films as well. Perhaps unsurprisingly, many of Schrader's early screenplays echo both film noir and his reading of it. Schrader-scripted films such as *The Yakuza* (1974), *Taxi Driver* (1975), and *Rolling Thunder* (1977) drew inspiration from the film noirs of the Forties and Fifties. His prediction about the growing importance of film noir to audiences and filmmakers proved prophetic. Given the importance of "Notes on Film Noir" and his later screenplays, that prediction would be, in part, a self-fulfilling prophecy.

## Backlash to the Sixties as Noir in *Joe* (1970)

Even before Paul Schrader's "Notes on Film Noir" began a self-conscious American critical and cinematic conversation about film noir, filmmakers had begun to use what Schrader would consider the language of film noir to capture and comment on what he would call the hardening political mood of the new decade. A film that strikingly anticipates Schrader's predictions about noir in the Seventies is the movie *Joe* (1970). The film started as a screenplay by Norman Wexler entitled *The Gap*. As originally conceived, the film focused on Bill Compton (eventually played by Dennis Patrick), a middle-aged advertising executive whose daughter, Melissa (Susan Sarandon in her film debut), has become a hippie and is living in the East Village with Frank Russo (Patrick McDermott), a drug-dealing would-be artist. Melissa ends up in the hospital following an accidental overdose and her parents decide to send her away to clean up her life. While clearing her stuff out of her apartment, Bill confronts Frank and, in a fit of rage, kills him. In a bar, he confesses his crime to Joe Curran (Peter Boyle), a factory worker who had been ranting about "Negroes," "queers," liberals, and hippies, who he believes are destroying America. Concerned that Joe might reveal his secret, Bill later seeks him out and the two develop an odd friendship. Despite their differences in class and attitude, Bill and Joe come from the same generation. They discover that they both fought in World War II. Both are, in very different ways, alienated from and fascinated by the youth culture represented by Melissa and Frank. Egged on by Joe, who embraces Bill's violent act more thoroughly than does Bill himself, the two men go downtown to search for Melissa. Victims of a robbery after doing drugs and sleeping with two hippie women, Joe and Bill eventually go on a killing spree at a hippie commune, gunning down all its residents. The movie concludes as Bill shoots his own daughter, whom he presumably does not recognize, as she attempts to flee the scene.

Norman Wexler's screenplay reflected both the cultural tensions in America at the turn of the Seventies and aspects of his own experience. Born in 1926, the child of Detroit factory workers, Wexler attended Harvard University before moving to New York in the early 1950s. *The Gap* would be his first screenplay. Like *The Gap*'s protagonist, he worked for a time as an advertising executive. John Avildsen, a young director and friend of Wexler's, whose previous experience was in exploitation films, took an interest in Wexler's story and convinced Cannon Films, a distribution company known for producing movies on the cheap, to finance the production. In a little over a week, Wexler wrote the screenplay and Avildsen shot the film quickly and cheaply.[16]

Wexler's story is almost classically noir: a normal, middle-class man, goes to a dangerous part of a city and through a combination of intent and happenstance commits a heinous crime. Although at first consumed by feelings of remorse and guilt, he discovers that he cannot return to a life of normalcy, and instead drifts further to the dark side, eventually

destroying that which he loves the most. Like many classic noir protagonists, Bill Compton is a World War II veteran. New York in the 1970s
is presented as a classic noir setting: an urban world that is losing its
moral bearings. But in 1970, most American audiences and critics were
not yet thinking in terms of film noir.

What would sell Avildsen and Wexler's film when it opened in
July 1970 was its sudden topicality. On May 8, 1970, in lower Manhattan, construction workers attacked a group of young people who were
protesting the recent Kent State shootings, resulting in dozens of inju-
ries and several arrests. What became known as the Hard Hat Riot
divided the city and the nation. Peter Brennan, the head of the Build-
ings and Construction Work Trades Council of Greater New York, publicly defended the rioters. While denying that the unions had in any
way organized the violence, Brennan told the New York Times that the
men "did it because they were fed up with violence by antiwar demon-
strators, by those who spat at the American flag and desecrated it."[17]
Demonstrations backing both sides of the May 8 events continued in
New York City. It became clear to The Gap's filmmakers that the character of Joe Curran, a hard hat fed up with liberals and hippies, was suddenly iconic, especially given the very strong performance that Peter
Boyle had turned in. The film was reedited to make Joe Curran a more
central character and retitled Joe to emphasize his importance.[18]

Enhancing the role of Boyle's Joe almost certainly improved the film.
Joe is, quite simply, the most compelling character in the movie and
Boyle's the strongest performance. Rather than focusing on the descent
of Bill Compton, a blandly ordinary, upper-middle-class American with
whom the audience was presumably supposed to sympathize, as The Gap
had originally done, Joe instead splits the audience's identification. For
its first fifteen minutes, Joe concentrates on Bill's daughter, Melissa, a lost
soul who is devoted to her drug-dealing abusive boyfriend, Frank. Only
when Melissa overdoses and ends up in the hospital do finally meet
her parents, who come across as caring but deeply ineffectual, a sort of
post-Sixties variation of Jim Stark's (James Dean) parents in Rebel without a Cause. Melissa then largely disappears from the film, returning
only briefly at a few key points in the action. We follow Melissa's parents to Frank's apartment, into which Bill goes alone, eventually confronting and killing Frank. Finally, about half an hour into the film, we

Fig. 2.2. *Joe* appealed both to audiences who cheered its title character's violent attack on hippies and to those who were revolted by it. (Credit: Cannon Film Distributors / Photofest © Cannon Film Distributors.)

meet Joe. The film cuts abruptly from a worried Bill, leaving Frank's place to a close-up of Joe, who is in the middle of delivering a rant about "the n——" to a bartender in a working-class bar.

*Joe* presents none of its three central characters—Bill Compton, Joe Curran, and Melissa Compton—in an entirely sympathetic light. Melissa spends the entire film as a victim, first of Frank, then of her father. The countercultural world to which she belongs features women who are sexually liberated but selfishly manipulated by the film's hippie men, who are all presented as petty criminals. Bill is weak, dull, and self-serving. Joe is by far the most vibrant character, but he is a bitter, violent racist. Unlike Bill, whose character undergoes a huge transformation from normal law-abiding citizen to cold-blooded killer, Joe, from the moment he appears on screen, is a bomb waiting to go off.

Especially in light of that spring's Hard Hat Riot, *Joe*'s new focus on Peter Boyle's working-class title character made the movie into a ripped-from-the-headlines social-problem film. What might have otherwise been an effective, noir-inflected exploitation film that used the generation gap as its backdrop, instead became a study of an emerging iconic American figure: the angry hard hat. The most positive reviews of *Joe* praised it for its extraordinary timeliness. Harlan Ellison, reviewing the film for the *Los Angeles Free Press*, declared that it was "a small artistic miracle" and compared it to Zola's *J'Accuse* and Harriet Beecher Stowe's *Uncle Tom's Cabin*. Ellison refuses to discuss the plot of the movie and instead openly declares that the sole purpose of his review is to get readers to see the film and to urge them to convince real hard hats to see it, too. And yet, he quite correctly understands the power of *Joe*'s vision of contemporary America to have been largely accidental: "No one conceiving this film, a year ago, could have known how loudly it would speak today."[19] Mark Goodman's review of *Joe* for *Time* magazine was similarly effusive about the film's social importance. Goodman begins with an extensive quote from Joe's introductory barroom rant. Declaring Joe to be "the ultimate hardhat," Goodman praised *Joe* as "a film of Freudian anguish, biblical savagery and immense social and cinematic importance."[20]

However, many other critics argued that *Joe* missed the mark. Penelope Gilliatt of the *New Yorker* thought *Joe* was a good idea for a film, poorly executed. The film's "intellectually interesting" conception "never grew, perhaps because it had its origins in simple pursuit of the current, and the end of the matter is a bad film disfigured by brute strokes of tendentiousness." Nevertheless, she noted the film's visceral effect on its audiences: "A group of youngish people at a midnight Broadway showing got up and yelled, 'We'll get you Joe!'" as the film reached its bloody conclusion.[21]

Many film reviewers emphasized the ambivalence of *Joe* toward its characters. Stanley Kauffmann, reviewing the film for *The New Republic*, admired its "neatly balanced viewpoint" toward its characters. "The outstanding aspect of the script is its ambivalence," wrote Kauffmann: "A coincidence highlights this. *Joe* is now playing in two New York theaters. On the East Side, where I saw it, Joe's mouthings drew laughs, and the East Village swingers drew applause. The very same night a friend saw the picture at its Broadway theater where, she reports, Joe was a hero to at least some and where one woman said, after the final shoot-up, 'We should kill 'em all.'"[22] Vincent Canby, on the other hand, was more critical of *Joe*'s ambivalence, describing the film as "convincingly schizoid" in his *New York Times* review. While noting that the film had received praise from "socially conscious critics on both the left and the right," Canby was largely dismissive of *Joe*, which he saw as terribly simplistic and the product of a screenwriter who was himself ambivalent about his title character, but not in terribly deep or interesting ways. Canby dismissed Joe as "a post-culture hero, like Ché, W.C. Fields and those two fornicating rhinoceroses" (the last was a reference to a famous poster of two copulating rhinos with the slogan "Make Love, Not War"). Far from being a searching piece of social commentary, *Joe* was, in Canby's view, just an exploitation picture.[23]

David Denby, reviewing *Joe* for the *Atlantic*, was harsher still. Like Canby, Denby argued that *Joe* was only a cheap exploitation film, barely disguised by a cultural pessimism that gives it an unearned sense of seriousness. Denby quotes from the critic Robert Warshow's negative assessment of Arthur Miller's *Death of a Salesman* to bolster his sense that pessimism is often mistaken in American culture for seriousness. Seeing in the film's conclusion a reference to, and a kind of inversion of, the Tate-LaBianca murders (the Manson trial had begun in June 1970), Denby accused the filmmakers of the worst kind of audience-pandering. "For many reasons," he argued, "incoherence, moral and emotional obtuseness, opportunism—*Joe* qualifies as a part of the social pathology it appears to condemn."[24]

The absence of any discussion of film noir in connection with *Joe* during the summer of 1970 is both unsurprising and striking. It is unsurprising because, as we have seen, neither the term "film noir" nor even the body of Hollywood films that the French had come to call by that name were yet the object of American critical discourse. It is striking because *Joe*, with its combination of social critique and tawdriness, its exploration of a society gone off the rails through the experience of a normal man who becomes a criminal, filled a narrative niche once occupied by classic noirs. Serious critics in the summer of 1970 felt the need to grapple with *Joe*: it was a surprise hit that had been successfully marketed for its topicality. But while some critics, like Mark Goodman at *Time*, found the film a satisfying, if disturbing, portrait of the hard hat in crisis, many other reviewers, like Stanley Kauffmann, Penelope Gilliatt, and David Denby, thought that *Joe* was cheap and exploitative.

The absence of noir as a critical category is particularly noticeable in Denby's review. Though he begins by quoting a 1952 essay by the great critic Robert Warshow on the false allure of cinematic pessimism, Denby argues that "now . . . for the first time the mainstream of American movie-making has turned toward a pessimistic view of American life." He never acknowledges the earlier period of pessimistic filmmaking represented by film noir. And Denby expresses his disappointment with *Joe* by suggesting that the movie is just "standard melodrama" and in some moral sense similar to the "nudies" for which Cannon Films and Avildsen had previously been known. Thinking about noir would probably not have led Denby to like *Joe* any better, but it would have at least led him to locate the film more precisely.[25]

Although it received a mixed critical reception, *Joe* was an enormous hit with audiences. It boosted the careers of Boyle, Wexler, and Avildsen. Wexler received an Oscar nomination for Best Original Screenplay for *Joe* and went on to write such films as *Serpico* and *Saturday Night Fever*. On this last film, Wexler worked again with Avildsen, who also benefitted greatly from *Joe*'s success. Quickly developing a reputation as a director of gritty, urban material, Avildsen would eventually win an Oscar for directing *Rocky* (1976). "*Joe* was the movie that changed everything," Avildsen would later remark. Cannon Films, the studio that produced *Joe*, was able to greatly expand its staff and became a much more significant player in Hollywood. *Joe*'s screenplay was issued as a trade paperback and there was even a *Joe Speaks* dialogue LP.[26] The extraordinary popular success of *Joe* helps explain Schrader's confidence in writing, just a year later, that noir would receive its due in the coming decade. Even before they had begun grappling with classic film noir as such, American filmmakers and audiences had returned to many of its moods and motifs.

## Neo-Noir and the New Hollywood

The success of a film like *Joe*—inexpensive, made by outsiders to Hollywood, exploring contemporary issues with levels of sex and violence previously associated with exploitation films—was indicative of larger aspects of American film culture in the early Seventies, a period of enormous change in Hollywood, both in the kinds of films being produced and in the structure of the industry that produced them. The old studio model had completed its long collapse in the Sixties. In the face of what seemed to be a losing effort to compete with other forms of entertainment, Hollywood began rapidly to change the way it did business. In the middle of the Sixties, the Motion Picture Association of America finally eliminated the Production Code, which had long since lost its enforcement mechanism, and, in 1968, introduced a ratings system, which for the first time formally distinguished between films intended for children and films intended for adults. Studios began to produce fewer and fewer movies in-house, instead focusing on financing and distributing independent productions. By the end of the Sixties, in an effort to appeal again to a youthful audience that they feared they had lost, studios began to fund directors, many fresh out of film school, whose approaches to cinema were edgier and more experimental than what had been seen in the Hollywood films of the past. The result was a period of moviemaking that, even at the time, was labeled the "New Hollywood." But if the Seventies began with the flowering of the New Hollywood cinema that grew out of these changes, by the end of that decade the studios had finally solved their financial troubles through a very different strategy: the blockbuster. Enormous hits like *Jaws* (1975) and *Star Wars* (1977)—each directed by a man who had gotten his start making small, New

Hollywood pictures—produced unprecedented profits, leading the studios to move away from funding small edgy movies and instead to focus on financing the next potential multimillion-dollar hit.[27]

The filmmakers who created the New Hollywood cinema of the late Sixties and early Seventies tended to have a distinctive professional background and, as a result, a particular relationship to the cinematic past. Earlier generations of filmmakers had come up through the old Hollywood studio system, or occasionally through overseas film industries before coming to the United States to work. Many of the key figures of New Hollywood filmmaking, on the other hand, were products of film schools and the culture of post–World War II American cinephilia. Film school graduates like Francis Ford Coppola, Steven Spielberg, Martin Scorsese, and Paul Schrader had a vast knowledge (and love) both of classic Hollywood cinema and of the critical and filmic responses to that cinema that had been produced outside the United States. Some older filmmakers associated with New Hollywood cinema did not go to film school but nevertheless learned their craft outside of Hollywood. Robert Altman, for example, cut his teeth on television. And, like the film school graduates, he combined a fascination with Hollywood's past with a desire to take American filmmaking in new directions.

New Hollywood filmmakers' interest in film history contributed to a great revival of genre filmmaking that took place in the 1970s. While these filmmakers were drawn to genre films out a desire to revisit, revise, and rework the material of Hollywood's past, the studios, in turn, saw genre as a way to simplify the marketing of movies.[28] Film noir played a very distinct role in the larger revival of genre filmmaking. While film noir had not functioned as a genre for American filmmakers in the 1940s and 1950s, who were, by and large, unaware of the category, rising American interest in noir during the Seventies led to a revival of film noir, this time as a self-conscious genre. Writing about Hollywood's "nostalgia craze" for the *New York Times* in late 1975, James Paris listed "film noir" as one of the classical genres Hollywood had lately tried to revive, though the term itself had first appeared in that newspaper only two years earlier.[29]

Today, critics usually see the movies of the American film noir revival that exploded in the Seventies as the beginnings of "neo-noir," a term used to distinguish these later films from the classic noirs of the 1940s and 1950s. However, this terminological division between "classic noir" and "neo-noir" did not come about until the 1980s, despite the fact that the notion that (classic) film noir had come to an end in the 1950s had been imported from French criticism into the American conversation about noir that began in the Seventies. The result was that, at the time of their creation, the neo-noir films of the Seventies were in what the film historian Foster Hirsch later called a "taxonomic limbo."[30] Nevertheless, what we now think of as the neo-noir films of the Seventies were part of the American cultural conversation about film noir that had begun with Paul Schrader's "Notes on Film Noir" and soon involved other critics, filmmakers, and audiences. Along the way, the term "film noir" itself became a common one in American culture. While Schrader's own noir-inflected screenplays of the 1970s are the most direct examples of the creative interplay between critical approaches to classic film noir and the production of neo-noir films, the general film-historical self-consciousness of New Hollywood directors' genre filmmaking inclined other filmmakers, too, to rework film noir.

Neo-noir proved to be an essential site in which cultural producers in the Seventies explored the pre-Sixties past. Indeed, the past played a central, distinctive, and multifaceted role in Seventies neo-noir. Like much of the rest of Seventies genre filmmaking, neo-noir grew out of filmmakers' deep engagement with Hollywood's cinematic past. New Hollywood filmmakers sought to emulate, rework, reappropriate, and critique classic film noir. Film noir's exclusive association with a partic-ular, bounded period of Hollywood's past—the Forties and the Fifties—in a sense deepened the pastness of neo-noir and its connections to pre-Sixties America.[31] Some Seventies neo-noirs, such as *Chinatown* (1974), *Farewell, My Lovely* (1975), and the remake of *The Big Sleep* (1978) simply set their action in this earlier period. But most Seventies neo-noirs were set in a Seventies present and used noir tropes to comment on the distance between that present and the pre-Sixties past in which film noir had been born.

Critics also understood the past to be a major theme and motif in clas-sic film noir itself, an aspect of the cycle that Schrader had emphasized in his "Notes on Film Noir." The protagonists of classic noirs were fre-quently trapped by their own pasts. Films like *Double Indemnity* (1944) and *Detour* (1945) take place almost entirely in flashback, as their already doomed narrators tell the audience of their seemingly inevitable fates. In *Out of the Past* (1947), Jeff Bailey (Robert Mitchum), who is living a quiet and normal existence running a garage in a small town in the Sierras, discovers that he cannot escape his own criminal past.

But while such films frequently featured, in Schrader's words, "an irretrievable past, a predetermined fate and an all-enveloping hopelessness," the past in question was most often a personal, not an epochal, one.[32] The fates of *Out of the Past*'s Jeff Bailey, *Double Indemnity*'s Walter Neff (Fred MacMurray), and *Detour*'s Al Roberts (Tom Neal) are all sealed by events or choices that they have made in the past. In each case, that past is quite recent. The world in which their fate catches up to them is very much the same world as that in which the fatal decisions that still trap them were made.

Private investigators (PIs) in classic film noir, and even more in the hard-boiled novels on which they were based, sometimes had a different relationship to the past. Hard-boiled and film noir PIs frequently embody values that the world in which they work seems to have lost. Raymond Chandler's Philip Marlowe, for example, has a sense of honor and integrity that is largely missing from the characters with whom he interacts. On occasion Marlowe seems to hint that his values belong to a different era.

As Schrader had suggested in "Notes on Film Noir," classic film noirs, especially from late in that cycle of films, often depicted a world that was suffering a kind of moral collapse. While some classic film noir protagonists themselves fall victim in one way or another to the social ills depicted in these films, other protagonists, drawing on the hard-boiled PI tradition, are islands of integrity in a sea of corruption. Jeff Bailey in *Out of the Past* and Dave Bannion (Glenn Ford) in *The Big Heat* (1953), for example, manage to operate in a corrupt world while maintaining their personal integrity.

Though often explicitly presented in mid-century hard-boiled novels and classic film noirs as out of step with the corrupt values of his time, the figure of the PI, had, by the Seventies, become associated in American culture with the values of the Forties and Fifties themselves.[33] Seventies neo-noirs with contemporary settings frequently feature protagonists whose personal integrity is contrasted with the corrupt society around them. Like the classic noir visions of the Fifties that Schrader so valued, the world of the Seventies in these neo-noirs was characterized by the collapse of moral order. But in these neo-noirs, the protagonists' integrity is often grounded in a vision of the Forties and Fifties, the period most associated with classic noir. What separates these characters' values from the values of the Seventies world around them are the Sixties, which represented a recent and vast change in American values. In a sense, Schrader's prediction in "Notes on Film Noir" that noir would see a new revival in the coming decade because "the Forties may be to the Seventies what the Thirties were to the Sixties" proved only half correct. While the hardening of the political mood and a desire to question the cultural changes brought about by the previous decade indeed helped encourage the creation of neo-noir, neo-noir films set in the Seventies frequently reimagined the Forties and Fifties in more positive and less ambivalent ways than classic noir had, even as they presented a vision of the Seventies that resembled in many ways the jaundiced classic noir image of the Forties and Fifties.

Another distinctive feature of the new noir cinema was a reworking of the role of violence in it. The moral economy of the Production Code had created limits on the narrative role of violence in classic film noir. Crime under the Production Code could not pay; murders needed to be met with punishment or even death. While plenty of classic noir protagonists achieve their goals through acts of violence, they pay for this success with their own lives. *Double Indemnity*'s Walter Neff shoots femme fatale Phyllis Dietrichson (Barbara Stanwyck), but she also shoots him; they both have to pay for the earlier murder of her husband with their deaths. In *Raw Deal*, escaped convict Joe Sullivan (Dennis O'Keefe) kills the sadistic crime boss Rick Coyle (Raymond Burr), but is himself killed in the effort. In *Out of the Past*, Jeff Bailey eliminates the malignant Kathie Moffat (Jane Greer) by driving her into a police roadblock, but he, too, dies alongside her.

In the post-Code Hollywood of the 1970s, on the other hand, extralegal violence did not need to be formally condemned by these sorts of karmic deaths. The many Seventies neo-noir protagonists who end up restoring order through extralegal violence do so with impunity, whether we are supposed to see their actions positively or negatively. And, of course, the acts of violence were themselves much more graphic than were shootings in classic noir.

## The PI as an Ambiguous Man from the
## Past in *The Long Goodbye* (1973)

One of the earliest, and most distinctive, Seventies reworkings of noir is Robert Altman's *The Long Goodbye* (1973), a film that remains fresh and surprising in part because its director's distinct style seems in many ways at odds with its genre. In fact, Altman was not the first director tapped to direct the film, which would be based on the last of Raymond Chandler's Philip Marlowe novels. David Picker, the head of United Artists, and producer Elliott Kastner had originally wanted Peter Bogdanovich to direct *The Long Goodbye*. They had asked veteran screenwriter Leigh Brackett, whose first screenwriting credit had been on the Bogart and Bacall version of the first Marlowe novel, *The Big Sleep* (1946), to write the screenplay. Kastner had wanted Robert Mitchum to star as Marlowe, but Picker wanted Walter Matthau or Elliott Gould. Matthau was not interested. Gould agreed. But Bogdanovich, who wanted to work with Mitchum, dropped out of the project. And Picker and Kastner turned to Robert Altman, who had found critical and popular acclaim several years earlier with *M\*A\*S\*H* (1970). Altman was, like most other New Hollywood directors, interested in reworking old genres; his previous film had been *McCabe & Mrs. Miller* (1971), a revisionist Western. But Altman was not particularly interested in reexploring the character of Philip Marlowe. He liked the Chandler novels well enough, as well as the film noirs based on them from the Forties, which included, in addition to *The Big Sleep*, *Murder, My Sweet* (1944), *The Lady in the Lake* (1947), and *The Brasher Doubloon* (1947). Altman was, however, unsatisfied with these movie versions of Marlowe. A different actor played Marlowe in each of these movies, but in each case, thought Altman, "they made him a kind of superhero," which the director felt was both untrue to the novels and uninteresting. Two things convinced Altman to sign on to *The Long Goodbye*, both of which cut against the grain of earlier movie Marlowes, especially the iconic Bogart performance from *The Big Sleep*.[34]

First, the director was intrigued by the choice of Elliott Gould, with whom he'd previously worked on *M\*A\*S\*H*, to play Marlowe. Gould had himself emerged at the beginning of the Seventies as a key New Hollywood figure. Following his success in *M\*A\*S\*H*, *Time* magazine had put him on the cover of its September 7, 1970, issue, declaring that Gould was a "star for an uptight age." Though arguing that Gould "does have star quality," *Time* emphasized the contemporary, urban-everyman qualities of his star persona, as well as its humorous dimensions: "Gould is the lowest comic denominator of everybody's worst opinion of himself." But though his early career had been built on comic roles like Trapper John in *M\*A\*S\*H* and Ted in *Bob & Carol & Ted & Alice* (1969), he was, already in 1970, branching off into drama; the *Time* article made much of the fact that Gould had been cast by Ingmar Bergman as the lead in his first English-language movie, *The Touch* (1971).[35] But following that film, Gould's career had stagnated.[36] Nevertheless, *The Long Goodbye*'s producer, Elliott Kastner, "loved the idea" of Gould as Marlowe because "he had a kind of dandruff on his shoulders, if you know what I mean."[37] Casting Elliott Gould as Marlowe, then, was both giving the role to a major young star and making a bold choice not to turn Marlowe into the "kind of superhero" that Bogart and other Hollywood actors had made him into in the past.

The second reason that Altman accepted the offer to direct *The Long Goodbye* was the ending that Leigh Brackett had written for her screenplay. In a departure from Chandler's novel, Brackett had Marlowe, at the end of her script, shoot his friend Terry Lennox in cold blood. "It was so out of character for Marlowe," Altman later noted, "I said, 'I'll do the picture, but you cannot change that ending! It must be in the contract.'"[38] The producers agreed.

The main plot of *The Long Goodbye* concerns Terry Lennox (played by baseball star and *Ball Four* author Jim Bouton), an old friend of Marlowe's who shows up late one night and demands to be driven to Tijuana. The next day, Marlowe is arrested by two police officers, who accuse him of aiding and abetting a murderer. It seems that Terry's wife, Sylvia, has been killed and the police suspect Terry. After several days in jail, Marlowe is abruptly freed as Terry has apparently committed suicide in Mexico, leaving a confession to his wife's murder. Papers report the case is closed. Marlowe, however, still thinks his friend is innocent of murder and doubts he committed suicide. Marlowe is then hired by Eileen Wade (Nina Van Pallandt) to locate her husband, Roger Wade (Sterling Hayden), a once famous novelist who has become consumed by alcoholism. Marlowe quickly finds Roger—he's staying at an expensive private rehab center—and brings him back to Eileen and their Malibu beach-front home. As he is leaving the Wade home, Eileen brings up Terry Lennox, expressing surprise that he killed his wife. Marlowe once again proclaims his friend's innocence. When he returns home, Marlowe is confronted by Marty Augustine (Mark Rydell), a Jewish gangster who demands that Marlowe produce the $355,000 that Terry Lennox owes him. Shortly thereafter, Marlowe receives a five-thousand-dollar bill in the mail with a note from Terry. He travels down to Mexico to investigate the supposed suicide. There he's shown photographs that seem to depict Terry's corpse, but Marlowe is still suspicious. Back in Los Angeles, Marlowe returns to the Wade house where he witnesses Roger commit suicide by walking into the Pacific Ocean. Eileen tells Marlowe that her husband was having an affair with Sylvia Lennox and killed her in a fit of jealousy. Marlowe visits Marty Augustine's office to clear the air, but Augustine threatens him again. Suddenly the money that Terry owes Marty Augustine arrives in Augustine's office. With Augustine satisfied, Marlowe is able to leave. Marlowe sees Eileen drive by in a convertible, but she does not stop for him and Marlowe gets hit by a car while running after her. After a short hospital stay, Marlowe returns again to the Wade house, which is now for sale, Eileen having left to an undisclosed location. Marlowe returns to Mexico where he bribes officials with the five-thousand-dollar bill and convinces them to tell him the truth about Terry, who is indeed still alive. Marlowe finally confronts Terry, who admits both that he was having an affair with Eileen and that he killed his wife. Furious at all that his friend has put him through, Marlowe pulls out a gun and shoots Terry. Walking away down a tree-lined road, Marlowe passes Eileen driving in a Jeep, presumably to meet Terry. The film comes to an end as Marlowe walks and dances jauntily down the road, away from the camera.

Though critics now recognize *The Long Goodbye* as one of the great Seventies neo-noirs, the film had trouble finding an audience at the time of its release. Among the problems the film faced was a botched marketing campaign, which tried to sell Elliott Gould as a traditional, tough-guy version of Philip Marlowe. After a poor opening, the film was withdrawn and then rereleased with a campaign featuring a poster by *Mad Magazine* cartoonist Jack Davis, which sold *The Long Goodbye* as a farce. The film then did very well in New York, but, according to Altman, "by the time that happened it was too late for Los Angeles and those other cities."[39]

Certainly the film is closer to a farce than a traditional Hollywood adaptation of a Chandler novel. But it is not exactly a farce either. Indeed, part of the power and charm of *The Long Goodbye* is that it seems more interested in undoing classic noir than in constructing anything entirely coherent to replace it. Altman, typically, gave his actors the space to bring their own ideas to their characters.

But two other choices made by Altman shaped *The Long Goodbye* into a meditation on Seventies America and the distance it had traveled from the pre-Sixties past depicted in Chandler's hard-boiled fiction and in classic film noir. First, while Brackett's screenplay is unspecific about the time in which the story is set, Altman set his film distinctly in Seventies Los Angeles rather than in the early Fifties, when the novel was set. Rather than living in a stucco house as he does in the book and the original screenplay, the film's Philip Marlowe lives in an apartment across from a group of young women who make hash brownies and perform yoga in the nude on their porch. Much of the action takes place in Roger and Eileen Wade's very Seventies Malibu beach house, represented in the film by a home that Altman himself was living in at the time he made the movie. In their clothing, hairstyles, and mores, the film's characters, other than Marlowe himself, also embody the culture of Seventies Los Angeles.

But while Altman set the film distinctly in the Seventies, he made his Philip Marlowe a man from the past. "I decided we were going to call him Rip Van Marlowe," the director later told an interviewer, "as if he'd been asleep for twenty years, had woken up and was wandering through this landscape of the early 1970s but trying to invoke the morals of a previous era."[40] Throughout the film, Marlowe is the only character who wears a suit and tie, which he pointedly refuses to take off, even while at the beach. He is also the only character who smokes, which he does constantly throughout the picture. Unlike all the other characters in the movie, he drives a car from the age of classic noir, a 1948 Lincoln Continental, which was, in fact, Elliott Gould's own car.[41] Marlowe even literally begins the film asleep: Altman added an opening sequence, which is neither in the novel nor Brackett's screenplay, in which Marlowe is woken by his cat, who demands to get fed and then leaves, never to return.

This contrast between Philip Marlowe, a figure from the past, and the often chaotic and inscrutable world of Seventies Los Angeles lies at

Fig. 2.3. Philip Marlowe (Elliott Gould) looking out of place in a Seventies Los Angeles supermarket in *The Long Goodbye*. (Credit: *The Long Goodbye*, directed by Robert Altman, 1973.)

the heart of *The Long Goodbye*. Marlowe's reputation as a tough-guy detective, which audiences would know even before the film begins, his conservative outfits, his smoking, and his car all suggest the Rip Van Marlowe figure of Altman's imagination. Though Gould later said that Marlowe is "the only character in the film with a conscience," his Marlowe rarely expresses to those around him the bygone values represented by Chandler's detective.[42] Instead, Marlowe spends most of Altman's *The Long Goodbye* mumbling to himself and telling all the characters around him who embody the new values of post-Sixties America "it's okay with me." Marlowe is certainly not at all inclined to become a part of the world around him, but he also seems disinclined to openly criticize it.

The most significant value that *The Long Goodbye*'s Marlowe clings to is loyalty to his friends. But, from the very start of the film, his loyalty is revealed to be misplaced. His cat abandons him in the film's opening minutes when he does not feed it the right food. His friend Terry Lennox abuses his trust. And Marlowe takes most of the movie to realize that Terry has done so. While casting Gould as Marlowe was in many ways a brilliant and creatively disruptive choice, the young star, who was seen as embodying both Seventies America and the spirit of the New Hollywood, was anything but a representative of an earlier age. Despite the suits, the '48 Lincoln, and the smoking, Gould's Marlowe often comes across as a kind of Jewish urban hipster.

How we ultimately understand *The Long Goodbye*'s Marlowe and what bygone values we see him as representing depends in large measure on how we read the film's ending. Having finally realized that his friend Terry Lennox, whom Marlowe has spent much of the film defending to other characters, killed his wife, lied to him, faked his own death, and is now living happily in Mexico, Marlowe tracks Terry down and kills him. The film's concluding shot of Marlowe, leaving the scene of this crime, walking down a tree-lined alley, self-consciously evokes the famous final shot of one of the classic film noirs, *The Third Man* (1949). In that film, Holly Martins (Joseph Cotten), having betrayed his former best friend Harry Lime (Orson Welles), stands dejectedly in a tree-lined alley after attending Lime's funeral as Anton Karas's mournful zither music plays the movie to a close. In contrast, Elliott Gould's Philip Marlowe, having killed his former best friend, kicks up his heels like Charlie Chaplin as *The Long Goodbye*'s soundtrack plays the song "Hurray for Hollywood!" The appearance of this tune is particularly striking as *The Long Goodbye* otherwise features an unusually single-minded soundtrack, which consists entirely of variations of the song "The Long Goodbye," a lush number written for the movie by Johnny Mercer and John Williams. Throughout the movie this title song appears and reappears, on car radios, played by doorbells, performed by a mariachi band in Mexico, as well as in many other variations. "Hurray for Hollywood!" is the only other music to appear in *The Long Goodbye*; it bookends the film, playing both over the opening credits and as Marlowe triumphantly walks off at the film's end.

The striking ending of *The Long Goodbye* is deeply ambivalent. On the one hand, it is a kind of artificial break with what has preceded it. As Altman says, there is something profoundly out of character about Marlowe, who has not so much as touched a weapon earlier in the movie, suddenly shooting the friend whom he had spent most of the film defending. But if Marlowe's action seems out of character, it does provide a satisfying ending to the film, especially if we see the film as satire and do not take the concluding violence particularly seriously. Terry's death at Marlowe's hand offers a satisfying narrative closure that comments on the figure of the PI and the role of gunplay in noir; it is somehow appropriate to the genre if not to the character. Seen another way, however, Marlowe's shooting of Terry, although surprising, is in fact very much in character. "There was, I felt, a certain sense of justice to this action by Marlowe," Gould later told an interviewer. "It fits with his having the only sense of conscience" in the film.[43]

However, the final shot of *The Long Goodbye* reminds us, by visually quoting another famous film about betrayed friendship while an upbeat old song about the wonders of Hollywood plays on the soundtrack, that this is only a movie. Marlowe's giddily walking away from the shooting after gunning down his former friend might suggest that *The Long Goodbye* is largely a film about movies and their distance from real life. Even film noir, that most apparently cynical and socially critical moment in American cinema, is, after all, Hollywood through and through. While *The Long Goodbye* seems to dismiss noir itself as nothing but a Hollywood myth, Altman made a point of telling interviewers that his and Gould's version of Marlowe was "closer to Chandler's character than any of the other [movie] renditions," though Altman also understood Chandler's Marlowe as "just a device to unite" his books, which were really "just a bunch of thumbnail sketches or thematic essays, all about Los Angeles."[44]

Marlowe's shooting of Terry Lennox also represents two important and connected ways in which violence functions differently in the neonoirs of the Seventies from the way it functions in classic noirs of the Forties and Fifties. Most obviously, and as noted above, under the Production Code's moral economy, Marlowe could not have shot Terry in cold blood without in some way being punished for his extralegal violent act. The second difference is less apparent, but more significant. As film noir scholar Paul Arthur has noted in a survey of the functions of violence in classic films noir, concluding acts of violence in those films rarely restore the protagonist or heal the broken world in which he acts. "What is crucially absent from most noir endings," writes Arthur, "is any sense of a 'regeneration through violence,' the consummatory act as '*necessary* and *sufficient* resolution of all the issues the tale has raised.'

While concluding violence in Westerns contributes to the reassertion of stable personal identity, in noir it often adds to the burden of self-abnegating loss, the final stage in a process of assuming the mantle of criminal 'other.'" In contrast to classic noir, but like many other Seventies neo-noirs, *The Long Goodbye* features a climactic act of violence that is thoroughly regenerative.[45]

Reviewers at the time picked up on the film's conception of Philip Marlowe as a man from the Forties trapped in the Seventies. George Anderson, in an admiring review of the film for the *Pittsburgh Post-Gazette*, notes that it "is not a faithful film version of Chandler's novel. Instead, it is a kind of 1970s updating of the book, as if Chandler's famous private eye were suddenly transported in a time machine from the '40s to the '70s."[46] But what the film was trying to suggest about the relationship of Forties values to Seventies America was trickier to say. And some of the critical disagreement over the film also hinged on what reviewers themselves felt about the relationship between the Forties and the Seventies.

Pauline Kael, one of the film's early defenders, praised it, in a long *New Yorker* review, as a film that essentially exploded the Marlowe myth, in both its original written and later cinematic forms. *The Long Goodbye*, Kael suggests, is a movie about movies that takes place in "the mixed up world of movie-influenced life that is L.A." She argues that the "sentimental foolishness" of Chandler's Marlowe, rather than any more solid set of Forties values, is the starting point for the Marlowe of *The Long Goodbye*: "The one-lone-idealist-in-the-city-crawling-with-rats becomes a schlemiel who thinks he's tough and wise. (He's still driving a 1948 Lincoln Continental and trying to behave like Bogart.) He doesn't know the facts of life that everybody else knows; even the police know more about the case he's involved in than he does. Yet he's the only one who *cares*."

Destroying the Marlowe myth is significant, suggests Kael, because the essentially cheap, mythic, and anti-intellectual sensibilities of pulp fiction become more virulent in cinematic form: "Suppose that through the medium of the movies, pulp, with its five-and-dime myths, can take a stronger hold on people's imaginations than art, because it doesn't affect the conscious imagination, the way a great novel does, but the private, hidden imagination, the primitive fantasy life—and with an immediacy that leaves no room for thought. . . . I suspect that people are reluctant to say goodbye to the old sweet bull of the Bogart Marlowe because it satisfies a deep need." The triumph of Altman's film, in Kael's view, is its successful transcendence of its underlying material's pulp sensibility. "Gifted filmmakers," Kael concludes, "are driven to go beyond pulp and to bring into movies the qualities of imagination that have gone in the other arts. Sometimes, like Robert Altman, they do it even when they're working on pulp material. Altman's isn't a pulp sensibility. Chandler's, for all his talent, was."[47]

The *Village Voice*'s Andrew Sarris, Pauline Kael's professional and personal rival and one of *The Long Goodbye*'s most significant detractors, also understood the film as attempting to call into question the verities of the PI films of the Forties and Fifties. But unlike Kael, Sarris felt that nobody ever had the kind of attachment to the Marlowe myth that Kael believed that the film criticized. Perhaps there were no verities to question. "The loud chorus of raves for 'The Long Goodbye' strikes one note most insistently, a kind of clarion call for growing up and not taking the private-eye genre too seriously," Sarris notes. "But when did we ever take the private-eye genre too seriously? . . . I remember the audience reaction to 'The Big Sleep' when it first came out, and no one I knew walked out of the theatre with the delusion that he had just witnessed a big slice of life in the raw." If anything, Sarris argued, the world of classic film noir was closer to reality in the Seventies than it had been in the Forties. "I am completely baffled by the argument that we have somehow outgrown the private-eye genre," Sarris concluded his review of the film, which had spread over two of his long weekly columns. "Today the front pages of the Times are full of genre stories. Dashiell Hammett's hallucinations in 'Red Harvest' and 'The Glass Key' are now the regular province of the city desk. Indeed, Watergate is more sordid and more scabrous and more sensational than any genre movie I have ever seen."[48]

But *The Long Goodbye* and its Rip Van Marlowe protagonist can also be read—and *were* also read—in a very different way: as a positive reassertion of the pre-Sixties myth of the noir PI. "*Film noir* has often used the character of the male private investigator to illustrate the alienated and paranoid nature of men in postwar America," wrote Elizabeth Ward, who would later become a significant independent scholar of film noir, in a series of screening notes for a 1974 showing of *The Long Goodbye* and *Hickey and Boggs* (1972) at UCLA. "As detectives these men become involved in dangerous situations that they feel compelled to control and change while attempting to reestablish morality in a world that appeared to ignore it." But, argues Ward, after thriving in classic film noir this version of the PI had largely disappeared in the 1960s and 1970s. *The Long Goodbye*, Ward argues, was an exception. While Gould's Philip Marlowe is "a man lost in a world he does not understand," he is still the heroic figure of Chandler's novels. "Marlowe can ignore the whacked-out girls next door or the rude market clerk, but he cannot ignore what he supposed is a convenient frame-up of his friend and, finally, he cannot be indifferent to his friend's exploitation of his trust." Rather than exploding the Marlowe myth, *The Long Goodbye*, especially in its violent climax, reestablishes it. After Terry Lennox calls Marlowe "a born loser," Ward argues, "Marlowe righteously kills him, because Terry is wrong. Marlowe is a loner but not a loser." Ward concludes that, like classic noir detectives, Marlowe lives by a code that is alien to the world in which he operates. But what distinguishes what Ward calls the "post-*noir*" films of the Seventies is that the world in which a character like Marlowe finds himself is one of total social indifference. Marlowe's clinging to the values of a bygone era both make him ineffectual for most of the film and lead him to shoot Terry, an act that Ward suggests is not about revenge but is rather about reestablishing moral order.[49]

These disparate contemporary readings of *The Long Goodbye* are interesting because they suggest both the importance of the Rip Van Marlowe trope and its ambiguity. The film clearly presents a jaundiced portrait of Los Angeles in the early Seventies. Indeed, Seventies Los Angeles in *The Long Goodbye* features the sort of moral collapse that Schrader associates with the social setting of late classic noir. In 1974, in one of the first critical surveys of what would later become known as neo-noir, Richard T. Jameson singled out *The Long Goodbye* as "one of the few Sixties-Seventies films to establish and make expressive use of a contemporary *noir* environment."[50] The movie just as clearly presents Marlowe as a figure out of step with Seventies Los Angeles who represents some version of pre-Sixties values embodied in the figure of the hard-boiled PI. But reviewers disagreed on the valence of this comparison. Does the film affirm those Forties, hard-boiled values or does it suggest that they are an illusion that we need to discard? And if it does the latter, is the film fair in accusing American audiences of having been under the spell of an outdated hard-boiled myth? Is the film's climactic moment of violence intended as a serious affirmation of those earlier values or an ironic undoing of them? While few other Seventies neo-noirs would be so ambiguous in the way they related the values of the pre-Sixties past to the world of the Seventies, that *The Long Goodbye* could so convince viewers of apparently opposite views on these matters suggests that cinematically celebrating the imagined pre-Sixties past of film noir could easily slip into cinematically criticizing it, and vice versa. One of the qualities of film noir that critics frequently remark upon is the moral ambiguity of its protagonists. Though utterly different in tone and devoid of the earlier film's reliance on sociological archetypes, *The Long Goodbye*, like *Joe* before it, took full advantage of noir's tendency to embrace moral ambiguity. The proximity of critique and celebration is worth bearing in mind as we turn to three films based on Paul Schrader screenplays that take strikingly different views of their heroes' uses of violence to solve the problems of Seventies social decay.

## Redemptive Violence in Paul Schrader's Neo-Noir Screenplays

Three early screenplays by Paul Schrader draw on the tradition of film noir and bear a striking resemblance to each other: *Taxi Driver, The Yakuza,* and *Rolling Thunder*. Each of these screenplays sets its action in the Seventies present. The protagonist of each film is a veteran, an ex-marine, who finds himself in a world from which he feels alienated. Indeed, society seems to him to have lost its sense of order. Criminal elements threaten or harm someone that the protagonist loves or at least thinks he loves. The protagonist responds by entering the abode of those criminal antagonists and committing brutal acts of violence that leave many people dead. As a result of this violence, the social order appears, at least to the protagonist, to be restored. This basic story structure both reflects the legacy of film noir and, in the potentially regenerative nature of the climactic violence, partakes of one of the distinctive Seventies neo-noir departures from classic noir that we have already seen in *Joe* and *The Long Goodbye*.

Though it was not the first of these movies to be filmed, *Taxi Driver* was the first to be written. In early 1972, Schrader was experiencing a profound personal crisis. Lacking clear professional prospects, having been fired from a position at the American Film Institute, and having been abandoned by a woman for whom he had left his first wife, Schrader took to driving aimlessly around Los Angeles. He became obsessed with guns and pornography. Drawing heavily on his own experience of loneliness, Schrader wrote *Taxi Driver* in just ten days, dashing off a draft in one week and revising it over the next three days.

In *Taxi Driver*, neither Schrader's screenplay nor director Martin Scorsese's movie provides much social, or even psychological, explanation for the behavior of its protagonist, Travis Bickle (Robert DeNiro). "Travis's is not a socially imposed loneliness or rage," Schrader told the film scholar Kevin Jackson, "It's an existential kind of rage."[51] Travis bears an ambivalent relationship to the New York in which drives. While he despises what he sees as social decay, he is a participant in that social decay. Early in the film, Travis expresses contempt for the city that he sees outside his cab and imagines a kind of apocalyptic cleansing of it: "All the animals come out at night—whores, skunk pussies, buggers, queens, fairies, dopers, junkies, sick, venal. Someday a real rain will come and wash all this scum off the streets." But Travis also spends much of his time attending pornographic movies. Travis's own contradictions are the most significant source of his problems. "Travis can't see that he is the one making himself lonely," Schrader notes. "He is the one making the world sordid."[52] Travis is not presented as a representative of the pre-Sixties past. And the problems of his world are not expressly presented as flowing from the changes in American culture brought about by the Sixties, though the world of the screenplay and the movie is distinctly the world of Seventies New York.

*The Yakuza* and *Rolling Thunder*, on the other hand, are both constructed around a conflict between a protagonist with values rooted in the past and a world whose new values create social disorder. Unlike *Taxi Driver*'s Travis Bickle, the protagonists of *The Yakuza* and *Rolling Thunder* are not themselves the principal sources of the problems that they face. Instead, the films present both as facing concrete and real problems that reflect actual social decay. Harry Kilmer (Robert Mitchum) in *The Yakuza* sets out to right a series of wrongs done to him and to his friends. Charles Rane (William Devane) in *Rolling Thunder* sets out to avenge the murder of his family and his own mutilation.

The difference in the three films' presentations of the sources of their protagonists' problems are mirrored in their presentations of their characters' climactic acts of violence. Travis's brutal acts of violence are horrific and driven more by a desire to lash out at figures by whom Travis feels personally wronged than by an attempt to right any real social evils. Far from being a hero, Travis is a psychopath. In contrast, Kilmer's and Rane's climactic acts of violence are presented as heroic attempts to right the wrongs that have been done to them, though, as we shall see, this was not entirely Schrader's intent when he wrote *Rolling Thunder*.

Both Kilmer and Rane are also presented as men whose values are rooted in the past. Kilmer is an American who believes in old Japanese values in a Seventies Japan that is rapidly rejecting them; Rane is a decorated military veteran in a Seventies America that seems only to pay lip service to honor, patriotism, and family, values to which Rane himself is deeply committed. In both cases, the past values in which the characters believe both contribute to their sense of alienation from the Seventies world in which they find themselves and lead them to the cleansing acts of violence with which they respond to this world. Both *The Yakuza* and *Rolling Thunder*, then, present stories about protagonists rooted in the past who confront Seventies social decay and successfully respond to that decay with violence. Like *The Long Goodbye*, they repurpose the legacy of film noir to comment on how America, and the world, have been changed by the Sixties.

After writing *Taxi Driver* in the spring of 1972, Schrader began driving around America, eventually ending up in North Carolina. There he received a letter from his older brother Leonard, who had spent some time in Kyoto, Japan, as a missionary while avoiding the draft. Leonard's marriage had fallen apart and he was spending his time watching yakuza—that is, Japanese gangster—movies. Fascinated by his brother's account of them, Paul called his agent and pitched the idea of the two brothers writing a version of a yakuza movie. Liking the idea, the agent paid for the two brothers to meet up in Los Angeles and write. The screenplay that emerged from their collaboration, *The Yakuza*, soon became the object of one of the most famous Hollywood bidding wars of the 1970s. Eventually the rights to the screenplay sold for $325,000, then an incredible sum.[53]

Sidney Pollack would eventually direct *The Yakuza*, with film noir veteran Robert Mitchum in the title role. In an effort to simplify the Schraders' apparently overly complicated screenplay and to increase the importance of the film's romantic subplot, Pollack brought in Robert Towne, the screenwriter who had written *The Last Detail* (1973) and *Chinatown* (1974), to rework the script, much to Paul Schrader's chagrin. Towne would later suggest that his alterations to the screenplay were principally about making the film more coherent. Towne's main goal in revising Schrader's screenplay was to make the protagonist's motivation more plausible. But Towne was apparently fascinated by the key themes of Schrader's screenplay, which survived his rewrite. Even with Towne's changes, the film's main weakness is exposition and character motivation, as the plot requires the audience to quickly understand a complicated backstory, while, in effect, sharing the protagonist's ignorance of central parts of that backstory.[54]

*The Yakuza* opens with a title crawl explaining the role of the yakuza in Japan, which highlights the two key themes of the film: the foundation of the yakuza in an ancient Japan, far removed from the contemporary world, and the importance of honor to the yakuza. The action opens in Japan, where George Tanner (Brian Keith), an American businessman, is in a dispute with a yakuza boss named Tono (Eiji Okada). Tanner owes Tono money and Tono has kidnapped Tanner's daughter and her boyfriend to pressure him. Tanner travels to Los Angeles and calls on his old friend and fellow Californian Harry Kilmer (Robert Mitchum) to go to Japan and rescue his daughter. A former PI, Kilmer had served with Tanner as marine military policemen during the occupation of Japan following World War II. Kilmer flies to Tokyo.

There, Kilmer reunites with Eiko Tanaka (Keiko Kishi). In 1949, Kilmer had saved Eiko from some American troops who were threatening her as she searched for penicillin for her daughter, Hanako. She agreed to live with, but not marry, Kilmer. Two years later, Eiko's brother, Ken Tanaka (Ken Takakura), a former imperial Japanese soldier, returned from the island on which had been hiding since the end of the war. Suddenly, Eiko refused to see Kilmer anymore. When Kilmer's tour of duty ran out, he left Japan, but first he bought Eiko a bar, which she named

Kilmer House and which she still runs. After arriving at her bar and surprising Eiko and her now grown-up daughter Hanako (Christina Kukubo), Kilmer explains that he's looking for Eiko's brother Ken, who Kilmer knows is a yakuza and who he believes will help him find Tanner's daughter out of a sense of obligation for his rescuing his sister decades earlier. Kilmer discovers that Ken has left the life of a yakuza and is now running a kendo dojo in Kyoto.

Kilmer visits Ken who does feel obligated to Kilmer, though the two obviously do not much like each other. Ken informs Kilmer that Tono is not a man of honor and expresses a willingness to help Kilmer recover Tanner's daughter. Back in Tokyo, a fellow American who sees that Ken doesn't like Kilmer asks Kilmer why he trusts Ken. *Giri* (obligation), Kilmer explains. Kilmer and Ken conduct a raid on the yakuza's den where the daughter and her boyfriend are being held. Following a bloody confrontation, in which Kilmer uses a gun but Ken, much more successfully, uses a sword, they release the daughter, whom they return to Tanner, who is himself now in Tokyo. Ken tells Kilmer that, so long as Tanner patches things up with Tono, none of them will be in any danger for the raid.

But the next day, Eiko tells Kilmer that Ken feels in danger. So she sends Kilmer to talk to Ken's older brother Goro (James Shigeta), a powerful yakuza of whom Kilmer was previously unaware. Meeting in a modern office building, Goro and Kilmer talk. Goro tells Kilmer that Ken long ago described Kilmer to him as a "strange stranger." "I took it to mean that you were a Westerner who had values consistent with ours," Goro explains. Goro suggests that Kilmer now has an obligation to Ken; why try to pass it on to Goro? Back in Tokyo, Kilmer is told that Tanner has been working with Tono to take over Goro's position.

Yakuza break into a house in which Kilmer is meeting with his friends and end up killing Hanako. Ken and Eiko are distraught. Ken and Kilmer go to Goro's house and agree to kill Tanner and Tono in revenge. Goro informs them that he has a wayward son who works for Tono and asks them to please spare him. They will recognize him by the spider he has tattooed on his forehead.

Goro pulls Kilmer aside and informs him that, while he is in fact Ken's brother, Ken is not Eiko's brother. In fact, Ken was Eiko's husband and Hanako's father. When Ken returned from the war, he was thus both grateful to Kilmer for saving his wife and enraged that he was living with her. Goro emphasizes that Ken's values are rooted in the past: "Ken is a relic left over from another age, another country."

Kilmer then goes alone to Tanner's office and shoots and kills everyone there, including Tanner. He then joins Ken in his raid on Tono's den. Once again, Ken arrives with a sword, Kilmer with guns: a shotgun in one hand, a pistol in the other. Ken kills Tono and informs the other yakuza present that they have come only for their boss. But it becomes clear that Ken and Kilmer will have to kill all of them. When Ken sees the man with the spider tattoo, he immediately recognizes him as the person who shot Hanako in the earlier raid. Ignoring Goro's request, Ken kills him.

The following day, Ken and Kilmer go to Goro's house. Goro informs them that the police believe that Tanner and Tono killed each other, so Ken and Kilmer have nothing to fear. Wracked with guilt over killing Goro's son, Ken takes out a cloth and a knife and cuts off his own pinkie finger. Ken ceremonially hands Goro the finger, wrapped in the cloth, and says "please accept a token of my apology." Goro just as ceremonially accepts the finger. Kilmer looks on in silent wonder.

In a cab on the way to the airport to catch his flight back to Los Angeles, Kilmer contemplates the fact that, in living with Eiko and bringing

Fig. 2.4. Harry Kilmer (Robert Mitchum), armed with two guns, and Ken Tanaka (Ken Takakura) carrying a sword, raid the yakuza Tono's headquarters in *The Yakuza*. (Credit: *The Yakuza*, directed by Sydney Pollack, 1975.)

about Hanako's death, he destroyed Ken's past and his future. Abruptly he orders the cab to turn around and drive to Ken's apartment. Once there, Harry repeats the finger cutting ceremony he saw in Goro's house. Handing Ken his finger wrapped in a cloth as a "token of my apology," Kilmer pleads with Ken to forgive Eiko as well as Kilmer. "No man has a greater friend," replies Ken. Together, each with his hand wrapped in a bandage, Ken and Kilmer go to the airport. As Kilmer boards the plane, he bows ceremoniously to Ken. The plane flies off and the film ends.

*The Yakuza* draws deeply on the legacy of film noir as Schrader understood and admired it. The film is not only an Americanized Japanese gangster movie, it is also a neo-noir. It is very much concerned with the relationship between the past, the present, and the future and is built on the "mood of *temps perdu*" that Schrader had identified as the key feature of film noir. Not only the protagonist's actions, but also those of other major characters, are determined, and many are doomed by, the characters' pasts: Kilmer's relationships to Eiko, Hanako, and Ken, as well as his loyalty to his old friend Tanner; Tanner's commitments to Tono; Eiko's dependence on Ken and Kilmer; Ken's sense of *giri* to Tanner and Goro; and of course the code of honor of the yakuza that ultimately underscores critical choices made by Ken, Goro, and even Kilmer. *The Yakuza* is also largely concerned with the issues that Schrader had identified in "Notes on Film Noir" as typical of the late-period classic noirs that he most valued: "the loss of public honor, heroic conventions, personal integrity, and, finally, psychic stability."[55] And, as in these classic noirs, the hero "goes bananas," slaughtering Tanner, Tono, and everyone around them.

As is often the case with Seventies neo-noir, the relationship between past and present in *The Yakuza* is figured in terms of changing values. From its opening title, the film lauds the ancient, "rigorous" code of honor of the yakuza. But we learn over the course of the film that Tono, despite being a yakuza, is not a man of honor. As characters in the film remind each other—and the audience—over and over again, the new Japan is not the old Japan. Indeed, it is not even the Japan of the American occupation, during which most of the film's backstory has taken place.

The crucial conflict of values in the film concerns past and present, rather than East and West. A film about an American in Japan that deals largely with Japanese values might be expected to revolve around the clash between American and Japanese values. And *The Yakuza*'s opening scenes, in which Tanner is confronted by a threat from Tono and turns to Kilmer for help, appear to draw just such a contrast between the American characters and the Japanese characters. However, it soon becomes clear that the real conflicts in *The Yakuza* involve the competition between old Japanese values and newer ones. The two major American characters, Kilmer and Tanner, turn out to have a very deep understanding of Japanese values that goes back to their time as marines in occupied Japan. While the film starts by suggesting an alliance between Kilmer and Tanner against Tono, by the end of the movie Kilmer and Ken, representing old Japanese values, are allied against Tanner and Tono, representing the corrupted values of contemporary Japan. Indeed, the very names of these characters suggest that Kilmer is a kind of American double for Ken, just as Tanner is an American double for Tono.[56]

We are repeatedly told in the film that Ken represents the vanishing values of old Japan. His reappearance within the film's backstory—belatedly returning from the war to find Eiko living with Kilmer in the early 1950s—was itself a kind of resurrection. And we are also told that Kilmer, peculiarly for a Westerner, shares these old Japanese values. While Kilmer certainly goes on a journey of discovery over the course of the film, that journey involves understanding his real relationship to Ken and finding a way to turn that relationship from one of hostile obligation to genuine affection. He has already discovered Japan long before the start of the movie.

But while Kilmer is a peculiarly Japanese sort of Westerner, he is also a variation of a protagonist common in classic film noir. We know little about Kilmer when we first meet him, but we soon learn that he is haunted by his past and a love that he has lost. We know that he is the sort of person someone would ask to recover a kidnapped relative. We soon discover that he is a loner, that he is an excellent detective, and that he is good with a gun. When we find out in the middle of the film, in a conversation between Kilmer and Ken, that Kilmer has, in the past, both been a policeman and a PI, we are not surprised.

Casting Robert Mitchum in the role of Kilmer underscores his character's affinity with classic noir protagonists. Mitchum's fame was largely based on his roles in classic noirs such as *Out of the Past* (1947) *The Big Steal* (1949), *Macao* (1952), and *Cape Fear* (1962), which some critics consider the last classic film noir. Along with *The Friends of Eddie Coyle* (1973), *Farewell, My Lovely* (1975), and *The Big Sleep* (1979), *The Yakuza* is one of a number of Seventies neo-noirs that employ Mitchum as a kind of found object, whose screen presence evokes both his earlier roles and the passage of time since them. As if to underscore his connection to these roles, in *The Yakuza*, Kilmer frequently wears a parka that resembles a trench coat, the most stereotypical film noir PI garb, the iconicity of which Mitchum himself helped establish in *Out of the Past*.

While Kilmer's status as a Westerner who sympathizes with old Japanese values seems to be a matter of character and temperament—as noir PIs' senses of honor generally are—Kilmer first discovers Japan in the late 1940s and early 1950s—that is, precisely in the era of classic film noir itself. Though the old yakuza values of honor and obligation go back centuries, for Kilmer they go back to the world just before the changes wrought by the Sixties, the world of the immediate postwar era. While the Seventies Japan of *The Yakuza* seems very unlike Seventies America, it nevertheless embodies stereotypically negative aspects of the Seventies in America: traditional values have been tossed aside and are being replaced by self-interest. While Kilmer and Ken's climactic acts of violence against Tanner and Tono cannot restore the old order, they can at least avenge the wrongs done by Tanner, Tono, and their henchmen. And Ken and Kilmer's self-inflicted wounds atone for the harms that each has done to their shared family (for Kilmer is very clearly part of the Tanaka family by the end of the film).

Although the film's setting and the specific, traditional values of the yakuza, especially the idea of *giri*, are explicitly Japanese and are presented in the film as exotic, *The Yakuza* bears a striking relationship to many Seventies neo-noirs set in America. An American character, with values grounded in the immediate post–World War II era, faces a corrupted contemporary world to which he seeks to restore moral order, eventually resorting to violence to do so. These films take very different attitudes toward these characters and their acts of regenerative violence. *The Yakuza* seems to wholly endorse its protagonist's violent acts. While the violence certainly won't restore Japan's old, noble values, it does restore order to the Tanaka family and defeats one major source of corruption.

Like Philip Marlowe in *The Long Goodbye*, Harry Kilmer, in returning to Japan after decades away, seems suddenly thrust into the corrupt,
contemporary world, making him, too, a kind of Rip Van Marlowe
figure. Early in the film, Kilmer tells an American friend how disori-
enting the new Japan is: "Everywhere I look, I can't recognize a thing."
His friend tries to reassure him: "It's still there. Farmers in the country-
side may watch TV from their tatami mats and you can't see Fuji
through the smog, but don't let it fool you. It's still Japan and the
Japanese are still Japanese." But Kilmer's concerns about change turn
out to be better founded than his friend suggests.

One function of the exoticism of the film's setting and values is that
they are used to blunt some of the horror we might otherwise feel at the
violence. The world of the yakuza seems to accept this violence. And
the film wants us to accept it as well, in part because it is a generic marker
of the Japanese yakuza movies on which the film draws. Critics at the
time, who were often deeply troubled by the escalating violence on
screens in the Seventies, were not wholly convinced by *The Yakuza's*
endorsement of mass killing and self-mutilation. *New York Times* critic
Lawrence van Gelder connected *The Yakuza's* violence to its attempt to
mix American and Japanese film genres, but remained nonetheless
disturbed by the film's bloodiness. *The Yakuza*, van Gelder wrote, "in
keeping with its [Japanese] genre, a movie of bloody gunplay and sword-
play, of death and dismemberment unreeled with such momentum that
the expectant and horrified mind's eye is sent hurtling repeatedly past the
audacious brinkmanship of the editing into unseen but imagined fresh-
ets of gore." Van Gelder praised *The Yakuza* for audaciously trying to
combine American and Japanese film genres and tropes, but criticized it
for not quite pulling off this cross-cultural feat: "To come upon it unsus-
pecting is a little like opening an Almond Joy wrapper and finding inside
the arrangement of fish, rice and seaweed known as nori maki. The effect
is surprising: the contents prove, upon examination, not unattractive; but
the product as a whole has a potential for evoking revulsion or ridicule
from anyone whose mind clenches at the exotic or whose heart is firmly
set upon an Almond Joy."[57] Roger Ebert, who gave the film one of its
most positive reviews, praised it as a largely successful American adaptation of the Japanese gangster genre, but warned his readers about the violence: "'The Yakuza' is a superior action movie, but all the same, it's for

audiences that have grown accustomed over the last few years to buckets of blood, disembowelments and severed hands flying through the air. It's very violent, and the fact that the violence has been choreographed by a skilled director . . . just makes it all the more extreme."[58] Ebert's enthusiasm for *The Yakuza* was, however, unusual. Although in ensuing years, *The Yakuza* has become something of a cult film, praised by many as a forgotten neo-noir classic of the Seventies, at the time of its release in late 1974, it received mixed reviews and performed poorly at the box office in the United States.[59]

*Rolling Thunder* (1977) was the last of the three early noir-inflected Paul Schrader screenplays to get produced. Like *Taxi Driver* and *The Yakuza, Rolling Thunder* features a lonely male protagonist who, in the film's climax, tracks the film's antagonist to his home base and engages in a graphic act of redemptive violence. *Taxi Driver* presented Travis Bickle's violence as a result of existential despair and psychological unraveling. Although Travis might see his violence as redemptive, the audience understands otherwise. *The Yakuza*, on the other hand, presented its violent protagonist as a righteous defender of older values in an increasingly anarchic and valueless world. Although he has just cut off his finger in an act of contrition for all he has done to hurt Ken Tanaka, Harry Kilmer in *The Yakuza* leaves Japan at that film's end having gained Ken's respect and, in a sense, found himself.

Schrader had intended *Rolling Thunder*, which features an even bloodier climax than the previous two films, to present a disturbing portrait of its protagonist like *Taxi Driver*, while understanding its protagonist's actions, as *The Yakuza* does, in terms of the shifting values of the 1970s, in particular the impact of the legacy of Vietnam. The success of *Taxi Driver* finally allowed Schrader's dark screenplay for *Rolling Thunder*, which he had written a few years before *Taxi Driver* was filmed, to get produced. At first, Schrader had hoped that it would be his directing debut, but eventually John Flynn was brought in to direct it. In the summer of 1976, while the film was in production, Schrader told the *New York Times* that the screenplay was a kind of reckoning with the Sixties: "It was meant to capitalize on our national frustration, our inability to face the fact that we had lost a war."[60] In *Rolling Thunder*, Schrader focused on the experience of the Vietnam War, which James Naremore would later correctly identify as the "structuring absence" in Schrader's

"Notes on Film Noir." *Rolling Thunder* was in fact part of the first wave of films about the Vietnam War to go into production after that conflict's end, along with *Coming Home* (1978), *The Deer Hunter* (1978), *Apocalypse Now* (1979), and a number of others.[61]

As it appeared on screens in 1977, *Rolling Thunder* (whose name evokes Operation Rolling Thunder, the sustained aerial bombardment campaign against North Vietnam that the United States conducted between 1965 and 1968) concerns Vietnam veteran Major Charles Rane (William Devane) who returns to San Antonio, Texas, following seven years held in captivity by the North Vietnamese. Rane's captivity happens to have covered the years of most intense social change in the late Sixties, so he returns to a different country from the one that he had left. Rane receives a hero's welcome but does not fit easily into the changed home to which he has returned. His wife (Lisa Blake Richards), assuming that he was dead, has gotten engaged to a policeman and old family friend, Cliff (Lawrason Driscoll). And his young son has no memory of him. Although Rane seems to bear no physical scars from his captivity, he is profoundly psychologically damaged. He has flashbacks of his time in captivity. And he tells Cliff of the horrors of torture and the psychological tricks that he had to learn to survive it. While Rane's private life is a mess, he is lauded publicly, receiving a new Cadillac as well as 2,555 silver dollars, one for every day he spent in captivity plus one for luck. These are presented to him by Linda (Linda Forchet), the young woman who had worn his POW bracelet.

However, Rane's silver dollars do not bring him luck. A gang breaks into his house to steal them from him. Finding Rane, but not the money, they try beating its location out of him. But Rane, who had resisted torture while a POW, refuses to talk. Frustrated, the gang pushes his hand into the garbage disposal in his sink and mutilates him. Rane's wife and son return and are also seized by the thugs. Eventually the son reveals the location of the money. The gang kills Rane's wife and son and leaves with the money.

While recovering in the hospital, Rane is visited by both Linda and his friend Johnny Vohden (Tommy Lee Jones), a fellow Texan and Vietnam veteran who comes all the way from El Paso to see him. Rane remembers his attackers, but refuses to tell the police what he knows. When he leaves the hospital, he saws off a shotgun, sharpens the tip of the hook with which his mangled hand has been replaced, and begins to seek revenge. He convinces Linda to join him, and they drive down to Mexico, where Rane believes he will find his attackers. The rest of the film consists largely of a series of violent set pieces, as Rane, initially with Linda's help, sets out to identify and exact revenge on the people who maimed him and killed his family. In the midst of this revenge spree, Linda bows out, and Rane goes to El Paso to gather his friend Johnny Vohden to join in a planned assault on the Mexican whorehouse where the remaining members of the gang are staying. Dressed in their uniforms, Rane and Vohden initiate an incredibly bloody firefight that results in the deaths of all the gang members. Wounded, but alive, Rane and Vohden leave the scene and the film comes to an end.

The violence of the film was so shocking to preview audiences—some of whom left the screening, others of whom became violent themselves—that Twentieth Century-Fox, which had produced the movie, decided to sell the film to exploitation film distributor American International Pictures, who eventually released it to mixed-to-negative reviews.[62] While some reviewers appreciated the film's first half, once Rane began to pursue his attackers, most saw it as little more than a gory revenge film. "The first half of 'Rolling Thunder' gives a perceptive portrait of the problems faced by a soldier who returns home spiritually and mentally scarred by the horrors of war and unable to adjust to a civilian existence," wrote Norman Dresser in the *Toledo Blade*. "At about midway through the picture, however, the character of 'Rolling Thunder' shifts gears abruptly and it becomes yet another exercise in blood and gore."[63] Some reviewers were less kind. "If you liked 'Death Wish' and the gory climax of 'Taxi Driver' (whose author, Paul Schrader, also wrote this), then 'Rolling Thunder' is right up your alley," opined United Press International's review of the film. "That should be warning enough for those who find this nastily exploitive stuff repellent and disgusting."[64] Declaring its Vietnam backdrop as entirely inessential to the film, C. Michael Potter, writing for the *Michigan Daily*, dismissed *Rolling Thunder* as "merely the latest installment in the rancidly enduring Revenge Film genre."[65] However, John Duvali, writing in the *Evening News* of Newburgh, New York, felt that the movie had something substantive, if disturbing, to say about Vietnam: "The film is not saying that war destroyed these men, it is saying it elevated them. It is the film's ultimate in irresponsibility. It is a sick movie."[66]

The *New York Times* had been anticipating the film for months, seeing it both as a kind of follow-up to *Taxi Driver* for screenwriter Paul Schrader and as one of the first movies to tackle the subject of Vietnam. But while Vincent Canby, in his review for the paper, found the protagonist interesting during the early part of the film, by the end Rane had become "not much more interesting than the fellow played by Charles Bronson in 'Death Wish.'" Ultimately, Canby was left puzzled by the film: "I can't believe that it was Mr. Schrader's idea merely to have Charlie reliving his Vietnam duty (and, anyway, Charlie was a flier, not a ground soldier) when he sets up the bloody series of executions that conclude the movie. This, however, seems to be the point. Something is missing, but what it is, I'm not sure."[67]

Canby's sense that something was missing was, in fact, on the mark. The screenplay, as Schrader wrote it, was highly critical of Major Charles Rane. But in the process of the film's going from screenplay to screen, a critical portrait had been changed to a celebratory one. "*Rolling Thunder* was really botched in the editing," Schrader told the writer Kevin Jackson years later:

> The main character of the film was meant to be the same sort of character as [*Taxi Driver*'s] Travis [Bickle], with that same antisocial edge. The character, as I originally wrote him, was a Texas trash racist who had become a war hero without even having fired a gun, and came home to confront the Texas Mexican community. All his racism from his childhood and Vietnam comes out, and at the ending of the film there's an indiscriminate slaughter of Mexicans, meant as some kind of metaphor for American racism in Vietnam.
>
> In order to get it made at Twentieth [Century-Fox], they insisted that the racist element be taken out, which is the equivalent of giving Travis Bickle a dog. Once you take out the perverse pathology of these characters, rather than become films about fascism they become fascist films, and that's what happened to *Rolling Thunder*.[68]

But a number of things stayed constant from Schrader's conception to the film that was eventually made. Whether criticizing or celebrating its protagonist, *Rolling Thunder* presented a tale that drew heavily on the legacy of film noir as understood by Schrader himself. The problems of Seventies America in *Rolling Thunder*, like those in Seventies Los Angeles in *The Long Goodbye*, and Seventies Japan in *The Yakuza*, resemble what Schrader saw as the "root causes" of the world depicted in late classic noirs: "the loss of public honor, heroic conventions, personal integrity, and, finally, psychic stability." They are certainly among the root causes of Charles Rane's behavior in *Rolling Thunder*. In addition, as in a classic noir, Rane's behavior is also determined by his past, or rather, two pasts: the pre-Sixties America that he left behind, but that no longer exists, and the North Vietnamese prison in which he was tortured. His attachment to the first past—pre-Sixties America—will prevent him from ever feeling at home in the country to which he has returned. His experience in the second past—the North Vietnamese prison—determines how he responds to the strange, new world of Seventies America.

When Rane arrives in San Antonio at the beginning of the film, he tells the crowd greeting him at the airport that "we knew all along, that everyone back home from the President on down was behind us 100%. It was God and faith in our families that kept us going. Speaking for myself, I'd like to say that the whole experience has made a better man, a better officer, and a better American out of me." There's a certain irony in this statement, of course. The audience—both in the film and at the movie—knows that Rane is wrong about everyone back home being "behind [Rane and his fellow POWs] 100%," as he will soon find out when he discovers that his wife is planning to leave him and when his home is invaded and his family slaughtered. In Schrader's original conception of *Rolling Thunder*, the irony of Rane's declaration would have been deeper still, as the action in the film would have also called into question Rane's statement that "the whole experience has made a better man, a better officer, and a better American out of me." As released, however, *Rolling Thunder* ends up affirming Rane's claim to have been improved by his captivity, though not perhaps in the way we expect at the movie's start. Rane's POW experience, *Rolling Thunder* ultimately suggests, has honed him into a kind of cold and efficient killing machine that the debased circumstances of the country to which he has returned demand.

Indeed, in Schrader's three noir-inflected screenplays that climax with violent outbursts from their protagonists—*The Yakuza*, *Taxi Driver*, and

*Rolling Thunder*—the line between order-restoring violence that expresses old, but still useful, values and purely destructive and pathological violence is disturbingly thin. In *The Yakuza*, Harry Kilmer is so impressed by Ken Tanaka's commitment to an old, Japanese code of honor that Kilmer not only joins Ken in a killing spree that flows from this code, but also mutilates himself as a way of atoning for the wrong that he discovers he did to Ken in the past. While the protagonist's violence in *The Yakuza* is justified not only by circumstances but by the rich and mysterious code of the yakuza, Travis Bickle's violence is clearly an expression of his pathology. Charles Rane's massacre of the men who invaded his home in *Rolling Thunder* was easily converted from the indictment of Rane's racism and of American militarism, which Schrader had intended, into a celebration of the regenerative power of violence.

## Conclusion: The Disruptions of the Recent Past and the Origins of a New Genre in the Seventies

In the January–February 1974 issue of *Film Comment*, Paul Schrader published another study of a genre that had previously been ignored by American film critics. "Yakuza-Eiga: A Primer" introduced American readers to the Japanese gangster film, a relatively recent, but important, film genre.[69] Timed to appear just weeks before the American premiere of *The Yakuza*, Schrader's article essentially marked the end of his career as a film critic and scholar. He had already been concentrating on screenwriting for a couple of years, and this essay would be the last work of film criticism that he would publish until the 1990s. Schrader says nothing about his own yakuza movie within the body of his essay, though he does present an excerpt from the screenplay—the scene in which Harry Kilmer cuts off his finger—as an illustration of "the finger-cutting," one of eighteen dramatic "set-pieces" that Schrader identifies in his article as appearing in many yakuza films.

However, anyone who watched *The Yakuza* and read Schrader's article would see the many ways in which the film reflected Schrader's understanding of the Japanese gangster genre. In addition to the finger-cutting, *The Yakuza* contains a number of the other set pieces that Schrader identifies as typical of yakuza films, including the yakuza introduction scene, the revealing of the tattoo, the disclosure scene, and the cemetery scene. His account of important stars of yakuza films begins with Ken Takakura, who plays Ken Tanaka in *The Yakuza*. And what Schrader identifies as the main theme of yakuza films—*giri-ninjo* (duty-humanity)—is one of the central themes of *The Yakuza*.

Schrader principally presents himself in "Yakuza-Eiga: A Primer" as a film critic, not a filmmaker. He never discusses the experience of *writing* a yakuza film within his article. However, the writer of *The Yakuza* is lurking behind every corner of the piece. The article's appearance as the cover story in *Film Comment* just weeks before the American release of *The Yakuza* served as a kind of advertisement for that film, though Schrader, in writing about yakuza films in a purely critical voice, does not specifically call attention to his film's upcoming release.

"Yakuza-Eiga: A Primer" concludes with some fascinating thoughts on the social meaning of film genres. Films in "strict" genres like yakuza-eiga, Schrader writes, "are not necessarily individual works of art but instead variations on a complex tacit social metaphor, a secret agreement between the artists and the audiences of a certain period. When massive social forces are in flux, rigid genre forms often arise to help individuals make the transition. . . . When a new genre comes into being, one immediately suspects that its causes run far deeper than the imagination of a few astute artists and businessmen. The whole social fabric of a culture has been torn, and a new metaphor has arisen to help mend it."[70] Schrader argues that yakuza films are a product of the Westernization of Japan and the growth of the Japanese economy since the end of the American Occupation. The yakuza film is all about whether or not the traditional virtues of Japan—embodied by the yakuza—can survive in this new world. This is, of course, also an important theme of *The Yakuza*.

Although Schrader—following most French critics—did not consider film noir to have been a genre, his thoughts about the relationship between film noir and America in the Forties and Fifties in "Notes on Film Noir" are similar to his arguments about genre in "Yakuza-Eiga: A Primer." But while yakuza-eiga, in Schrader's understanding, was a way of helping the Japanese audience make the transition to a modern, Westernized Japan, the rise of film noir, in the Forties and Fifties, was more simply a reflection of the post–World War II audience's sense of disillusionment "The war continues," wrote Schrader in "Notes on Film Noir, "but now the antagonism turns with a new viciousness toward the American society itself."[71] And, as Schrader suggests in that essay, what was true of the Forties and Fifties might again be true of the Seventies.

The effective emergence of neo-noir as a self-conscious genre in the 1970s suggests that Schrader might have been right. And it is that very self-consciousness, along with nostalgia for Hollywood's classic film noirs, as well as the world that created them, that ultimately distinguishes the neo-noirs that began in the 1970s from the film noirs of the 1940s and 1950s. If classic noir was, among other things, a way for Hollywood filmmakers to represent and analyze some major social tensions of post–World War II America, neo-noir was, among other things, a way for New Hollywood filmmakers to represent and analyze some major social tensions of post-Sixties America. The added element of the past-ness of classic film noir itself helped neo-noir foreground the changing values of America during and immediately after the Sixties. Filmmakers used Rip Van Marlowe figures like *The Long Goodbye*'s Philip Marlowe, *The Yakuza*'s Harry Kilmer, and *Rolling Thunder*'s Charles Rane to imaginatively toss the values of the pre-Sixties past into the world of the Seventies, which filmmakers portrayed as suffering from many of the same ills that Schrader had associated with the post–World War II America that appeared in classic noirs. Though the neo-noir films of the Seventies provided more opportunities for violence to be redemptive than classic noir had done, the moral ambiguity of classic noir was generally reproduced by Seventies neo-noirs. The values of the pre-Sixties past might have a nostalgic attraction, but they could provide no easy answers in these films.

# 3

## "A Committee of 215 Million People"

### Celebrating the Bicentennial in the Wake of the Sixties

In 1976, America would mark its Bicentennial. But this major anniversary arrived at a fraught moment in American life. "What a crazy time to hold a bicentennial celebration!" the liberal public intellectual Max Lerner wrote in an April 1975 syndicated column.[1] "No one really wants it, no one's heart is in it. There is nothing to cheer about and little to celebrate. So why go through the motions?" Given events of the recent past, Lerner thought, America was in no place to reckon with its origins: "The trouble with trying to take a long, 200-year look at American history right now is that so many Americans are looking at the 20-year history with a short-range despair that distorts the long-range look."

Lerner insisted that he was "fiercely proud" of those two hundred years. And that even those wrenching twenty years had "facets . . . that belie our prevailing despair":

[Americans] lived through the scarred and scarring '60s; they proved themselves flexible and resilient enough not to be destroyed by the inner tensions of that decade. After their first dazed surprise they followed the Watergate spoor to the end, suffered the constitutional passion of the republic and are likely to survive the batterings of the oil cartel, the Vietnam collapse and the revelations about the shenanigans of the intelligence services.

Those who feel thus about American survival power despite its whopping blunders—and there must be many who do—don't feel like parading either their hopes or despairs in public. The trouble with the bicentennial hoopla is that what is surfacy about it will be meretricious, and what is deeper can't be presented in tableaux and pageants and cooked-up TV specials.

Lerner concluded that Americans found themselves in a "crisis of national identity" that couldn't be resolved by public celebrations. The answer, he concluded, had to be personal rather than social: "It is like someone in a crisis of his personal history, who must find himself. As a people we have suffered scars, have had illusions stripped away. The effort to find ourselves must be quiet rather than noisy, inward rather than outward, reflective rather than celebrative. Let's skip the bicentennial and do some self-exploring." Of course, Lerner knew that this was a fantasy. Federal plans for the celebration had been underway for a decade. And countless state and local efforts were in the works as well. Skipping the Bicentennial was not a possibility. But the problem Lerner identified was real and broadly understood: How could America celebrate its Founding in the wake of the upheavals of the Sixties and early Seventies? With so many aspects of American life, including even its system of government, seemingly in crisis, Lerner was not alone in wondering whether celebrating the Founding was sensible or even possible in the mid-1970s.

America's plans for the Bicentennial had begun in the 1960s. But, as Max Lerner suggested, the shadows of that decade complicated these plans from the start. Congress authorized the creation of an American Revolution Bicentennial Commission (ARBC) in 1966 to plan for the celebrations a decade later. However, the Johnson administration did not devote much time or resources to it, presumably because it had more immediate problems to deal with. Nixon saw ARBC as an opportunity for both political patronage and propaganda, which in turn mired it in scandal, eventually leading to ARBC's dissolution and replacement by a new agency, the American Revolution Bicentennial Administration (ARBA). Long before the Bicentennial arrived in 1976, the idea of a single, big national event—like 1876's Centennial Exhibition in Philadelphia—had been shelved. And the reasons were not only bureaucratic. By the mid-1970s, Americans seemed far from embracing unifying narratives about their nation's founding.

Nevertheless, when the Bicentennial date of July 4, 1976, arrived, the celebrations felt, to the surprise of many, like a success. This chapter will explore the nature of this success. As we will see, Lerner's suspicion that the celebrations were being built more on "bicentennial hoopla" than on any deep reckoning with the American past was largely correct. But Lerner, in effect, underestimated the power of bicentennial hoopla. Celebration itself proved a powerful force of national unity, a kind of substitute for any real national consensus about the meaning of the American Revolution in the wake of cultural upheavals of the Sixties and early Seventies.

The chapter begins with the story of a popular narrative of the American Revolution: the musical *1776*. A huge success on Broadway in 1969, *1776* failed, with both audiences and critics, when transferred to the movie screen just three years later. That failure was less cinematic than political: a narrative of America's founding that had seemed compelling just a few years earlier no longer did so by the 1970s. And no other competing grand popular narrative of the Revolution emerged in the run-up to the Bicentennial, though there were certainly attempts to forge one. The People's Bicentennial Commission (PBC) tried to construct such a narrative out of the radical legacies of the Sixties. Though it generated a lot of attention and even arguably contributed to the downfall of the ARBC, the PBC's New Left version of the American Revolution ultimately gained few adherents. Most Americans seemed content to mark the Bicentennial through the kind of cultural ephemera that the historian Jesse Lemisch at the time labeled "Bicentennial schlock."

Nonetheless, a patriotism grounded in the American past retained cultural power, even in the absence of a strong consensus about what the American Revolution was about. In Robert Altman's movie *Nashville* (1975), characters frequently turn to the past to find comfort amid the social crises of the day. Set in the near-future Bicentennial year of 1976, *Nashville* presents a vision of a society that uses the past as the basis of a kind of patriotic stoicism, though the film—and critics in their generally positive reviews of it—seemed unsure whether such sentiments are worryingly empty or a viable anchor in a time of social and cultural turbulence.

The federal government's ARBA propounded a more positive, though also oddly empty, vision of the past. Created in the wake of the collapse of its predecessor, ARBC, and starting work in the midst of the Watergate crisis, ARBA claimed that the Bicentennial celebration was in the hands of the American people, each of whom could draw their own conclusions about the precise meaning of the American Revolution. Though ARBA and its director, John Warner, frequently invoked the Declaration of Independence, the Constitution, and the Bill of Rights in almost liturgical ways, what precisely these documents meant or how they could guide the nation forward was largely left to the "committee of 215 million people" who were ARBA's audience.

Academic historians were frustrated by this approach. During the years leading up to the Bicentennial, historians had forged a new "republican synthesis" that sought to explain the ideological origins of the American Revolution and had explored the social history of the revolutionary era. But they and their work were largely ignored by ARBA, which, in turn, felt that historians were being unreasonable in demanding more say in the federal government's Bicentennial planning. In the twenty-first century, historians have seen in the success of ARBA's diffused, commercialized, and celebratory observation of the Bicentennial an anticipation of the revival of patriotism of the Reagan years and the beginnings of the late twentieth-century's "age of fracture," a time in which American culture's relationship to the past was simultaneously immediate and fragmented. But in one important way, the Bicentennial was unlike the way Americans would most often relate to past in the decades to come: for a moment at least, ARBA's approach to the American past seemed more to unite the nation than to spark a culture war.

## The Musical *1776* and Shifting Popular Narratives of the American Revolution

On March 16, 1969, the musical *1776* premiered on Broadway. A dramatic retelling of the story of the framing of the Declaration of Independence, the play was an enormous popular and critical hit, running for over 1,600 performances and winning three Tony Awards, including Best Musical. Sherman Edwards, who conceived the show and wrote the music and lyrics, and Peter Brook, who wrote the book, made a point of emphasizing the historical accuracy of the musical. "The first question we are asked by those who have seen—or read—*1776* is invariably: 'Is it true? Did it really happen that way?' The answer is: 'Yes,'" the two wrote in an historical note appended to the published version of the script.[2] Critics loved the new musical, both for its theatrical effectiveness, which some found surprising given the topic, and its sense of history. "The authors have really captured the Spirit of '76," wrote Clive Barnes in the *New York Times*'s rapturous review.[3] Writing a year later, in 1970, in the *Journal of Higher Education*, Hans Rosenhaupt, a literary scholar and then president of the Woodrow Wilson National Fellowship Foundation, saw great significance in the play's popularity, declaring that it might be, according to the title of his article, "a bridge at generation gap":

> The musical *1776* is playing to standing room only audiences in New York every night. There are no belly dancers in it, everybody is wearing clothes, and the few ribald jokes are tame by comparison to the prevailing climate. What carries this remarkable show to thrilled and even tearful audiences is something so old and corny that one hesitates to mention it before an academic audience—love of country. What might patriotism in America today be? Martial music? The Stars and Stripes? Pledges of allegiance? Uniforms? The national anthem?
>
> Yet *1776* has none of these. Nor does the author, a high school teacher of history, by the way, poke fun at love of country. Rather, he builds his play around the simple facts known about the drafting and adoption of the Declaration of Independence.[4]

By focusing on the very humanity of the participants in the drama of the framing of the Declaration, Rosenhaupt argued, the musical *1776* might point the way to a solution to the divisions facing the country as the 1970s began. Like the success of the musical *Hamilton* over four decades later, that of *1776* seemed to portend a broader public interest in understanding the Revolutionary past and its connections to contemporary American life.

Impressed by the musical and its popularity, an aging Jack Warner, one of the last of the old-time movie moguls still producing films in Hollywood, bought the rights to the show and produced the film version of the musical. It would be Warner's last production credit. Warner put the play's Tony Award–winning director, Peter Hunt, in charge of the film, who in turn got many in the Broadway cast to recap their roles. The result was a handsome and effective film, true to the stage musical. The movie now has a deservedly positive critical reputation. But when it was released in 1972, the movie 1776 was a critical and popular failure. "An insult to the real men who were Adams, Jefferson, Franklin and the rest," declared Roger Ebert in the *Chicago Sun-Times*.[5] Pauline Kael concluded her long and bitter review of the film with a question: "Have we lost the capacity to know when we've been insulted?"[6]

What accounts for 1776's extraordinary change in fortune? In many ways, the musical is a culmination of a form of popular history that thrived in mid-twentieth-century U.S. culture. 1776's view of history is, in certain ways, old-fashioned. Its principal characters are almost all members of the Continental Congress, the "Great Men" who framed the Declaration of Independence. Two of their wives—Abigail Adams and Martha Jefferson—also appear. Though Mrs. Adams is portrayed as a

Fig. 3.1. Howard Da Silva, Ken Howard, and William Daniels, who played, respectively, Ben Franklin, Thomas Jefferson, and John Adams, in the original Broadway production of 1776, reprising those roles in the movie version of the musical. (Credit: 1776, directed by Peter H. Hunt, 1972.)

strong woman with a revolutionary agenda of her own, both she and Mrs. Jefferson primarily serve in the play and the movie as figures of emotional support and representations of the homes from which John Adams and Thomas Jefferson are absent. The average people of Revolutionary America are largely represented by Andrew McNair, the custodian of Congress, whose historical fame is connected with his being the official ringer of the Liberty Bell. McNair is given one, brief scene with a Courier and a Leather Apron that highlights the concerns of the common people fighting the war outside of Independence Hall. But 1776 presents a largely top-down view of American independence.

While 1776 focuses on Great Men, it also goes out of its way to humanize them, to make the Great Men seem, in important ways, just like you and me. The film presents its major characters—Adams, Jefferson, and Franklin—in a manner that emphasizes their foibles. Adams is irritable. Jefferson suffers from writer's block. And while the play—and film—generally try to portray its major characters in historically accurate ways, its minor characters, like Richard Henry Lee and Lewis Morris, are often played entirely for comic relief. "Stone and Sherman seem to view the Continental Congress as an early version of *Animal House*," complained the novelist and historian Thomas Fleming some years later.[7]

But 1776's single largest departure from historical fact, in both its stage and film versions, is its portrayal of the American Revolutionary War itself. During the early spring and summer of 1776, when the action of the musical takes place, the war was going well for the Patriots and their Continental Army, under the command of George Washington. But in 1776, the deliberations of the Continental Congress are repeatedly interrupted by dire reports from the field. In the play and film, the war seems to be going badly, with Washington's army on the brink of collapse.[8] And though delegates in Congress joke about what a gloomy personality General Washington is, the show gives a sense that the war itself is failing and that the Declaration is necessary simply to keep the Patriot cause alive.

Of course, in 1969, when 1776 premiered, unlike in the months during which the action of the play takes place, the United States was in fact in a war that was going very badly. By the end of the 1960s, the Vietnam War had come to be seen, by both its opponents and supporters, as largely about credibility. Opponents warned of a "credibility gap," between the statements of the Johnson and, later, Nixon administrations and what was actually happening on the ground in Vietnam. Supporters of the war, on the other hand, argued that continued American involvement in Vietnam was essential to U.S. credibility around the world. "A nation cannot remain great if it betrays its allies and lets down its friends," warned President Nixon in the November 1969 address to the nation best known for its conjuring the image of a "great silent majority" of Americans who continued to support the United States fighting the Vietnam War. *1776*'s imaginary bad news from the Revolutionary War itself—and its characters' staunch patriotism in the face of that bad news—no doubt resonated with much of its audience in 1969.

But if *1776* presented a message on the need to support America's troops, the show was not politically conservative. Indeed, one of the play's centerpieces was a number performed by Pennsylvania delegate John Dickinson and a chorus of the other members of Congress who shared Dickinson's opposition to independence. "Cool, Cool, Considerate Men" presents the American opponents of independence as implacable, wealthy conservatives:

We have land,
Cash in hand . . .
We'll dance together to the same minuet
To the right, ever to the right
Never to the left, forever to the right.[9]

Although *1776* is suspicious of the right, associating it with opposition to the creation of an independent United States of America, the musical does not present the revolution as particularly radical. Another major scene in the show involves Congress's decision to remove Jefferson's language denouncing slavery from the draft of the Declaration. The show presents slavery as an evil but makes clear that compromising with it was necessary for national unity and American independence. And in the song "Molasses to Rum," South Carolina's Edward Rutledge points out that New England, too, is bound up in the slave economy, despite the vocal opposition to slavery by delegates from New England. In *1776*, even at the moment of independence, slavery is not simply a regional problem, but rather an American dilemma. Though the musical wears its own politics rather lightly, taken together its presentations of war, conservatism, and slavery embody a kind of post–World War II "vital center" liberalism that went over better in 1969 than it would even a few years later.

When the film came out in 1972, critical reviews focused on many of the aspects of the show that had drawn acclaim in 1969. Pauline Kael attacked both the film's tone and its politics. *1776*, she suggested, "degrad[ed]" its characters into "yokel jokers." It "doesn't even have enough spirit to be campy." Its coverage of slavery was a cheap effort to be "relevant," made worse by the easy way with which the show puts the issue to rest. "I guess this is a movie for people like the Sally Kellerman nurse in 'M*A*S*H' before she snapped out of it," Kael suggested, "for the Regular Army clowns and their liberal-clown cousins."

Richard Nixon, on the other hand, so disliked the "Cool, Cool, Considerate Men" number that equated conservatism with opposition to the American Revolution itself that he personally convinced Jack Warner to remove it from the film. Warner did so without so much as consulting the director Peter Hunt and even told Hunt that he'd ordered the negatives of the scene to be shredded. In fact, the negatives survived. Warner reportedly said on his death bed that his one regret was listening to Dick Nixon on cutting that scene. "Cool, Cool Considerate Men" has been restored in recent rereleases of the film.[10]

## Confusion, Disorder, and "Bicentennial Schlock"

While *1776*'s "vital center" vision of America's Founding had lost much of its cultural purchase in the aftermath of the Sixties, no other popular narrative of the Revolution met great success, either. Indeed, Americans seemed surprisingly indifferent to narratives about the American Revolution. The film of *1776* stands virtually alone among Hollywood movies made in the first half of the 1970s in having a Revolutionary-era setting. The closest thing to a television hit involving the Revolutionary era was the PBS miniseries *The Adams Chronicles*, which ran weekly from January 1976 through April 1976 (though only the first six episodes of the thirteen-part series dealt with John Adams, and the Revolution is over after the first three). Despite a publishing boom of material concerning the Revolution, only two books with Revolutionary-era content made the *New York Times* weekly bestseller lists during 1976: Jack Shepherd's *The Adams Chronicles*, a book written to accompany the aforementioned PBS series, and Alex Haley's *Roots*, a subject of chapter 4 of this book.

Indeed, *The Adams Chronicles*, both the miniseries and the book, form an interesting contrast to *1776*. Though an American production, the show was most deeply influenced by quasi-high-minded, character-driven BBC soap operas like *Upstairs, Downstairs*, which had been an enormous hit for PBS during the early 1970s. When the *New York Times* devoted much of its "Book Ends" column on March 14, 1976, to the success of *The Adams Chronicles* book, it made no mention whatsoever of the Bicentennial, instead explaining its popularity entirely in terms of other successful publishing tie-ins to notable series airing on PBS, such as *Alistair Cook's America*, *Civilization*, and *The Ascent of Man*. Though certainly a reflection of the Bicentennial, *The Adams Chronicles* built its popularity as much on its genre as on its subject matter.

The activist Jeremy Rifkin hoped that a radical understanding of the Founding might capture public support in the Seventies. Rifkin founded the PBC as a kind of counterweight to ARBC, the body originally constituted during the Johnson administration that had been charged with creating the national Bicentennial celebration. Rifkin charged ARBC with concocting a "Tory" view of the American Revolution and proposed instead a reading of the Revolution as a truly radical event that might lead to a new American revolution against the corporate domination of American politics and life.

Rifkin did not invent the tactic of packaging New Left politics in American Revolutionary garb (Abbie Hoffman, Jerry Rubin, and the Yippies had been among the pioneers of this), but the PBC was unusually effective at getting its message noticed through a combination of publishing, protest, and street theater. Amid accusations of corruption at the ARBC, the irritant of the PBC played a role in the eventual decision by the Nixon administration to disband and replace ARBC. But while the PBC certainly generated a lot of publicity for itself, it was not successful in remaking the popular vision of the American Revolution. Rifkin did, however, generate pushback. The Senate Judiciary Committee held very hostile hearings about the PBC in March 1976. And the Heritage Foundation published a pamphlet entitled *The Great Bicentennial Debate*, which reprinted a debate at St. Olaf's College in Minnesota between Rifkin and the conservative journalist Jeffrey St. John. Rifkin's talk, as one might expect, is an elaboration of the PBC's reading of the Revolution and a call to political action. But rather than proposing a fleshed-out alternate reading of the Revolution, St. John focuses on attacking the politics of Rifkin and the PBC. Perhaps St. John realized that, for most American audiences in the mid-1970s, it was easier to tear down a particular political reading of the Revolution than to construct a viable, popular alternative one.[11]

A kind of Bicentennial spirit did seem to grip the public. But it did so without a more serious grappling with America's past, which in turn contributed to the emptiness of this emerging patriotic rhetoric. The commercial appropriation of the past, what the historian Jesse Lemisch at the time labeled "Bicentennial schlock," dominated the public representation of the Revolutionary era during the Bicentennial. Americans bought teddy bears that recited the Declaration of Independence, liquor bottles featuring the images of Revolutionary war heroes, and shot glasses, clothing, food items, and other pieces of disposable memorabilia branded with the Bicentennial. To Lemisch, who curated a museum exhibit of such objects at the State University of New York at Buffalo in 1976, these disposable knickknacks were unfortunately "the Bicentennial's most pervasive manifestation and perhaps its most enduring heritage."[12]

The federal government's ARBA, which spent most of its energy and limited resources promoting local efforts and licensing its Bicentennial logo, would defend this commercialism. The market, ARBA director John Warner repeatedly suggested, would police those who sought to cheapen the celebration: "No item will be made for long for which there is not a buyer. . . . The citizens will hold the seller accountable, exercising rightfully good taste and good judgment."[13] Besides, as Warner also would repeatedly argue, "the founding fathers fought just as hard for freedom of enterprise as they did for freedom of speech, freedom of religion and freedom of the press."[14]

ARBA's diffuse approach to encouraging often commercialized commemorations did little to encourage reflection on the meaning of the occasion. Looking back on the Bicentennial in 1977, the historian Milton M. Klein recalled an enormous flurry of commemorative activity, but little consensus around what any of it meant: "With the Bicentennial year securely behind us, we may legitimately ask why there was so much confusion and disorder about the commemoration of so important an event in our history. Superficially, there seems no disagreement that July fourth marks our birthday as an independent political community. But beyond that, the matter becomes less clear."[15]

## The Ambiguous Stoicism of Robert Altman's *Nashville*

While neither books nor films about the Revolution galvanized the public in the run-up to the Bicentennial, one film did capture the national mood around the celebration. Robert Altman's *Nashville* opened in June 1975 to critical acclaim and at least modest popular success. Though the Bicentennial itself is not the focus of any of the film's many plots and subplots, the film is set in 1976 and the Bicentennial frames Altman's sprawling motion picture. The relationship of the characters of *Nashville* to the American past and their effort to find meaning and solace in that relationship is one of the many themes of the movie. Part of *Nashville*'s power is that its portrait of these things captured important, larger aspects of the place of the American past during the Bicentennial.

The film is framed by representations of patriotism amid tragedy. *Nashville*'s second sequence is set in a recording studio, as country star and music mogul Haven Hamilton (Henry Gibson) begins recording a new, Bicentennial-themed ballad, "200 Years." And the film concludes with a patriotic political event gone horrifically wrong. Hamilton's opening song grounds the American experience in war, sacrifice, God, and patriotism. In one verse the singer notes the many wars his family has fought in, from Bunker Hill to World War II. In another he lists hardships, like biblical plagues, that he and the country has survived ("I've lived through two Depressions / And seven dustbowl droughts / Floods, locusts, and tornadoes . . ."). But the song's refrain affirms that America's very survival indicates its essential goodness: "We must be doing something right / To last two hundred years." While the song certainly celebrates the United States, it oddly fails to associate many concrete positive values with the nation, beyond patriotism, faith, and perseverance itself. The song concludes by suggesting that the struggles at its heart are never-ending: "It's been hard work / But every time we get into a fix / Let's think of what our children face / In two-ought-seven-six / It's up to us to pave the way / With our blood and sweat and tears / We must be doing something right / To last two hundred years." The singer has no question that the country will continue for another century, but his vision of the future is driven as much by fear as by hope.

With its slow march tempo and slightly plaintive tone, "200 Years" is oddly grim for a patriotic song. Like so much else in *Nashville*, the film presents "200 Years" in a way that suggests that Altman's intent is largely ironic. The song itself, like much of the music in the film, skirts close to self-parody. The recording session fails to come to a successful conclusion. Hamilton is dissatisfied with his backup band, eventually dismissing the pianist with a rant that makes the singer look petulant and high-handed. Over the course of the movie, Hamilton is revealed to be self-important and self-interested in very unattractive ways. But like so much else in *Nashville*, it is unclear how deep the irony goes. For all of the ridiculous qualities of the song and the recording session, "200 Years" works as a patriotic ballad. As Vincent Canby noted in a glowing review of *Nashville* for the *New York Times*, "The movie is amused by the song's maudlin sentiments and rhyme schemes, and by Haven's recording-studio tantrums. But it also appreciates the song's stirring beat and the vast, earnest public for whom it will have meaning."[16]

*Nashville* concludes at a rally for independent presidential candidate Hal Philip Walker. Walker's campaign forms a constant backdrop for the action of the movie. Indeed, the first shot of the film, after the opening title sequence, features a campaign van driving through the streets of Nashville, with the recorded voice of Walker booming from its loudspeakers. Only then does "200 Years" begin to play on the soundtrack and the film cut to Haven Hamilton in the recording studio. *Nashville* features an ensemble cast with two dozen major characters. And almost all of them—and almost all of the film's various plotlines—converge at the Walker rally at Nashville's Parthenon with which the film concludes. As country star Barbara Jean (Ronee Blakley), one of a number of musical acts scheduled to perform before Walker's appearance, concludes her nostalgic hit "My Idaho Home," brooding loner Kenny Frasier (David Hayward), who is in the crowd at the Parthenon, unlocks the violin case he's been carrying throughout the film, pulls out a handgun, and shoots Barbara Jean. Kenny is tackled by obsessive Barbara Jean fan and Vietnam vet Private First Class Glenn Kelly (Scott Glenn). Chaos reigns on the stage in front of the Parthenon. Shot in the arm himself, Haven Hamilton grabs the microphone. "This isn't Dallas," he tells the crowd, "This is Nashville." He hands the microphone to Albuquerque (Barbara Harris), a would-be country singing star who has seemingly aimlessly wandered through the film, unable to get her music heard. With a dazed look on her face, Albuquerque starts to sing "It Don't Worry Me," an upbeat song that we have heard on a number of occasions earlier in the film. Soon she is joined by a gospel choir on stage. And the audience at the rally sings along. As Hal Philip Walker and his motorcade drive away, order, on stage and in the crowd, is restored. The film concludes as the song ends, the camera showing the whole scene at a distance: the Parthenon, with an enormous American flag and Hal Philip Walker signs,

Fig. 3.2. "This isn't Dallas. This is Nashville," Haven Hamilton (Henry Gibson) insists to the crowd that has just witnessed the shooting of country star Barbara Jean (Ronee Blakley) at the rally for presidential candidate Hal Phillip Walker that concludes the movie *Nashville*. (Credit: *Nashville*, directed by Robert Altman, 1975.)

dwarfs Albuquerque and the other remaining characters on stage. Those attending the rally listen, sing, and clap. Finally, the camera tilts up heavenward and the film fades to black.

Politics is only one of the thematic strains in *Nashville*, but with Altman beginning and ending with the Hal Philip Walker campaign, it frames the film. As with many of its other themes, *Nashville* seems to have something to say about politics, but it is elusive and ambivalent. The assassination of Barbara Jean feels political—it takes place at a campaign rally—but Kenny's motivation in shooting her remains mysterious. Haven's plea that "this isn't Dallas," however, captures the mood of the act: it feels like yet another in the string of public shootings of political figures inaugurated by the President Kennedy assassination, acts that by the mid-1970s were among the darkest things marking the division between the present and the pre-Sixties past.

But what are we to make of Albuquerque's musical response to the shooting? It is unquestionably emotionally powerful. As Roger Ebert noted in his 1975 review of the film, "At this late date after November 22, 1963, and all the other days of infamy, I wouldn't have thought it possible that a film could have anything new or very interesting to say on assassination, but 'Nashville' does, and the film's closing minutes, with Barbara Harris finding herself, to her astonishment, onstage and singing, 'It Don't Worry Me,' are unforgettable and heartbreaking. 'Nashville,' which seems so unstructured as it begins, reveals itself in this final sequence to have had a deep and very profound structure—but one of emotions, not ideas." On the one hand, Albuquerque and her song instantaneously bring back together, at least for the moment, a community that had just been torn apart by an act of horrific violence. The moment feels like a triumph over tragedy, in part because that is the mood of the song, whose lyrics are similarly hopeful in the face of hardship. "It Don't Worry Me" largely lists social challenges, such as high taxes, inflation, and, ultimately, the lack of freedom itself, to which the singer responds with the song's title phrase:

Economy's depressed not me,
My spirits high as they can be
And you may say I ain't free
But it don't worry me

But as hopeful as those lyrics are, they are also profoundly evasive. Rather than confronting the problems in her world or her life, the singer simply proclaims that she is unconcerned.

The origin of the song "It Don't Worry" within the world of the film, however, complicates its anti-political message of indifference. Long before Albuquerque performs it in the film's concluding moment of tragedy, we learn that "It Don't Worry Me" is a hit song written by Tom Frank (Keith Carradine) and recorded by his folk rock trio, Bill, Mary, and Tom. The song plays, presumably on a car stereo, amid the chaos of an early scene in the film in which a multicar accident produces a huge traffic jam on a Nashville expressway. And later in the film, when Bill, Mary, and Tom, in town to record an album, make a surprise appearance at a club, the audience spontaneously sings the song as they come on stage. But by this point in *Nashville*, we know that Bill, Mary, and Tom are not what they seem. Bill and Mary are a couple, but Mary is secretly having an affair with Tom. And there are four women in the audience at the club that the film's audience has seen Tom sleep with, each without knowledge of any of the other three. Like his other songs in the film, Tom Frank's "It Don't Worry Me" presents a positive image that thinly covers Tom's quite despicable behavior.

"It Don't Worry Me" is a perfect finale for *Nashville* because its attitude toward the present is very like the attitude of "200 Years," the film's patriotic opening number, toward the past. The nation survives despite hardship, and that is as good a source of meaning and solidarity as anyone in the world of *Nashville* can find. The only real source of hope is that we survived the past and we are now surviving the present. In between, *Nashville* is full of songs like "My Idaho Home" that nostalgically evoke the innocence of simpler personal pasts. "Country music is about a longing for roots that don't exist," Pauline Kael proclaimed in her celebratory review of the film, explaining the pertinence of Hal Philip Walker's slogan "New Roots for the Nation," visible in both the opening and closing scenes of the film.[17] But though John Triplette (Michael Murphy), the smooth-talking visiting Walker campaign worker, manages to convince a number of characters to tentatively support his candidate, the hope of new roots seems less attractive, or at least less durable, than the narcissistic stoicism of "200 Years" and "It Don't Worry Me."

The sentiment of these songs also bears an interesting similarity to the phrase mumbled repeatedly by Philip Marlowe (Elliott Gould) in Altman's earlier *The Long Goodbye* (1974): "It's okay with me." As we discussed in chapter 2, Altman and Gould's version of Philip Marlowe was explicitly intended to be a bearer of old values out of place in the 1970s. And that film is ambiguous about whether Marlowe—and his values— are ultimately still effective in the new world of post-Sixties America. But the explicit association of that phrase with the American past in *The Long Goodbye* suggests something implied by the stoic attitudes of "200 Years" and "It Don't Worry Me" in *Nashville*, songs that come from musical genres—country and folk—that are themselves self-consciously grounded in the past. Both films suggest this form of indifference is an old American stance. It is not only an attitude toward the past, but a legacy of it as well.

Like Max Lerner, whose op-ed about the Bicentennial that began this chapter was published just two months before the release of Altman's movie, *Nashville* suggests that America's national mood in the run-up to the Bicentennial was dominated by the experience of having survived the crises of the 1960s and 1970s. But while Lerner argued that, in the wake of these crises, Americans must now individually take part in a period of introspection about the meaning of the American experience, *Nashville* presents a world in which nobody is willing to engage in such introspection. To the extent *Nashville* offers any hope, its characters find it in survival itself and its collective acknowledgment.

Indeed, some film critics felt that *Nashville* suggested that there was something practically impossible about a national coming to terms with the past. In their dialogic, positive, but critical review of the film for the *Village Voice*, Andrew Sarris and Molly Haskell explored the film's evocation of the American past. Haskell felt that Barbara Jean's assassination did not work as a reckoning with the national past because the most immediate traumas of that past could not be captured artistically: "The assassinations that we have lived through are both too specific and too elusive to be appropriated in the nightmare vision of any one artist." But Haskell concludes that the film's ending works: "The fatalism does seem apposite on the individual, or religious level. As Blakley—whose character is apparently loosely based on the real-life country singer Loretta Lynn—sings a song of lost innocence (and, did you notice, the sun that shines on her is actually blocked momentarily by a cloud?) we feel not so much that America was a paradise, now corrupted, but that each of us must experience his own personal loss of innocence, as we 'outgrow' the roots, the family, the 'folk heritage' that spawned us."[18] Like Lerner, Haskell argued that we need to settle for individual reckonings with the past; unlike him, however, she suggests that this may not involve anything more concrete than a loss of innocence.

Pauline Kael argued that *Nashville* depicted an inclusive but critical vision of Americans as a people who misunderstand the lessons of the recent past, especially Watergate:

> For the viewer, "Nashville" is a constant discovery of overlapping connections. The picture says, This is what America is, and I'm part of it. "Nashville" arrives at a time when America is congratulating itself for having got rid of the bad guys who were pulling the wool over people's eyes. The movie says that it isn't only the politicians who live the big lie—the big lie is something we're all capable of trying for. The candidate, Hal Philip Walker, never appears on the screen; he doesn't need to—the screen is full of candidates. The name of Walker's party doesn't have to stand for anything, that's why it's the Replacement Party.[19]

*Nashville*, according to Kael, presents an America that is without resolutions or even many visible conflicts. Its characters are "frauds who are halfway honest, true to their own characters" living their lives in collision with each other. Like Haskell, Kael loved *Nashville*, but, even more than her fellow critic, saw its invocations of the American past as intentionally empty.

## ARBA and the Official Understanding of the Bicentennial

While thinkers from historians like Jesse Lemisch and Milton M. Klein to film critics like Andrew Sarris, Molly Haskell, and Pauline Kael worried about America embracing a kind of empty patriotism during the Bicentennial, it fell to ARBC and its successor agency ARBA to forge an official understanding of the Bicentennial and bring the American people on board its celebration. Almost from the start, the crises of the long Sixties interfered with this task.

The story of America's official national celebration of the Bicentennial began badly.[20] In 1966, Congress authorized the creation of ARBC to plan for and oversee the celebration a decade later. But ARBC languished. Presumably because he was dealing with much more pressing matters, President Johnson took six months to appoint members of the commission, though his eventual appointees would include major figures like Daniel Boorstin and Ralph Ellison. The underfunded ARBC met only twice during the Johnson years and little had been accomplished by the time Nixon became president in 1969. Johnson's commissioners submitted their resignations, which gave Nixon a chance to appoint an ARBC of his choosing. But Nixon too waited six months to appoint commissioners. Although he reappointed seven of Johnson's seventeen public ARBC members, he also began to use the ARBC, in the words of a 1972 *Village Voice* exposé on favors received by contributors to the Nixon campaign, as "a sort of clearing house for political payoffs."[21]

By the summer of 1972, ARBC had become steeped in controversy. Not only was it widely seen as a center for Nixonian cronyism, the agency seemed to have accomplished little. With support from both Presidents Johnson and Nixon, ARBC toyed with the idea of a major, national Bicentennial Exposition to be held in Philadelphia. While such an exposition had been the centerpiece of the Centennial celebrations in 1876, there seemed to be little enthusiasm for it this time around. Over the objections of at least one Pennsylvania congressman, in May 1972, ARBC eventually voted overwhelmingly to reject the Philadelphia exposition, a little over a year after Nixon had reauthorized the idea.[22] In 1971, hoping to take advantage of more vigorous efforts at the state level, ARBC chairman David Mahoney, CEO of Norton Simon, proposed fifty "bicentennial parks," one of which would be located in each state. But the commission, worried about costs, shelved that idea, too.[23]

ARBC did propose structuring the federal celebrations around three program areas: "Heritage '76," which focused on history; "Festival '76," which focused on domestic and foreign tourism; and "Horizon '76," which challenged Americans to imagine the country's future. And in 1971, ARBC adopted a striking logo—a star defined by the

Fig. 3.3. One of the few major accomplishments of the American Revolution
Bicentennial Commission, the federal agency initially in charge of the celebration, was
the creation of this striking logo, which its successor agency, the American Revolution
Bicentennial Administration, would eventually license widely as part of its
decentralized approach to the Bicentennial. (Credit: Wikimedia Commons.)

negative space created by red, white, and blue stripes—before descend-
ing into internal disagreements over how to use it and a moratorium
on the licensing of it, pending internal review of the matter, only six
months after the logo's creation.[24]

The overall impression that ARBC gave was that it utterly lacked
momentum. Charles Mathias, the liberal Republican senator from
Maryland who, as a member of the House of Representatives had introduced the legislation that created ARBC in 1966, proclaimed in Decem-

ber 1971 that "the commission has, thus far, come forth with nothing—no plan, no program—capable of genuinely arousing the entire nation in the celebration of its two-hundredth anniversary." "There is what might charitably be described as a haziness of definition in the broad purposes the commission has provided itself," wrote the journalist Anthony Neville in a July 1972 *Harper's* magazine piece that did much to ramp up public criticism of the effort.[25] In August 1972, the Senate held investigative hearings into ARBC's operations.

Finally, in February 1973, President Nixon proposed dissolving ARBC and replacing it with ARBA, which was designed to be more efficient and more focused than ARBC had been on coordinating the commemorative efforts of others in state and local government and in the private sector. In December 1973, Congress authorized the new agency. Early in 1974, ARBA began its work. Nixon appointed Secretary of the Navy John Warner to be its director. While ARBC had had three executive directors between 1968 and 1972—and had been without one since Jack Levant resigned in August 1972 in the face of accusations of political favoritism— Warner would direct ARBA from the time of his confirmation in March 1974 through September 1976, after the bulk of ARBA's business had been concluded. With no centralized, national celebration planned, ARBA served as a clearinghouse and sponsor of events large and small around the nation. And Warner acted as a steady figurehead for the effort. This was no easy task. Nixon had appointed Warner as the Watergate scandal was reaching its climax. The spring and summer of 1974 was a difficult moment to convince Americans that the anniversary of the creation of the nation's political institutions was a cause for celebration, especially when the effort was led by a Nixon appointee. With the American public rapidly losing faith in governmental institutions, the *official* celebration of the Bicentennial seemed to many especially problematic, even had ARBC not become such an object of criticism.

On May 11, 1974, just two months into his job as director of ARBA and just two days after the House Judiciary Committee had begun formally considering impeaching Nixon, John Warner traveled to Terre Haute to give the commencement address at Indiana State University (ISU). Given a decade of campus unrest, college and university audiences might have been expected to be particularly skeptical about the upcoming Bicentennial. The official records of this visit provide a fascinating snapshot into both the political situation ARBA found itself in and War-ner's response to it.

In April, ARBA had sent its program officer for Ethnic and Minority Heritage, Martin Goldman, to Terre Haute to explore the mood of the campus in preparation for Warner's visit. Not surprisingly, Goldman found a campus that was not focused on the Bicentennial. Like many other large public universities, ISU had been altered by the Sixties. Dur-ing that decade, ISU had expanded its physical plant, but the students never arrived, leaving empty high-rise dorms ("the butt of some cam-pus humor," Goldman would report to Warner). The students, Gold-man found, were largely apathetic. Only "parties, good grass, and rock music" excited them. The students were largely conservative and from working-class families. They were often the first in their family to go to college. Most had supported Nixon in 1972. Only one student brought up Watergate. There was a general feeling that their education was meaning-less. Liberal arts majors worried about their employment prospects.[26]

The faculty also "expressed a general feeling of discouragement." Most were from Indiana and had been educated there. "The thing that struck me most about the ISU faculty," Goldman would write to Warner, "was their feelings of hopelessness about the future. Many had come through the campus revolutions of the 1960's intact—but the wars seem to have worn them down; and many were deeply scarred." The biggest issue among the faculty was tenure. Declining student enroll-ments led the administration to threaten to eliminate some faculty lines, which increased the sense of anxiety among the faculty.[27]

The ISU administration, for its part, was "definitely under the gun . . . beleaguered, to say the least." Issues of racial and gender discrimination dominated administrative concerns. Goldman was impressed with the administrators he spoke with, who seemed "extremely concerned with the quality of education in the college" and felt misunderstood by the faculty. Not surprisingly, "other problems seemed to outweigh Bicenten-nial considerations at this moment." Among the staff, those in the library seemed most excited about the Bicentennial. "Like the other con-stituencies in this community," Goldman would write, "an air of pessi-mism pervaded the administration with whom I met."[28]

Finally, Goldman investigated a fourth "integral part of the ISU community": Black students, who "in many ways, make up a separate faction on the ISU campus and perceive things in a starkly different light." Black students did not seem to lack direction. ISU had a successful Afro-American Studies program, which attracted white as well as Black students. Unlike other humanities disciplines on campus, the program was experiencing growing enrollments and bred "a healthy spirit of cooperation and inter-disciplinary participation." But there were two separate student communities at ISU. "One is black and the other is white," Goldman would tell Warner, "and whether this is the result of racial hostility that has continued from the 1960's or is simply the result of the natural inclination of human beings to seek out familiar people and surroundings this, unfortunately, is the way it is."[29]

Ultimately Goldman would paint a bleak picture of the ISU community in 1974 in his memo to Warner:

> The spiritual malaise at ISU is not untypical of other university communities. Unlike the generation that emerged from World War II or even the generation of the early 1960's the ISU community senses certain meaninglessness in their education and in their very lives. They seem to be drifting, searching for something that will provide some centrifugal [sic] force to people in limbo.
>
> It is important to remember that these are not radical students. I did not come across any traditional malcontents on this campus.... These students and faculty are internalizing their distress. There are no organized protest rallies to point out the general depression this community seems to feel with the current state of their educational experiences. Nevertheless, the depression is evident in every conversation.

Though Goldman cautioned that "it would be glib to conclude that the ISU campus is a microcosm of the current American scene," that was clearly the implication of the memo that he wrote to John Warner on April 30, 1974: "I see a distinct relationship here between the academic malaise that this Indiana educational community is facing and the current lack of Bicentennial spirit in other more diverse communities." Grappling with the situation at ISU reflected the broader challenges facing ARBA.[30]

In the context of a sense of meaninglessness and fear for the future among the white student majority, hopelessness and concern for their future employment among the faculty, and fears that they would be unable to fulfill ISU's educational mission in a period of retrenchment among the administration, Warner's task at ISU, then, would be to suggest that the newly reformulated federal Bicentennial effort might help provide meaning and direction to all their lives. Goldman's memo to Warner concludes with a vision that the Bicentennial's focus on the pre-Sixties past might heal the wounds of recent change in Seventies America:

> Americans moved too rapidly through the 1960's—the growth of the ISU campus is a case in point. It is time for a re-examination of our past. The Bicentennial is a fantastic opportunity to institutionalize a spiritual rebirth in America. What better place to start than a small college campus in the heartland of America where spirit seems to be at such a low ebb? Using the American Revolution as a central point of reference and the founding fathers as examples, your May 11 commencement address should point out the need for re-vitalization of the American spirit, re-examination of where we all have been and most important, some thoughts on where we all are going. If the Bicentennial era does nothing else it should help America and Americans to recover from the shocks of the sixties and the seventies with a new and revitalized spirit.[31]

Goldman's conclusion makes explicit a theme that ran, usually implicitly, through both official and unofficial thinking about the Bicentennial as 1976 approached, that reflection on the history of the country's founding might help America overcome the changes wrought by the Sixties and the ensuing crises of the Seventies.

When Warner and his staff put together the ISU speech, they did not want to shy away from acknowledging the problems that seemed to be weighing on the nation. Indeed, another staff memo to the new ARBA director urged him to address the graduates as "raised in the peace of the 50's, schooled in the revolution of the 60's, and graduated in the crises of the 70's." And Warner eventually concluded his speech by directly discussing "the tragic, tangled bundle of issues known as Watergate." After offering the "historical perspective" that the United States is "now the oldest continual existing republic on earth operating under its original constitution," Warner argued that the success of the United States could be found in the "lasting blueprint of government" laid out in "three immortal documents": the Declaration of Independence, the Constitution, and the Bill of Rights. That system, Warner said, had often been tested and had always survived. "Those three great instruments," Warner argued, "will permit us to resolve the current tragedy in an orderly process of law and justice." Though the Bicentennial is "above and beyond politics" and "will never be used as a vehicle to divert attention from the issues of our time, Watergate or any other," the solution to these problems will "flow from the three great foundation documents upon which our Bicentennial observance is centered."[32]

This invocation of the "three great foundation documents" as a kind of secular scripture that could simply transcend the problems of the present would be typical of ARBA's presentation of the Revolutionary past, despite the fact that two of the documents—the Constitution and the Bill of Rights—arrived long after the period officially celebrated by ARBA, which would end with the observation of the two-hundredth anniversary of the signing of the Declaration in July 1976. Warner and his agency put more effort into invoking the power of these documents than into exploring their meanings. "When Americans begin in March of next year to celebrate their Bicentennial," Warner himself told the U.S. Conference of Mayors on June 24, 1974, "they will be celebrating that Declaration of Independence which, with the Constitution and the Bill of Rights, form the three great pillars on which our system of government so firmly rests."[33] Other ARBA officials echoed these sentiments. "The real celebration," ARBA senior assistant administrator Robert W. Miller told the annual convention of the National Retail Merchants Association on January 6, 1975, "is for 200 years of growth under the three great cornerstones of this Nation: the Declaration of Independence, the Constitution, and the Bill of Rights."[34] In testifying to a House appropriations subcommittee on February 2, 1976, Warner wove a complicated mixed metaphor that both defended ARBA's extremely decentralized efforts and proclaimed the centrality of these documents:

Our Nation derives its strength not from huge pavilions, sky-scrapers or freeways, but from a diversity of its cultures and heri-tages, and, above all, from a guarantee of its freedoms. Against this legacy of richness of diversity, why should we expect a single "centerpiece"? My response is that the "centerpiece" of our Bicen-tennial will be in the form of a unique mosaic of these thousands of little cornerstones.

This mosaic "centerpiece" will rest on the same foundation which has enabled this Nation to become the oldest surviving democratic republic on earth—the Declaration of Independence, the Constitution, and the Bill of Rights.[35]

These documents, treated more as totems than as texts, would also play a central role in the opening event of the Bicentennial Weekend, co-sponsored by ARBA and the National Archives. On July 2, 1976, these "three basic documents of democracy" were honored in ceremonies at the National Archives featuring President Ford, Vice President Rockefeller, Speaker of the House Carl Albert, and Chief Justice War-ren Burger. Intended to "set a reflective tone for Bicentennial celebrations around the country," the ceremony began a "76-hour vigil" during which the documents were put on public display. Members of the public who saw the documents could sign an official register, which was put in a time capsule to be opened at the Tricentennial in 2076.[36]

In addition to the foundational documents, ARBA statements tended to emphasize the "revolutionary spirit." Unlike the PBC, which called for a *new* revolution against forces in twentieth-century American life that it likened to the British monarchy in 1776, ARBA saw the *original* revolu-tion as an ongoing process. ARBA statements invoked the language of revolution not so much to urge change as to raise the spirits of a nation that ARBA—and others—felt had entered a period of malaise. Neverthe-less, rhetoric supporting this vision could sound unintentionally radical. "Cultural Revolution Gains Momentum in America" announced one 1974 ARBA press release promoting Bicentennial arts programs.[37] Another press release began with an exemplary quotation from a seventeen-year-old high school senior in Connecticut: "The American Revolution didn't begin on Lexington Green and didn't end in Yorktown. We need much more than a big party on the Fourth of July, 1976—we need a continuing program to maintain the spirit of a permanent revolution dedicated to human freedom."[38]

Warner told the U.S. Conference of Mayors that he detected "an exciting mystique" in the "ever-increasing surge for Bicentennial celebration and commemoration." Out of the "dismal swamp" of Watergate and a rededication to the "great instruments" of our democracy—the Declaration, Constitution, and Bill of Rights—would come a renewal of the revolutionary spirit, a fact that Warner suggested had even taken him by surprise:

> As one of your constituents said only recently to me, "You, Mr. Warner, have the opportunity to be a revolutionary hero." I snapped back and retorted that I entertained no such ambitions whatsoever for heroic worship. I desired only to achieve a reputation for public trust in a Bureaucrat; further, I didn't believe we needed another revolution. He came right back at me: "Either lead or step aside for we are in a revolution—not one of force and violence but one of the hearts and minds seeing greater fulfillment." His final awakening punch to me was: "In 1776 the cry was 'Give me Liberty or give me death.' Today it is 'Give me greater fulfillment for the liberty I have.'"[39]

But while emphasizing that a renewed revolutionary spirit was essential, to counteract the malaise that many felt was gripping the country, ARBA, in marked contrast to the PBC, made a point of saying that the Bicentennial would not be about further social reform.

What almost never appeared in ARBA statements was history that went beyond generalities about founding principles, and even these were not discussed in depth. Indeed, ARBA managed to generate some bad press for itself when a pamphlet it published for children told a false story of James Madison signing the Declaration of Independence.[40] Far from producing a definitive vision of what the Bicentennial was celebrating, ARBA frequently emphasized that the celebration was a collective effort and that each individual American had to come up with his or her own view of what was being celebrated. In response to a letter from Ronald Van Nostrand, who was trying to promote the public's signing of a new Declaration of Americans, Warner wrote to disagree with the proposal:

"No single statement, it seems, can entirely encompass the meaning to all Americans of what the Bicentennial commemorates. For that reason we are extremely reluctant to select any one declaration as official in the context of the entire commemoration."[41] Indeed, ARBA often emphasized that every single American had a role to play in defining the Bicentennial. "The American Bicentennial is in reality the activity of a committee of 215 million people with each American taking part according to his or her own interest or inclination," declared Warner in October 1975.[42]

ARBA's vision of the Bicentennial was certainly more positive than *Nashville*'s emphasis on its characters'—and the nation's—stoic perseverance in the face of tragedy. But Warner's habit of gesturing toward the "spirit of revolution" and the "three basic documents of democracy," the precise meanings of which he rarely discussed, shared some of the emptiness of *Nashville*'s invocations of the American past. Both ARBA and *Nashville* saw in the celebration of the Bicentennial a possible path out of conflicts and social doubts that each associated with the changes wrought by the Sixties. But, in both cases, what the past offered was largely sentimental. While *Nashville*'s characters found strength to carry on by recalling surviving past crises, ARBA presented the past as offering a spirit of revolution and foundational documents the very existence of which was supposed to inspire patriotic faith. Neither offered a coherent account of the Founding that the Bicentennial celebrated. And Warner went out of his way to deny that such an account was even necessary.

## Academic Historians and the Bicentennial

ARBA's vision of the Bicentennial did not much appeal to professional historians. Jesse Lemisch dismissed as "Bicentennial schlock" what John Warner saw as the wonders of free enterprise. And while Warner celebrated 215 million Americans each having their own understanding of the meaning of the Bicentennial, Milton M. Klein found troubling the lack of a consensus over what the American Revolution meant. However, even in the absence of such a consensual narrative, the Bicentennial year saw an explosion of books and articles about the history of the Revolutionary era.[43] On the eve of the Bicentennial, the *New York Times* even feared that this "deluge" of books might be "a bit too much."[44] With the help of grants from ARBC and, later, ARBA, local history projects flourished, though the historian Michael Kammen worried that, even among scholars themselves, local historians and historians of the American Revolution as such were not much communicating with each other.[45]

During the decade or so leading up to the Bicentennial, professional historians produced a plethora of important work on the American Revolution, much of which fell into two strands. On the one hand, historians like Gordon Wood (*The Creation of the American Republic, 1776–1787* [1969]). Bernard Bailyn (*The Ideological Origins of the American Revolution* [1967]), and Pauline Maier (*From Resistance to Revolution* [1972]) focused on the ideological origins of the Revolution. Overturning the older view that Lockean liberalism, plain and simple, had provided the ideological content of the Revolution, these historians argued that a republican tradition, concerned with virtue, corruption, and power, provided a much more important ideological basis for Revolutionary political culture. By 1972, the historian Richard Shalhope declared in the pages of the *William & Mary Quarterly*, the premier journal in early American history, that a new "republican synthesis" had emerged. "Hopefully," Shalhope concluded, "an understanding of republicanism might open the door to new insights about American society."[46]

Meanwhile, a second strain of important new scholarship on the Revolutionary era emerged from the new social history, which was arguably the most significant methodological movement in the academic field of history during the late 1960s and early 1970s. As Laurence Veysey described it in a 1979 review essay, the new social history held "that history should be viewed in terms of the processes affecting the great majority of people alive at any given time, with special attention to the anonymously downtrodden, those whose standard of living and prestige are the lowest (this corollary helped build a specious bridge toward Marxism), and that the historian should be intensely skeptical of literary sources of evidence, always the product of a small elite, instead making use of whatever bare quantitative data exist to assure that one's conclusions are truly representative of the social aggregate being discussed."[47] While social historians wrote frequently about the Revolutionary period during the decade leading up to the Bicentennial, they did not produce a new, general understanding of the Revolution itself to rival that of the intellectual and political historians associated with the republican synthesis.[48] Nevertheless, the new social history also helped encourage academic work on the Revolutionary period.

But these exciting developments in the professional study of the American Revolution had relatively little impact on the federal government's Bicentennial celebrations. "The entire historical profession is waiting impatiently and with increasing skepticism for [ARBC] to do something that bears a direct relationship to Independence and the American Revolution," wrote Stephen Kurtz, the director of the Institute of Early American History and Culture (now the Omohundro Institute of Early American History and Culture) at the College of William and Mary, in June 1971, to David Hansen, the program officer for the ARBC's Heritage '76 initiative, the aspect of the planned Bicentennial celebration to focus on history. Although describing himself as "entirely kindly disposed" toward Hansen and the ARBC, Kurtz was obviously upset at the apparent lack of effort to reach out to historians.[49]

Eventually, ARBC did assemble an advisory committee for the Heritage '76 initiative. ARBC considered inviting an extraordinarily wide and impressive—and at times surprising—array of scholars and intellectuals to take part, including Theodore Lowi, Jackson Turner Main, Forrest McDonald, Gary Nash, Oscar Handlin, Bernard Bailyn, Mary Maples Dunn, John Hope Franklin, Alan Heimert, Robert Dahl, Peter Gay, Jack Greene, and Hannah Arendt. A number of scholars with strong ties to the left, including Staughton Lynd, Jesse Lemisch, Aileen Kraditor, and William Appleman Williams, even seem to have been considered as members.[50] The twelve-person Heritage '76 advisory committee eventually included, among its members, three professional historians: Mary Maples Dunn, Richard McCormick, and George A. Billias.[51] But little came of its efforts. After ARBC gave way to ARBA, which focused less on generating national celebrations and more on fostering local ones, this committee languished.

A session devoted to the Bicentennial celebrations at the 1974 Organization of American Historians Meeting in Denver, Colorado, which took place that April, shortly after the creation of ARBA, proved quite hostile to the new federal Bicentennial agency. Dr. James Robertson, chair of the Virginia Tech History Department and the final speaker at this session, was particularly incensed, repeating the ugly history of accusations of cronyism associated with the recently disbanded ARBC. Attending the event as ARBA's representative, program officer Martin Goldman, who that very month had also visited ISU in preparation for Warner's visit, became so frustrated with Robertson that at one point he interrupted the presentation from the audience and, by his own account, declared about one accusation, "Sir, that is a damnable lie." After the session, Goldman's complaints to the organizer that ARBA had not been invited to take part apparently fell on deaf ears.

As frustrated as historians were with the federal agency responsible for the Bicentennial, ARBA, in turn, felt frustrated by them. Goldman completed his memo to his superiors on the Organization of American Historians session with a few choice words about academic historians:

> As an historian and a former member of the academic community, I believe that the historians have an extremely narrow focus of [sic] what the Bicentennial era really is about. The profession seems to be under the impression that all the Bicentennial means is that scholars will get together and hack over the American Revolution, once again, by publishing or republishing long, dead doctoral dissertations, or newly conceived histories. While I am not at all against such activity, the scholarly community must be made, somehow, to realize that the Bicentennial is far more than rewriting the history of the American Revolution. It consists of far more than rehashing, at scholarly symposia, their theories of the American Revolution ad nauseum. Such a narrow focus, whether on the state or national or even local level, only involves historians and excludes the wider community of Americans that is ARBA's goal to include in the Bicentennial era. While I am not sure what the Bicentennial is, I am quite sure of what it is not—and it is not the exclusive preserve of the American historical profession no matter how loudly they scream.[52]

Goldman's admission that he was "not sure what the Bicentennial is" is especially interesting. The disagreement between ARBA and academic historians was not so much over the meaning of the Bicentennial as it was over whether arriving at any sort of agreement over its meaning was necessary and whether academic historians should be seen as anything more than an insignificant minority of the "committee of 215 million people" that John Warner suggested should direct the celebration.

From ARBA's perspective the problem with academic historians was not merely their exclusive claim to expertise. While ARBA was, above all, interested in highlighting heroic and positive aspects of the American past, all the better to work through the crises facing America in the 1970s, academic historians usually saw unheroic aspects of the past through the lens of those contemporary crises. Edmund S. Morgan, one of the most distinguished historians of the period, summed up the situation nicely at the beginning of his review of Bernard Bailyn's *The Ordeal of Thomas Hutchinson* for the March 21, 1974, issue of the *New York Review of Books*:

> As the bicentennial of the American Revolution approaches, historians are in no mood to celebrate. On the left, they are busy seeking out the role of the inarticulate masses who were somehow forgotten or betrayed by the gentlemen who ran the show. On the right, historians who survived the activities of would-be campus revolutionaries in the Sixties have difficulty seeing the merits of the Boston Tea Party. And the hard-core liberals who make up most of the academic establishment, if they honor the wisdom of the founding fathers, wish to dissociate them as far as possible from the morally bankrupt government that claims its descent from them.

Indeed, Morgan continued, as the book he was reviewing suggested, many historians from across the political spectrum had begun to feel sympathy for the "losers in the American game, whether of the 1970s or the 1770s."[53]

## Conclusion: Looking Back and Looking Forward from the Bicentennial

When July 4, 1976, arrived, despite years of concern on the part of many about the way America was planning for the occasion, the celebrations of the Bicentennial were surprisingly successful. "Nation and Millions in City Joyously Hail Bicentennial" read the banner headline in the *New*

*York Times* the following day. Looking back four decades later, the historian Rick Perlstein has noted both the felt success of the celebrations and the expressions of surprise about that success on the part of many observers. Perlstein argues that July 4, 1976, was a kind of sentimental tipping point for the nation, a moment when, suddenly, Americans discovered that "it wasn't so hard to unapologetically celebrate America, after all."[54]

Like all anniversaries, the Bicentennial was, in the first instance, about looking backward. However, historians who have studied it in recent years see the seeds of the immediate future in its success. Tammy Stone Gordon, author of *The Spirit of 1976*, the first scholarly monograph on the Bicentennial, is, like Perlstein, upbeat in her assessment of the celebration. Both Gordon and Perlstein see the cultural tone of the Reagan years as flowing from the powerful, but diffuse, patriotism that characterized America's Bicentennial celebrations. Not only were Americans brought together, Gordon suggests, but they also felt empowered to think historically. The very decentralized nature of the national Bicentennial celebration under ARBA as well as the "do-your-own-thing" spirit of the 1970s led people to understand that "individuals working in groups . . . controlled the meanings of history."[55] The historian M. J. Rymsza-Pawlowska places the Bicentennial celebrations and the public debate about them in the middle of a shift in America's public historical consciousness from a "logic of preservation" focused on material evidence of the past and the study of historical narratives that stand apart from the present to a "logic of reenactment" that produced knowledge affectively and experientially, a shift that opened up new spaces for historical expression.[56] The historian Daniel Rodgers has identified a similar shift in the way that Americans viewed the past during the last quarter of the twentieth century. Rodgers argues that, by the 1980s, Americans of all different political stripes came to see the past in ways that were immediate and often uncomplicated. Historical time, Rodgers argues, became "wrinkled" and "compressed," allowing the past to be brought to bear directly on the present, in, among many other cultural spaces, Reagan's speeches, originalist Supreme Court jurisprudence, Civil War reenactments, and national history education standards.[57]

But one thing was very different about the Bicentennial's relationship to the American past from what was to come in the 1980s. "However one tried it," writes Rodgers, "by the end of the 1980s, bringing the historical past into the present meant ending up in a nest of controversies."[58] This was not yet the case in 1976. Controversies certainly attended Bicentennial planning in the United States. And observers, including the leadership of ARBA itself, well understood that the divisions and crises of the 1960s and early 1970s made the task of bringing the nation together through the celebration of its founding tricky. Nevertheless, by farming out much of the celebration to a diffuse "committee of 215 million" and by keeping its pronouncements about the meaning of the American Revolution and its legacy extraordinarily general, ARBA managed to a great extent to transcend the divisions and controversies and encourage a celebration that brought much of the nation together, albeit one that left historians like Jesse Lemisch and Milton M. Klein frustrated about its emptiness.

# 4

## Family Stories and the African American Past in Alex Haley's *Roots* and Octavia Butler's *Kindred*

Among the groups that often felt excluded even from the very generalized patriotism of the Bicentennial celebrations were African Americans. Beyond ritual invocations of Crispus Attucks, the Black sailor who is often considered to be the first American killed in the Revolutionary War, fitting the African American experience into the broad-stroke, upbeat stories about the nation's founding that dominated the Bicentennial proved challenging. Indeed, one of the most frequent criticisms leveled at the Nixon and Ford administrations' planning for the Bicentennial involved their failure to engage African American history and the African American community. This criticism was one of the areas explored during the August 1972 Senate hearings that helped lead to the dissolution of American Revolution Bicentennial Commission (ARBC), though the Nixon administration proudly emphasized that one in ten members of ARBC was Black.[1] Although both ARBC and its successor agency, the American Revolution Bicentennial Administration (ARBA), put African Americans—including eventually Malcolm X's widow Betty Shabazz—on official committees, to many in the African American community, these efforts never seemed to rise above the level of tokenism. In February 1973, Barbara Diggs, an African American program officer with ARBC, even wrote to the Schomburg Center for Research in Black Culture in New York to express her frustration with ARBC's efforts in incorporating the Black experience in its planning.[2] Outside of the auspices of the official Bicentennial celebrations, a number of private organizations, including the Association for the Study of African American Life and History, planned Black-oriented Bicentennial programming.[3]

One of the most celebrated Black responses to the Bicentennial more directly expressed anger at the celebration. Stand-up comedian Richard Pryor won a 1977 Grammy for his album *Bicentennial N——*, which was released in September 1976. The title track begins with Pryor's asking, "Y'all know how Black humor started? It started in the slave ships, you know. Cat was on his way here rowing. Dude say, 'What you laughing about?' 'Yesterday, I was a king!'" While Pryor begins with this bitter, private joke within the African American community, he quickly switches to imagining a performance for the white community: "They're having a Bicentennial. 200 years! Gonna have a Bicentennial N——. They will. They're gonna have some n——, two-hundred years old, in blackface. With stars and stripes on his forehead. . . . And he'll have that lovely white-folks expression on his face. But he's happy! He happy 'cause he's been here 200 years!" For the rest of the routine, Pryor performs as this character, shuckin' and jivin' his way through the horrors of African American history, laughing all the way. The bit is powerful, but despairing. It suggests a deep connection between African American humor and African American history, but also suggests that white Americans cannot take seriously Black suffering in that history. Pryor suggests that, while Black humor for African Americans has always been a survival mechanism, for white Americans it can be a way of papering over the past.[4]

But despite the fraught relationship of the Black experience to the Bicentennial itself, 1976 would prove to be a crucial year for the public memory of the African American past. In August 1976, a little over a month after the nation celebrated its two-hundredth birthday, Alex Haley's *Roots: The Saga of an American Family* was published. As a noted journalist and the author of *The Autobiography of Malcolm X* (1965), Haley was already a nationally known figure; indeed, President Ford had named him to the ARBA advisory council in 1975. But his second book would catapult him to a new level of fame. The product of more than a decade of work, *Roots*—first as a book and, five months later, as a television miniseries—quickly became a cornerstone of the public memory of the African American experience, in general, and of slavery, in particular. Although Haley had originally hoped to publish the book in the late 1960s, he ended up dedicating it "as a birthday offering to my country." In a year in which the nation focused on its founding, it would become far and away the year's best-selling book that touched on that period of the American past.

Haley's *Roots* not only presented his family's story as a representative saga of the African American experience, but it also made an argument about the promise of history for contemporary African Americans. In *Roots*, Haley foregrounded his family's preservation of its own history through oral traditions that stretched back to Africa before slavery and concluded his book with his own tale of researching the details of that history. Family history, Haley suggested, is a more available resource for African Americans than they had generally thought it to be. And, properly understood, his family's story, and by extension the African American experience, is a story of preservation of tradition and triumph over the abomination of slavery. In *Roots*, the African American past is legible and empowering. Haley suggests a much more affirmative view of the relationship of the Black past to American history than more pessimistic figures like Richard Pryor did. African Americans, *Roots* suggests, by uncovering their family histories and celebrating stories of surviving and overcoming slavery, can both develop deeper senses of Black identity and—as the book's subtitle, *The Saga of an American Family*, suggests—lay claim to participating in a larger American narrative of perseverance like that embraced by the mostly white characters of Robert Altman's *Nashville*.

Three years later, in 1979, the African American science fiction author Octavia Butler would publish *Kindred*, a novel that, through a plot involving time travel, explores the relationship of a present-day African American woman to her family's past under slavery. While *Kindred* was not the immediate publishing phenomenon that *Roots* had been, it became—and remains—Butler's most critically acclaimed and commercially successful work. The narrator and protagonist, Dana Franklin, finds herself mysteriously transported into the past. For Dana, the history of slavery is even more palpable and immediate than it is for Alex Haley in *Roots*. But her encounters with history produce the opposite effect. Facing the past in *Kindred* is both psychologically and physically destructive. Dana's very sanity, the novel ultimately suggests, is dependent on her ability to put it entirely behind her.

This chapter will explore Haley's and Butler's very different arguments about the meaning of the African American past for Black Americans in the 1970s. Both *Roots* and *Kindred* present the family histories of their Black protagonists as quintessentially American stories. And both suggest that Black identities in the 1970s are bound to the history of enslavement through which the families in each book pass. Where they differ most profoundly is in their sense of what knowledge of that past is possible and what the impact of that knowledge might be for African Americans in the 1970s. Haley sees the African American past as surprisingly legible. Knowledge of that past, for Haley, is profoundly liberating, allowing him to find a deeper sense of identity by connecting to his family's culture in Africa prior to his ancestors being kidnapped, enslaved, and sent to America. One foundation of the enormous popular success of *Roots* was that it offered the promise of such liberatory, identity-forming knowledge to other African Americans as well. In *Kindred*, Octavia Butler presents a much more pessimistic sense of the possibilities of the past for her African American contemporaries. Despite literally traveling back in time, *Kindred*'s protagonist Dana Franklin ends up with a much murkier understanding of her family's past than Haley claims to achieve of his. And what knowledge she does attain is not at all liberating. If anything, it troubles her sense of identity. Despite these crucial differences, one other factor binds these two books together and to the larger theme of this book: both *Roots* and *Kindred* grew out of their respective author's grappling with, and largely rejecting, the politics of race in the Sixties.

## *Before This Anger* and the Roots of *Roots*

In an interview published early in 1977, the freelance journalist Paul Bernstein asked Alex Haley about the connection between *Roots* and the Sixties, the decade in which Haley had begun to work on the project: "Going through the civil rights movement and the urban riots and the rise of black nationalism during the long period you worked on *Roots*— did those processes affect your thinking on the book?" Haley's response began with a simple denial: "No, those things which are happening here didn't. My mind was so thoroughly in the 1700s that I wasn't concerned in that sense." But hints of some of the connections between Haley's book and the decade in which it was conceived appeared in the rest of Haley's reply: "I was aware, needless to say, of what was going on here, and in some ways was part of it. I wrote *The Autobiography of Malcolm X*. But I think that being a sort of historical buff by nature, tending to see what was happening in the '60s in the context of its having evolved from the 1700s, I was seeing the natural cries and protests of the descendants of the people I was writing about."[5] Haley's response reflects the complicated connection between his initial conceptualization of *Roots* and the politics of race in the decade in which it was born, but it significantly understates the relationship between the upheavals of the Sixties and the project that became *Roots*.

In 1964, while still working on *The Autobiography of Malcolm X*, the book that would first make him famous, Haley was already thinking seriously about his next major project. Haley had spent much of his early childhood in the 1920s in Henning, Tennessee, his mother's hometown. His maternal grandfather, Will Palmer, ran a local lumber company, an unusual position for an African American in the segregated South. As Haley's biographer Robert J. Norrell notes, despite Henning's being a typical Mississippi Delta town in which African Americans lived under conditions of extraordinary discrimination punctuated by bouts of deadly violence, in Haley's youthful experience "blacks were not treated harshly but were just considered to be different from whites."[6] As battles over racial justice grew in intensity during the 1950s and early 1960s, Haley grew interested in writing about the Henning of his youth, first in short stories and later, he hoped, in a novel. By 1964, this project had become an idea for a novel about racial relations in the South in the 1930s and had acquired the title *Before This Anger*. In August of that year, he pitched it to his editor at Doubleday, Kenneth McCormick. Haley contrasted the world in which his novel would be set to the urban unrest dominating the news that summer. McCormick liked the idea, noting that it would be "a book Southerners will read with appreciation. . . . A book that exposes the warmth and love of the south."[7] Doubleday gave him an advance contract for the project.

Over the course of 1964, however, Haley became interested in exploring the deeper history of his family. When Haley was a child, his older relatives in Henning had told stories of an African ancestor kidnapped into slavery named "Kin-tay." And the family had passed down some of the African words that he was said to have used. By early 1965, *Before This Anger* had transformed into a work of family history. On January 30, 1965, Haley wrote a long, excited letter to his literary agent Paul Reynolds about his new project. Haley had just returned from Kansas, where his younger brother, George, had been sworn in as a state senator. At the family gathering in Kansas, Haley had spoken at length with "some of the family's elders." And he'd already assembled a sweeping account of his family's journey from freedom in Africa, to slavery in the United States, to renewed freedom—and success—after slavery. Though the four-thousand-word synopsis of this family story provided to Reynolds early in 1965 differs in important respects from the narrative that would eventually appear in *Roots*—for example, he had yet to identify Kunta Kinte by name, calling him "the Mandingo" in these early exchanges with Reynolds—the general shape and purpose of the project were already substantially in place. "You know, Paul?" Haley concluded, "In America, I think, there has not been such a book. 'Rooting' a Negro family, all the way back, telling the chronicle, through us, of how the Negro is part and parcel of the American saga. Without rancor, which I do not feel, which has not been my experience in any influencing way. It is a book which I so deeply feel that America, the world, *needs* to read. For its drama, for its authentic image, for other reasons. I shall write it, when I get to the writing, with love."[8] This statement of purpose shows Haley very much thinking about the project that would become *Roots* as bearing a particular relationship to the heated racial politics of his day, which would only intensify during the second half of the decade. Though no longer focused on an idealized portrait of the 1930s South, *Before This*

*Anger* was still conceived as an answer to the racial conflicts of the 1960s. Avoiding rancor and writing with love were key components of what Haley had in mind for this new project, as his retention of the book's original title suggested.

In early correspondence about *Before This Anger,* Haley expressed a hope of finishing the book quickly, so its appearance could mark precisely two centuries since his family arrived in America. "It must get published in 1966," Haley wrote Reynolds in the middle of 1965, "the even 200 years since the Mandingo was landed."[9] But work on the book dragged on, as Haley expanded his research and his expected completion date slowly crept forward. Haley's agent and editors at Doubleday and *Reader's Digest,* which was funding much of Haley's research in exchange for publishing condensed excerpts from the book, remained enthusiastic about the project, even as it never seemed to get finished.[10]

## The Publication and Impact of *Roots*

While the book was not completed in time to mark the two-hundredth anniversary of his family in America, when it finally appeared in the middle of 1976, the United States was celebrating its own two-hundredth anniversary. This was a happy accident and Haley seized on it in the book's dedication: "It wasn't planned that *Roots'* researching and writing finally would take twelve years. Just by chance it is being published in the Bicentennial Year of the United States. So I dedicate *Roots* as a birthday offering to my country within which most of *Roots* happened."[11] *Roots* finally appeared in American bookstores in August 1976. James Baldwin began his lyrical and largely celebratory review of *Roots* for the *New York Times Book Review* on a note of concern regarding how Haley's book would be received:

> I cannot guess what Alex Haley's countrymen will make of his birthday present to us during this election and Bicentennial year. One is tempted to say that it could scarcely have come at a more awkward time—what with conventions, the exhibition of candidates, the dubious state of the particular and perhaps increasingly dubious union, and the American attempt, hopeless and predictably schizophrenic, of preventing total disaster for white people

and for the West, in South Africa. There is a carefully muffled pain and panic in the nation, which neither candidate, neither party can coherently address, being themselves, but vivid symptoms of it.[12]

Baldwin's concerns proved largely unfounded. As Haley's biographer Robert J. Norell notes, *Roots* in many ways could not have arrived at a better time. The Bicentennial had spurred interest in American history in general. Jimmy Carter's surprising ascendency to the Democratic nomination had helped increase public fascination with the South. And *Roots* also appeared as Americans had begun searching for their family's origins and reinterpreting their identities based on what they found. *World of Our Fathers*, Irving Howe's popular history of Eastern European Jewish immigration to America, had appeared earlier in 1976, to much popular and critical success.[13] Theodore Solotaroff, reviewing Howe's book for the *New York Times Book Review*, recommended the volume to non-Jewish readers—calling it "a great book . . . a work of history and of art"—but thought that it would have special meaning for Jewish Americans: "If you are Jewish you will also realize that Howe has written a necessary book, particularly for those of you who need its blow on the head to deliver you from your amnesia or, better, to help you begin to rescue yourself. . . . For this life, as you will see, still lives—right behind your sense of your own distinctive mind and heart and face. And slowly you will begin to understand."[14] Solotaroff's hopes echoed the broader ways in which history had become personal and local during the Bicentennial.

Despite Baldwin's concerns, *Roots* became an enormous popular and critical success. *Roots* entered the general nonfiction bestseller list in October and by November was the number-one nonfiction bestseller in America. The book's sales would get a huge boost in January 1977, when the ABC miniseries based on it became a surprise sensation. The standard practice for miniseries before *Roots* was to run one episode a week for a couple months. But Fred Silverman, the innovative president of ABC who had already rescued that network from the ratings doldrums through the success of *Happy Days* and *Laverne & Shirley*, decided to air the show in episodes of one or two hours in length on eight consecutive nights, from January 23 to January 30. This transformed *Roots* from a normal miniseries into a special television event.

Nevertheless, the strategy was risky. Though *Roots* was already a best-selling book that had reached both Black and white readers, would viewers appreciate eight consecutive nights of television on such a potentially controversial topic as slavery, which television had up until then largely avoided? By scheduling *Roots* for January, Silverman was, in effect, hedging his bets; the show would end before February's ratings sweeps period. But *Roots* succeeded as a miniseries beyond anyone's hopes. Audiences, large from the first night, continued to grow over the course of the series. It was the top-rated show each night of its initial run. Its average rating was 35.5 percent (i.e., an estimated 35.5 percent of all televisions in America were, on average, showing *Roots*). The finale of the miniseries received a 71 percent share (i.e., 71 percent of all televisions in use were tuned to *Roots*), making it, at the time, the all-time highest-rated entertainment program. No fewer than 135 million people, out of a total U.S. population of around 220 million, had seen at least some of the show. These were extraordinary numbers. But they only hinted at the cultural phenomenon that *Roots* became.[15]

Since 1977, *Roots*, as both book and television show, has remained a vital text in American culture. Though *Roots* was seen at the time as transforming television, its impact beyond that medium has, if anything, been even greater. For many readers and viewers, *Roots* provided an unusually intensive exposure to African American history in general and the history of slavery in particular. Educational researchers found that *Roots* had an enormous positive impact on children who had viewed the program, noting that it increased interest in and knowledge of African American history, encouraged students to critically examine their own racial attitudes, and even encouraged the development of "inquiry skills to recognize and evaluate bias in the treatment of complex and controversial issues."[16] Almost immediately, colleges began to build curricula around *Roots*, both to encourage interest in the history of slavery and to encourage students to explore their own families' genealogy.[17] Beyond the classroom, too, *Roots* encouraged Americans, and especially African Americans, to delve into their family histories. The African American historian and literary critic Henry Louis Gates Jr.'s PBS television show *Finding Your Roots*, which began airing in 2012, is a direct descendant of Haley's book. "You can say I had a severe case of *Roots* envy," Gates has said.[18] The book itself has been continuously in print; the miniseries has been repeatedly rerun, was widely available on videocassette, and is now widely available both on physical media and via streaming services. In 2016, the History Channel remade the miniseries.

## Controversies over the Truth of *Roots*

But despite its canonical role in American culture, *Roots* was, for decades, largely ignored by academics. Excerpts from *Roots* have never appeared in any of the three editions (1996, 2004, 2014) of the nearly three-thousand-page-long *Norton Anthology of African American Literature*, of which the *Roots*-envious Henry Louis Gates Jr. was and is general editor.[19] And until the second decade of the twenty-first century, there was very little scholarly work on Haley. The first serious biography of the author came out in 2015. There are a variety of reasons for this scholarly neglect, despite the text's obvious impact. First, *Roots* is distinctly middlebrow, in its style and sprawling form. Though Haley's writing can be effective in places, even critics who praised the book often criticized Haley's stiff dialog and awkward habit of introducing historical background material through conversations among his enslaved characters. The book's essential connection to a television show at a time in which that entire medium was still often casually dismissed as a vast cultural wasteland probably hurt its scholarly reputation as well.

The book's erstwhile critical neglect also reflects a set of controversies that have swirled around *Roots* nearly from the moment of its publication.[20] First, the accuracy of *Roots* was called into question. British journalist Mark Ottaway decided to go to Gambia to research a story about the effect *Roots* was having on the country in which Haley had done much of his research and from which Kunta Kinte had been kidnapped. While there, he became convinced that Kebba Fofana, the Gambian who had been the source of much of what Haley claimed to know about Kunta Kinte, was not a true griot and was unreliable. Furthermore, Ottaway argued, Haley had done a poor job checking the facts that he was told. Ottaway began to chase down other pieces of Haley's research and he discovered that it was similarly sloppy. On April 10, 1977, Ottaway's article "Tangled Roots" appeared in *The Times* of London.

To these apparent problems of accuracy were soon added accusations that Haley had plagiarized material from other books. First, the African American novelist Margaret Walker accused Haley of lifting up to thirty-five passages from her literary novel *Jubilee* (1966), about an enslaved woman during the Civil War. Soon she was joined by the folklorist and novelist Harold Courlander, who claimed that there were over eighty instances of theft from his novel *The African* (1967), which concerns a young African boy kidnapped into slavery and brought to the Americas. Each author took Haley to court. In September 1978, Walker's case was summarily dismissed. The Courlander case began that November and dragged on for six weeks. Apparently concerned that the ongoing suit was itself hurting his reputation, Haley settled with Courlander out of court on December 14, 1978. Haley admitted to accidental borrowing; Courlander was paid an undisclosed amount.

Over the years, accusations that *Roots* was inaccurate grew. In 1981, Gary Mills, a historian at the University of Alabama—and according to Haley biographer Robert J. Norrell an active neo-Confederate—and his wife, Elizabeth Shown Mills, a genealogist, called into question many of the details of the Virginia portion of the family history that Haley recounts in *Roots*. That same year, Donald R. Wright, a historian of Gambia at the State University of New York at Courtland, spoke with Kebba Fofana about Kunta Kinte and doubted what he was told, much of which also contradicted what Fofana had told Haley.[21]

But Norrell suggests that the single most decisive piece in discouraging scholarship on Haley has been Philip Nobile's "Uncovering Roots," published in the *Village Voice* in 1993, a year after Haley's death.[22] Nobile accused Haley of knowingly passing on fiction as truth. *Roots*, Nobile argued, was "a hoax . . . a Piltdown of genealogy." Though Nobile's piece made scholars wary of *Roots* and was taken up by some conservative culture warriors, Norrell argues that it has had little effect in the popular assessment of the book and the miniseries.[23]

## The Importance of Telling the Family Story in *Roots*

*Roots* is a book about many things, most obviously the African American experience, especially slavery, and Alex Haley's family history. But it is also about the importance of the past and one's relationship to it.

From the beginning of the book, the central characters tell and are told stories of their family's past. Early in the book, when Kunta Kinte is still a young child in Africa, sick in a time of famine, his Grandma Yaisa tells him "slowly and softly" about his grandfather, Kairaba Kunta Kinte, who died before Kunta was born and who was a Muslim holy man originally from Mauretania. Yaisa narrates his story in some detail, right up to the point that he meets and marries Yaisa herself and she gives birth to Kunta's father Omoro.[24] Haley underscores the importance of this moment through Kunta's reflections on it:

> That night in his mother's hut, Kunta lay awake for a long time, thinking of the things that Grandma Yaisa had told him. Many times, Kunta had heard about the grandfather holy man whose prayers had saved the village, and whom later Allah had taken back. But Kunta never truly understood until now that this man was his father's father, that Omoro had known him as he knew Omoro, that Grandma Yaisa was Omoro's mother as Binta was his own. Some day, he too would find a woman such as Binta to bear him a son of his own. And that son in turn . . . [25]

This moment captures many of the essential elements of the role that family history plays in *Roots*. First, the story is transmitted orally, relative to relative. Haley draws attention to the oral nature of this history by having Yaisa gesture at a pile of Kairaba Kunta Kinte's books in her hut. There is writing in Kunta's home village of Juffure; Kunta Kinte will later learn to read and write Koranic verses.[26] But *history* in this culture is oral. Part of what gives Yaisa's narrative its power for Kunta is that the speaker is transmitting experiences that she herself has had with people that she knew personally, but that the hearer could not have had and could not have known. Kunta knows Yaisa and Omoro. And knowing them, his hearing Yaisa tell her personal experience of his grandfather brings him closer to Karaiba Kunta Kinte, a figure whose deeds he had heard about many times before but whom he never had "truly understood" in relation to himself. Finally, the story of Karaiba Kunta Kinte, transmitted to Kunta Kinte by an older relative who knew him, makes Kunta understand that he himself is part of this river of family history. And he realizes that one day he, too, will have a wife and a child, and presumably they will hear history from him.

Kunta's dream of continuing the Kinte clan in Juffure will be dashed by his being kidnapped into slavery. But that horrific experience only makes his transmission of the family history that much more important. Kunta resists all aspects of the culture he finds in America. He avoids speaking English, he refuses to eat pork, he rejects Christianity and secretly practices Islam. Though given the name "Toby," he continues to call himself Kunta Kinte. And he constantly plots escaping to freedom. Only when he turns thirty-nine does he fall for Bell, the plantation cook whom he had already known for years. Kunta's continuing attachment to things African becomes a source of constant tension in their marriage. Eventually, he teaches her some Mandinka words.

When their daughter is born, he insists on giving her an African name, Kizzy, which means "stay put," in the hopes that she won't be sold away. Bell resists the idea, fearful that Massa Waller will disapprove, though she eventually relents and convinces Waller to let her use the name, which she claims comes from *her* family. And Kunta vows that, though her last name will be "Waller," he will make sure that she "grow[s] up knowing her own true name."[27] As if to underscore this point, Kunta later reflects on the death of an old gardener on the Waller plantation, whose name Kunta had never known until he hears it at his funeral (it was "Josephus"). But Kunta "wondered what the gardener's true name had been—the name of his African forefathers—and to what tribe they had belonged. He wondered if the gardener himself had known. More likely he had died as he had lived—without ever learning who he truly was."[28] For Kunta, knowing one's African name and family history is the key to identity, without which one cannot be one's true self.

Kizzy's own connection to Africa through familial oral tradition becomes central to *her* identity, as well. Kunta teaches Kizzy African words in her infancy. One day, she suddenly calls him "fa" (father), to his great delight.[29] This is, in fact, the first moment in which Kizzy appears as anything but a rather distant object of Kunta's concern. Her speaking Mandinka in effect turns her into a human being. As Kizzy grows up, Kunta feels his greatest love for her immediately after he teaches her Mandinka words for various things in the Virginia landscape.[30] He tells her about her ancestors and Juffure.[31] But ultimately, she gets sold away, suddenly and horrifically, in punishment for trying to help her boyfriend Noah escape.

Kizzy's connection to her family's African past allows her to survive the trauma of being raped by her new enslaver Tom Lea, a rape that occurs immediately after she becomes the protagonist of *Roots* following her being sold away.[32] From this rape, a child is born, whom Kizzy does not even get to name, as Lea insists that she call him "George" after "the hardest working n——I ever saw."[33] Lea's insistence on the name "George" leads Kizzy to reflect on her own Africanness, knowledge of which she had received from her parents:

> She lay thinking of how she never understood why her pappy had always felt so bitter against the world of white people—"toubob" was his word for them. She thought of Bell's saying to her "You's so lucky it scare me, chile, 'cause you don' really know what being a n——is, an' I hopes to de good Lawd you don' never have to fin' out." Well, she had found out—and there seemed no limit to the anguish whites were capable of wreaking upon black people. But the worst thing they did, Kunta had said was to keep them ignorant of who they are, to keep them from being fully human.
>
> "De reason yo' pappy took holt of my feelin's from de firs," her mammy had told her, "was he de proudest black man I ever seed!" Before she fell asleep, Kizzy decided that however base her baby's origins, however light his color, whatever name the massa forced upon him, she would never regard him as other than the grandson of an African.[34]

Thus, like her father before her, Kizzy relates the history of the family's African roots to her son. By the time George is three, Kizzy is telling him the stories about Kunta Kinte and Africa, passing on the Mandinka words that she remembers. As with her father, Kizzy's parental love seems wrapped up in her telling the stories of the family's origins to her child. And George himself, even as a three-year old, takes ownership of the stories: "Even beyond what she had hoped, George seemed to be building up his own image of his gran'pappy, and—to the limits of her endurance—Kizzy tried to help it along with tales from her own rich store of memories."[35]

By the time he is twelve, George, too has embraced his African identity. He presses Kizzy to tell him still more about Kunta Kinte, and promises to pass the story on himself:

> She said softly now, "Whole lot o' times I done tried to scrape in my min' if it's sump'n 'bout yo' gran'pappy I ain't tol' you, an' seem like jes' ain't no mo'—" She paused. "I knows you don't forget nothing'—but I tell you again any part of it if you says so."
>
> George was again quiet for a moment. "Mammy," he said, "one time you tol' me gran'pappy give you de feelin' dat de main thing he kep' on his mind was tellin' you dem Africa things—"
>
> "Yeah, it sho' seem like dat, plenty time," Kizzy said reflectively.
>
> After another silence, George said, "Mammy, I been thinkin'. Same as you done fo' me, I gwine tell my chilluns 'bout gran'pappy."[36]

And, indeed, Kizzy and George work to pass on the story even before the next generation is born. When, years later, George's wife Matilda becomes pregnant for the first time, Kizzy tells her all of her memories, both about herself and more importantly about her father: "Tilda, how come I'se tellin' you all dis, I jes' want you to understan' how I wants dat chile in yo' belly an' any mo' you has to know all 'bout 'im, too, on 'count of he's dey great-grandaddy." And as soon as the child, a son named Virgil, is born, Chicken George (as he's now known, since he trains Lea's fighting cocks) sweeps the child up in his hands, tells Kizzy that he is going to fulfill his promise to her, and once again narrates the story of Kunta Kinte.[37]

With each new birth, in each generation, this ritual is repeated. Chicken George tells his second son and his third son, sitting down the whole family to hear the story again.[38] Eventually, when his fourth son is born at a time of great strife between George and Tilda, Virgil takes the lead in suggesting that the story be told again. Though George begins at his eldest son's urging, eventually Virgil takes over from him, adding at the end, "Gran'mammy say de African make us know who we is!" This makes George suddenly feel at home again.[39]

When George is forced to go fight cocks in England to pay off one of Tom Lea's gambling debts and further financial trouble leads Lea to sell off half the family, Kizzy gathers George's children and again makes them promise to remember their roots.[40] When Chicken George returns, one of the first things he does is tell his first grandson, Uriah, the story of the family and of Kunta Kinte's African heritage.[41] Though George has gotten his freedom, he cannot stay with his family in North Carolina, where they now live, as a free Black man. But before he leaves, he makes his fourth son, Tom, who is now the center of the narrative, promise him to tell his child, who is about to be born, the story.[42] And Tom does so a few pages later.[43]

The Civil War comes and slavery ends. Chicken George moves the family to Henning, Tennessee. Cynthia, Tom's youngest child and Alex Haley's eventual grandmother, marries Haley's grandfather, Will Palmer. When Haley's mother, Bertha Palmer, is born, Cynthia assembles the family and tells the "the whole story back to the African, Kunta Kinte, just as Tom Murray had told it to his children."[44]

Eventually, Alex Haley himself is born. His mother, Bertha, had been very much her father's child and seemed to inherit his resentment of her mother's family narrative. So Haley heard the stories when he visited Henning from his grandmother and great aunts. Just to drive the point home, Haley, for the first time in the book, repeats the entire narrative as he more or less remembers hearing it as a child.[45] This, in turn, becomes the seed from which *Roots* grows. The book ends with Haley briefly telling the story of his search for the details of his family's history.[46]

## The Importance of the Recoverability of the African American Past in *Roots*

Though *Roots* is the story of Haley's family, the telling and retelling of that story *by* Haley's family is the book's most important action, the thing that allows Haley's ancestors to survive slavery, maintain their identity, and, eventually, thrive in freedom. *Roots* itself is a grand, final instantiation of the act of telling the family history back to Kunta Kinte in Africa. Implicit in the way the book presents this telling and retelling of the family history are a number of propositions. First, one's family history—and, for African Americans, one's African roots—are one's identity. Without knowing them, one cannot be oneself. Secondly, knowledge of one's family history and one's African roots could survive generations of slavery. Almost all of the other enslaved African American families that we encounter in *Roots*, however, seem to have lost all memory of and connection with the particularities of this past. The unusual success of Haley's maternal ancestors in Henning, Tennessee, the book implies, reflects the family's strong sense of identity, grounded in its understanding of its roots.

The key to the survival of the family history among Haley's ancestors was a peculiarly African art: oral history, the art of the griot. In *Roots*, it is crucial that the tradition of passing on the family story by word of mouth, though well suited for a world of slavery where reading and writing would be punished, was part of an African tradition that Kunta Kinte himself knew in Juffure. In America, the integrity of the story in Haley's family is only really imperiled in freedom. Will Palmer is the first person to marry into this family who feels threatened by the story, and Bertha Palmer Haley, Alex's mother, does not pass it on to her son herself. He needs to hear it at the feet of older relatives. Inspired by seeing the Rosetta Stone in the British Museum, Alex Haley uses modern, Western tools of research to vindicate the family tradition and add details to his narrative. But the most crucial facts about his last African ancestor Kunta Kinte come from a griot. Haley presents *Roots* itself as the proof of the power and importance of the oral narrative, preserved since Kunta Kinte's time, on both sides of the Atlantic.

Much of the power of this representation of African American memory, familial cultural connection to an African past, and preserved identity is its explicit rejection of an image of slavery and post–Civil War African American culture that was dominant in American public culture during most of the 1960s. Well into the 1950s, the ascendant voice in the historiography of slavery had been Ulrich Bonnell Phillips. A Southerner by birth, Phillips's work presented slavery as an economic problem for the South—plantation agriculture slowed the development of industry in the region—but a benefit to enslaved African Americans, who, according to Phillips, had been treated well by their enslavers and gained civilization and Christianity that their African forebears lacked.[47]

In 1959, Phillips's benign view of slavery was challenged by Stanley Elkins's *Slavery*.[48] Drawing on Bruno Bettelheim's portrait of life in Nazi concentration camps, Elkins suggested that African Americans were infantilized by the experience of slavery, making them psychologically dependent on their enslavers and incapable of building organized resistance or even forming meaningful interpersonal connections, and effectively robbing them of their individuality and culture.[49] Unlike Phillips's, Elkins's portrait of slavery was accurately harsh. But his implication that the pathologies caused by slavery might still exist in the African American community of his own time became controversial, especially as this premise found its way into Daniel Patrick Moynihan's *The Negro Family: A Case for National Action* (1965), better known as the Moynihan Report.[50]

Moynihan wrote *The Negro Family* in his capacity as assistant secretary of labor in the Kennedy and Johnson administrations. He presented African American families as burdened with a "tangle of pathology" that was the legacy of slavery. Drawing in part on Elkins's view of slavery, Moynihan argued that the formation of properly masculine men had been impeded for generations in the African American community. The result was a matriarchal family structure that burdened women while creating generations of failed men. Merely giving African Americans formal equality, Moynihan argued, could not solve these problems. Indeed, these problems were getting worse, even as legal segregation was being dismantled. The only solution, Moynihan suggested, was to directly address the pathology of Black family structure "so as to enable it to raise and support its members as do other families." The Moynihan Report set off a fierce debate. While Moynihan was advocating vigorous national action to improve the lot of African Americans, his portrait of them was seen by many as highly pejorative and, in effect, blaming African American culture for the problems of African Americans.

*Roots* was, among other things, a kind of response to Elkins's depiction of slavery and the Moynihan Report's vision of Black family life. While slavery was depicted as horrifically brutal in *Roots*, Haley's enslaved forebears in his book are utterly unlike Elkins's infantilized automatons. Despite constant threats to their bodies, lives, and families, Kunta Kinte, Kizzy, Chicken George, and the others are fully formed, adult human beings. Their families are vibrant and gain strength from the continuity of African cultural traditions that survive generations of enslavement. Despite the unusual horrors of slavery, Haley's book suggests that African Americans, like most other Americans, triumphed over adversity in the United States by finding strength in traditions from the old country and adapting them to new circumstances. The subtitle of the book—*The Saga of an American Family*—highlights its suggestion that despite the extraordinary horrors of slavery, Black families by the late twentieth century were, in important ways, much more like their white counterparts than Moynihan had suggested.

*Roots* arrived just as the historiography of slavery was undergoing another shift, led by historians like Eugene Genovese (*Roll, Jordan, Roll* [1974]) and Herbert Gutman (*The Black Family in Slavery and Freedom* [1976]). As Robert J. Norrell notes, it is not clear that Haley was familiar with this emerging work as he wrote *Roots*, but, if he was not, "he should be credited for his intuition in addressing the same questions" that they did.[51] Moreover, the consilience between *Roots* and this emerging historical scholarship was noted by reviewers, who would suggest that an encounter with *Roots* might lead readers to grapple with Gutman, Genovese, and other recent scholars of slavery.[52]

Haley and his publisher, Doubleday, insisted on marketing *Roots* as nonfiction.[53] And it was the nonfiction bestseller list that *Roots* ruled in late 1976 and early 1977. But the Ottaway article in *The Times* of London created a controversy over the truth of *Roots* in the spring of 1977. Both the National Book Award and the Pulitzer Prize juries awarded special prizes to *Roots* that avoided having to place the book in any of the categories of history, general nonfiction, or fiction. Much of the ensuing controversy over the book revolved around the fact that its author and publisher had presented it as nonfiction.[54] In his biography of Haley, Norrell concludes that it was simply a mistake to market the book as nonfiction. Had Haley called the book a novel, Norrell argues, he would have avoided the controversy and the book would have had the same cultural impact: "The power of *Roots* ultimately lay not in its adherence to historical fact but in its being a new story of blacks' past that included African origins. The book was not competing with empirical studies for the attention of the popular mind but with myths about slavery established by works of pure fiction."[55]

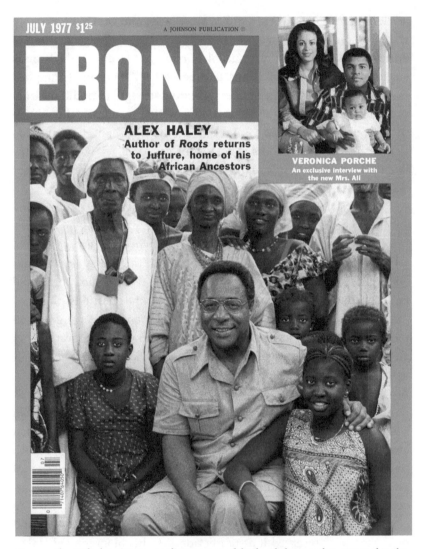

Fig. 4.1. Alex Haley's insistence on the accuracy of the family history that appeared in the pages of his book *Roots* was a critical part of the book's reception and success, as this July 1977 cover of *Ebony* magazine suggests. (Credit: Special thanks to Ebony Media Group, LLC.)

In his fascinating study of the making of *Roots*, the historian Matthew F. Delmont makes a similar argument. Though Haley tried to finesse the issue by referring to roots as "faction" (a portmanteau of "fact" and "fiction"), Delmont argues that Haley's "insistence on the accuracy of the people, places, and dates in the Gambian part of his story painted him into a corner." Haley himself understood that his portrait of Africa had mythic qualities to it. Defending the imaginative aspects of his portrait of Kunta Kinte's village, Haley himself noted in 1977 that "I, we, need a place called Eden. My people need a Plymouth Rock." And though Ottaway's article affected journalistic and scholarly reception of the book, it seemed to have little effect on the book's popular reception. Thus Delmont, like Norrell, seems puzzled by Haley's insistence on the essential truth of the book's details. "Haley could have staved off some of the criticism of *Roots*," Delmont suggests, "if he had made his desire to write a mythic history more clear in the book."[56]

But both Norrell and Delmont underestimate the importance of Haley's claims for the truth of *Roots*. Because of the importance of its representation of an African American family accurately preserving two centuries of memories through oral tradition—and of Haley's self-presentation as having been able to confirm and elaborate on this family story—the essential truth of *Roots* was a vital part of its impact. In calling the book "faction," Haley admitted from the start that aspects of the book, such as the dialog and details of day-to-day life, were fictionalized. But the truth of the genealogy and of his family's preservation of its outlines were critical to the book's cultural power and to the claims that it made about African American life under slavery and the possibilities of contemporary African Americans' recovering their families' pasts. Haley understood the importance of the core of his story being true and he always insisted on its veracity.

Reactions to *Roots* captured the centrality of its truth claims to its appeal. For example, Roger Paschall and Leo Pochinkas Jr., who performed as Roger Paschall and Leo Charles, wrote a tribute song, "Ain't That Roots," that focused on the truth of *Roots*:

> Roots with proof.
> Roots with truth. . . .
> Mister Alex Haley, went across the sea.
> He went to Africa, in search of you and me.
> The black man's true identity, started 'cross the sea.[57]

In the context of America in the mid-1970s, *Roots* marketed merely as a work of historical fiction could not have had this effect. And the power of the story of "the African," passed down from generation to generation by members of Haley's family, preserving the essential truth of their identity, would have been significantly blunted were this family ritual a mere literary device and not a Rosetta Stone to the African American past. As the historian M. J. Rymsza-Pawlowska notes, "*Roots* was a book about the process of discovery as much as it was about the history that it recounted."[58] While Haley's book presented that process of discovery as heroic, it also suggested it was reproducible by other African American families. Haley's vision of African American history did not shy away from the horrors of slavery. But he suggested precisely through reestablishing a connection to African history, those horrors could be transcended. Indeed, *Roots* argues that, through their attachments to their own history, even enslaved African Americans had been able to maintain a sense of cultural identity and to pass it on to future generations. This was a vision that appealed to both white and Black audiences in the 1970s. And it stood in stark contrast to Richard Pryor's suggestion in *Bicentennial N——* that the history of slavery had created a permanent division between the ways Black and white Americans understood the nation's past.

## Octavia Butler's *Kindred*: A More Fraught View of Slavery and the African American Past

As Matthew F. Delmont has argued, thanks to its enormous popular success, *Roots* "provided a baseline from which to create and appreciate more nuanced and challenging treatments of slavery."[59] One of the first such works to appear in print after roots was Octavia Butler's novel *Kindred* (1979). Though a work of fiction, with fantastical elements, *Kindred* shares with *Roots* not only a focus on the history of slavery, but also a concern with the meaning of that history to African Americans in the 1970s. But while *Roots* suggests that knowledge of their families' pasts is, in principle, accessible to African Americans and that such knowledge is deeply empowering, *Kindred* is much less optimistic. Only literal, involuntary time travel—the existence of which the novel never explains—gives *Kindred*'s protagonist Dana Franklin knowledge of her family's past in slavery. That knowledge complicates Dana's sense of identity, and her experience of the past ultimately maims her.

Just as Haley's growing up as the child of an upper-middle-class African American family in the Jim Crow South had a profound impact on *Roots*, Butler's very different background shaped *Kindred*. Octavia Butler was born in 1947, in Pasadena, California. She was raised primarily by her mother, who worked as a housecleaner, and her grandmother. Her father was largely absent. Her four siblings, all brothers, had died before she was born. Butler lacked the sort of large extended family that had played a major role in Haley's youth. In childhood, Butler was, in the words of her literary biographer Gerry Canavan, "solitary and lonely; extremely, almost cripplingly shy; and a dreamer."[60] From a very young age, she began to write stories. When she encountered science fiction in her early adolescence, it became her genre of choice. Years later, she would explain, "I was attracted to science fiction because it was so wide open. I was able to do anything and there were no walls to hem you in and there was no human condition that you were stopped from examining."[61] Throughout her life, Butler also kept extensive notes on, among other things, her writing and her attempts at self-development. Written in commonplace books and scraps of paper, they provide a remarkable record of Butler's often painfully introspective account of her writing process.

Butler began to try to write for publication as a teenager, but her career began to take shape in the early 1970s. Science fiction was going through a period of transformation. Writers like Ursula K. Le Guin, John Brunner, Samuel R. Delany, and Philip K. Dick pushed the genre in ever more literarily and intellectually sophisticated directions. But science fiction still often struggled to be taken seriously as literature. And the world of science fiction was dominated by white and male writers. Women like Le Guin and African Americans like Delany were very rare. Feeling that writing was impractical, Butler's mother and aunt discouraged her career choice. And, despite support early in her career from Delany and Harlan Ellison, both already successful science fiction writers, Butler was often wracked with self-doubt. Though throughout her career Butler explored issues of race and gender in her work, she was wary of Ellison's suggestion to market herself on the basis of her African American background. While the wildly successful Haley had connections, in *The Autobiography of Malcolm X* and *Roots*, respectively, with both the Black nationalist and integrationist tendencies in Black politics, Butler felt alienated from both schools of thought.[62]

By the time she published *Kindred* in 1979, Butler had enjoyed a certain amount of success from her first three published novels: *Patternmaster* (1976), *Mind of My Mind* (1977), and *Survivor* (1978). Although early versions of what became her fourth novel had more clearly science fictional elements, by the time she completed it, *Kindred* was not in a conventional sense science fiction. The narrator, Edana Franklin, who goes by Dana, is a struggling, young African American writer in Southern California who is married to Kevin, a slightly more successful, white writer. We first meet Dana in a hospital in July 1976. She has just lost her left arm and the police are concerned that Kevin is somehow responsible, though she insists he is not. The bulk of the novel is a flashback that explains that missing arm.

On June 9, 1976, her twenty-sixth birthday, Dana suddenly finds herself transported to the bank of a river in which a white, red-haired boy is drowning. Dana rescues him, but his mother, who stands helplessly on the bank, accuses her of harming her son, whose name is Rufus. A white man arrives and points a gun at Dana. Still wet and muddy, she is just as suddenly transported back to her house in California, reappearing, just seconds after she disappeared, before Kevin's eyes.

Over the course of the novel, Dana repeatedly makes such leaps in time and space. They are never explained. But she soon discovers that she is being transported across the country and back in time to Maryland in the early nineteenth century. Over the course of the novel, Dana makes a half dozen such leaps to the past. Sometimes her stays there are short; sometimes they last for months. Once Kevin is touching her when she leaps back, and he is thrust into the past with her. She always appears in the past at a moment at which Rufus's life is threatened and she must rescue him; and she is returned back to 1976 whenever her own life is threatened in that past. Though days sometimes pass in 1976 between these jumps back in time, Dana always arrives back in her present just moments after she had left.

Rufus, who grows into adulthood over the course of the novel, turns out to be the brutal, frequently disobedient, and deeply dislikeable son of a plantation-owning family, the Weylins. Yet Dana and he find themselves bound together by circumstance and they develop an odd closeness. Dana realizes fairly early in the novel that both Rufus and a free Black woman who lives near the plantation named Alice are her ancestors.

Eventually, Rufus tries unsuccessfully to rape Alice and later asks Dana to convince Alice to sleep with him. Dana, realizing that her own existence depends on this union, relents. Alice and Rufus have a number of children, one of whom, a girl named Hagar, is Dana's ancestor. But Alice eventually hangs herself in response to Rufus abusively—and falsely—telling her that he had sold her children into slavery. Dana refuses Rufus's request that she replace Alice as his sexual partner. Furious, he attempts to rape Dana. She stabs and kills Rufus, who even in death continues to grip her left arm. Dana travels, for the last time, back to Los Angeles in the present. But this time, her left arm, starting with the spot at which Rufus had gripped it, is painfully fused to the wall of her house, forcing its amputation. Her final leap and return have taken place on July 4, 1976.

*Kindred* presents a distinct vision of the relationship of the present to the past. History is extraordinarily immediate to Dana, but her relationship to it is almost entirely involuntary. Unlike Haley, who presents himself as uncovering the past through a heroic search for his family's roots, Dana is thrust into her family's past against her will. She nevertheless has the advantage of knowing how things will turn out, that slavery will end and that she will eventually be born. At first, this makes her feel apart from events she experiences in antebellum Maryland: "I began to realize why Kevin and I had fitted so easily into this time. We weren't really in. We were observers watching a show. We were watching history happen around us. And we were actors. While we wanted to go home, we humored the people around us by pretending to be like them. But we were poor actors. We never really got into our roles. We never forget that we were acting."[63] But shortly after observing this, Dana feels that sense of distance eroding and a sense of helplessness replacing it. She tells Kevin: "You might be able to go through this whole experience as an observer. . . . I can understand that because, most of the time, I'm still an observer. It's protection. It's nineteen seventy-six shielding and cushioning eighteen nineteen for me. But now and then . . . I can't maintain the distance. I'm drawn all the way into eighteen nineteen, and I don't know what to do. I ought to be doing something. I know that."[64]

The novel's view of the past is connected to its view of slavery and its relationship to the present. Over the course of the novel, Dana's complicity in the often brutal events in her family's past grows and she repeatedly notes how easy it seems to be for people, even for her, a woman born in freedom, living over a century after the end of slavery, to accommodate themselves to slavery.[65] And slavery itself fosters "strange relationships," like the one between Rufus and herself, relationships that Kevin, even after he himself spends years in the past, cannot wholly understand.[66]

## Conclusion: The Present and the Past in *Roots* and *Kindred*

Haley and Butler present very different views about the meaning of the past to African Americans in the 1970s. In *Roots*, history liberates those who remember it. Haley's enslaved ancestors remember their family's past in Africa, which allows them to never fully accommodate themselves to slavery. For Haley himself, as for them, history establishes a more solid and noble sense of identity. Throughout *Roots*, right up to the account of Haley's own research with which the book ends, history appears through acts of will, of remembrance and of telling. This view of history, in turn, linked the African American experience to the experience of white Americans. Though *Roots* certainly emphasizes the distinctive qualities of African American history, it also suggests that, like Americans of European descent, African Americans can find out about their families' past in an "old country," can derive meaning from that cultural identity, and can take part in modern, pluralistic American culture while embracing that identity. Part of the appeal of *Roots* to white readers—and later white television audience members—was its suggestions that, despite not being Black themselves, they could understand and relate to the African American experience and that the experience of slavery, though truly horrific, created no persistent barriers to the full integration of African Americans into the nation's life in the present.

In *Kindred*, history forces itself on Dana. Far from clarifying her identity, it complicates it. History in *Kindred* protects no African American from slavery. Instead of history providing a psychic and spiritual lifeline out of slavery, Dana's encounter with the past suggests how easily people slip into slavery's habits of mind and how thoroughly slavery binds slavers and the enslaved into disturbing, but close, relationships. And, as a white man, Kevin can never entirely understand Dana's experience or her relationship to Rufus, even though he, too, comes to spend time in the past.

Both Haley in *Roots* and Dana in *Kindred* are descendants of an African American woman who is coerced into having sex with the white man who is enslaving her. In *Roots*, Kunta Kinte's daughter, Kizzy, is violently raped by her enslaver Tom Lea. Though Lea is certainly biologically Haley's ancestor, *Roots* treats him as existing outside the family line that forms the spine of the book's narrative. In *Kindred*, Rufus's relationship to Alice, while at least as brutal, is more subtle and complicated. *Kindred* fully treats Rufus as Dana's ancestor, and the novel makes Dana utterly complicit in forcing Alice to have sex with Rufus. *Roots* treats Lea's rape of Kizzy as nothing more than an assault on her and—by extension—Haley's family. *Kindred*, on the other hand, emphasizes that the forced union of Rufus and Alice was necessary for Dana to have come into being at all. And while Kizzy lives through the rape, becoming stronger through her survival of it, Alice eventually takes her own life because of Rufus's brutality toward her. In *Kindred*, the sexual violence of enslavers toward African American women is even more destructive for those women that it is in *Roots*. Yet, it is also much more constitutive of African American identity for Butler than it is for Haley.

Butler's decision to make her protagonist a woman was also significant. Reflecting later on her first, failed attempts to write the novel that became *Kindred*, Butler noted that her protagonist had originally been a man: "But as I wrote, I began to see that a black man would never survive the mistakes he would be certain to make traveling from the present to the antebellum past. He might, for instance, look people in the eye when he talked to them. Such a simple thing—but an act of defiance. His whole manner would be wrong, and he would be perceived as dangerous. He would be killed—more likely soon than late."[67] Butler wanted a subtle weakness of character to contribute to Dana's survival. In a letter to her friend and fellow science fiction author Marjorie Rae Nadler, Butler describes Dana as "a somewhat watery little person." This, Butler suggested, was "a survival characteristic, as it made her malleable."[68] This is a very different model of survival from Kunta Kinte's intensely masculine form of resistance, which reflects Haley's general commitment to African American history as largely patriarchal.[69]

In *Kindred*, Dana's relationship to the past literally maims her. As she is a writer, Dana's loss of an arm is of special significance; it is a kind of silencing.[70] Once again, this image stands in stark contrast to *Roots*, in which history repeatedly makes its characters whole. Dana's loss of her arm results from an attempted rape that she survives. And the book begins with Dana, having, we later discover, repeatedly been threatened and beaten by white men in the past, having to defend her white husband from the false accusation that he has harmed her.

Butler began work on what would become *Kindred* in 1975. One earlier treatment of the story, then called *Switchback*, had her protagonist make her first leap back in time on the day Martin Luther King Jr. was assassinated in 1968.[71] Her eventual decision to set the novel in the summer of 1976 and to have it end on July 4 most obviously served as a commentary on the Bicentennial celebrations. The central plot of *Kindred* begins on Dana's birthday and ends on the nation's. Like Richard Pryor, Butler suggests that the Black experience of the American past was fundamentally different from the largely white version of history presented by the Bicentennial celebrations.

But the setting of *Kindred* has another, less obvious, significance. The novel takes place just weeks before the appearance of *Roots*, which would fundamentally alter American popular understandings of slavery. When Dana and Kevin, between her leaps back in time, attempt to find out about slavery, *Roots* is thus not among the books they turn to. Although *Roots* is not mentioned in Butler's notes on writing *Kindred*, she was, of course, well aware of Haley, his book, and its extraordinary success. Indeed, Butler kept a clippings file on Haley, which contained pieces published in the *Los Angeles Times* and in national magazines. Judging from these clippings, Butler seems to have been particularly interested in the public impact of Haley's book and in the author's extraordinary popularity, the latter doubtless related to Butler's own desires for and anxieties about commercial success. On one clipping about the controversies about the veracity of *Roots*, Butler wrote a note defending Haley: "Here, Reporters magnanamously [*sic*] forgive Haley for errors they do not prove he has made."[72] Butler's decision to set the present-day portions of *Kindred* before the publication of *Roots* is significant. Had the novel been set any later, *Roots* would have almost certainly been made to play a role in the way in which Dana and Kevin tried to understand her experiences.

Dana's ignorance of slavery at the start of the novel reflected an important fact about Butler's own relationship to history. Unlike Alex Haley, who had enormous faith in his abilities as a historical sleuth—and who was perfectly happy to invent details when he had no facts to go on— Butler questioned the very possibility of writing historical fiction, which seemed to her to lack some of the freedom she found in science fiction. While on a bus trip to Maryland to research *Kindred*, Butler wrote a note to herself that reflected these anxieties:

> I don't want to recreate historical worlds—or at least not that historical world. I don't understand how people have the arrogance to write historicals—doubtless more filled with inaccuracies than other kinds of fiction. And how can anyone possibly do enough research to avoid such errors.
>
> Of course . . . people do. They avoid large errors and are fully aware of the liberties they take with historical fact. They may begin small—that is by handling a culture no one knows much about. Or they may begin big and turn out to be born researchers.[73]

Though she did extensive research for *Kindred*, Butler never felt like a "born researcher." She later noted that she had "used [her] own ignorance" by creating a protagonist and narrator in Dana who shared it.[74]

*Kindred* concludes with a short epilogue in which Dana, having come home from the hospital, and Kevin fly to Maryland to seek out what historical evidence remained of the things they had experienced in the past. They discover little. The Weylin house is gone. All they find are a couple newspaper articles. One notes Rufus's death in a fire that partially destroyed the house; Dana assumes that one of the slaves set it to cover up the real cause of his death. Another newspaper article notes the sale of Rufus's slaves, listed by name, after his death. But a number of the Weylin slaves are missing from the list, including Alice's daughter—and Dana's forebear—Hagar. The scraps of information they find do not contradict their experiences in the past, but they raise new questions and leave the fates of key players in the story unresolved. Dana realizes that she will never entirely know what occurred in the aftermath of Rufus's death by her hand.

The novel ends with Kevin and Dana standing outside the Maryland Historical Society and questioning their desire to find out more about Rufus Weylin and the past they had experienced. Dana asks Kevin, "Why did I even want to come here. You'd think I would have had enough of the past." Kevin offers an answer: "To try to understand. To touch solid evidence that those people existed. To reassure yourself that you're sane." Dana responds by noting, "If we told anyone else about this, anyone at all, they wouldn't think we were so sane." Dana (and Butler) give Kevin the last word: "We are. . . . And now that the boy is dead, we have some chance of staying that way."[75]

History in *Kindred* is palpable and immediate, but ultimately mysterious and destructive. Though, as a visitor from the future, Dana at first feels like an observer who can stand apart from the world of antebellum Maryland in which she finds herself because of her general knowledge of how history will unfold, this feeling turns out to be illusory. The past exacts a terrible toll on Dana's body, for reasons that remain mysterious to her and Kevin and to the novel's readers. The knowledge she has gained of her family's past is far from positive; if anything, it disrupts her sense of identity. She discovers that her very existence depends on acts of sexual violence in which she herself is complicit. Dana and Kevin's inexplicable experiences cannot be shared with anyone else; nobody would believe them, and little evidence is available in the present to back up their story. They need to be satisfied with their imperfect understanding of the past. As Kevin notes in the novel's concluding sentence, their continuing sanity is dependent on their ability to put the past permanently behind them, though he seems more capable of doing so than Dana does.

Butler presents an almost total inversion of Haley's vision of history. In *Roots* the past is legible and liberatory. Research allows Haley to fill in the details of the story handed down to him by his family. And in doing so, he deepens his sense of identity. Kunta Kinte's memory of Africa and of the family histories he was told before being kidnapped into slavery sustains him through his darkest hours in bondage. His story provides hope to his descendants still in slavery. And Haley turns this family history into a public act.

Haley spent the better part of a decade before *Roots* was published telling his family's story on the lecture circuit. Matthew F. Delmont argues that these lectures were key to the later success of the book and the miniseries. Haley was by all accounts a riveting lecturer. He saw his family's story as an opportunity to buoy Black self-esteem and the lectures as a way of building an audience for the book to come.[76] While Kevin and Dana's experience of her family's past demands their silence, Haley's story demanded publicity.

Neither *Roots* nor *Kindred* are works of nostalgia, though, as originally conceived, Haley's *Before This Anger* had grown out of a kind of nostalgia for the segregated world of Henning, Tennessee, in which his family had prospered during the first half of the twentieth century. But both *Roots* and *Kindred* make the imaginative move that, I have argued, played such an important role in 1970s American culture and that is the subject of this book. The past is made immediate to each book's protagonists. And both authors suggest that the encounter with the past can have a profound impact on the present.

Both books are also responses to the Sixties, and especially to political divisions within the African American community that grew during that decade. Haley's original title, *Before This Anger,* reflected this desire. *Roots* attempts to resolve the tensions between the integrationist and nationalist strains of Black politics by, in the words of Robert J. Norrell, "offer[ing] a softer and more palatable expression of black nationalism."[77] As Delmont notes, Haley "believed in affirming black culture, appreciating black history, and fostering black pride. But he also believed that all of these should be pursued with the least possible conflict or confrontation."[78] In *Roots,* Haley managed to craft a Black nationalist narrative that even white audiences could find uplifting. *Roots* suggests that, despite its long history of oppressing African Americans, the United States could be a functional, multiracial polity with Black racial pride as one of its foundations.

*Kindred*'s relationship to the Sixties is more subtle and complicated. Butler never felt at home in either the integrationist or Black nationalist strains in African American politics. Indeed, she was deeply suspicious of both tendencies.[79] *Kindred* reflects these political discomforts. Butler later remarked that "the germ of the idea for *Kindred*" came from a confrontation she had with a fellow student in the mid-1960s:

When I got into college, Pasadena City College, the black nationalist movement, the Black Power Movement, was really underway
with the young people, and I heard some remarks from a young
man who was the same age I was but who had apparently never
made the connection with what his parents did to keep him alive.
He was still blaming them for their humility and their acceptance
of disgusting behavior on the part of employers and other people.
He said, "I'd like to kill all those old people who have been holding us back for so long. But I can't because I'd have to start with
my own parents."[80]

Butler's biographer, Gerry Canavan, argues she rejected this view because
she believed that "survival is not necessarily the same thing as defeat-
ing your enemy, or even fighting back or standing up for yourself, but
simply means that you (and, crucially, your children) have continued into
the future."[81] For African Americans, survival had often meant accommodating themselves to the degrading and oppressive circumstances of
slavery and segregation. In Butler's view, for the present generation to
simply denounce those accommodations was profoundly unrealistic and
might even endanger future survival.

Kindred, like Roots, is an affirmation of the Black past, but it is an alto-
gether less optimistic one. Understanding that past as best she can gives
Dana a more realistic sense of self than the Black nationalist that Butler
argued with in college had had. But far from promising a new cultural and
psychic wholeness, as Haley's presentation of family and African
American history does, the past in Kindred disrupts even Dana's physical well-being. The Sixties visions of Black politics that Butler rejects are
not replaced in the novel by a new, positive vision of African American
identity. Instead, the past teaches the necessity of survival, which, for
African Americans, has always involved acknowledging and even at
times accommodating the seemingly unalterable facts of oppression.

# Afterword

As we have seen in the preceding chapters, American culture in the 1970s engaged with the past in intense and myriad ways. Yet academic historians have played only a small role in these chapters, which reflects a paradox about Americans in the Seventies and their engagement with the past: in that decade, while the public seemed to be fascinated with the past, the formal study of history appeared to be on the wane. Despite the fervent and growing public interest in the American past during the Seventies—seen, among many other places, in television shows like *Happy Days*, the emerging movie genre of neo-noir, the broad success of the Bicentennial celebrations, and the publishing sensation of *Roots*— high school history courses were being replaced by social studies classes and colleges and universities were also seeing rapidly declining enrollments in history. And those enrollment declines were contributing to an academic job crisis that was felt particularly strongly by professional historians.[1] The exclusion that so many academic historians felt from the Bicentennial celebrations, which I discussed in chapter 3, was part of a more general sense of crisis that pervaded the discipline in the 1970s.

The paradox of a culture fascinated with the past but uninterested in studying history was noted, often with alarm, by professional historians in the 1970s. I conclude this book with a glance at these historians' reactions because I think they help highlight what was distinctive about American culture's attitudes toward the past in the Seventies. Historians in the twenty-first century have also tried to understand and characterize the ways Americans engaged with the past in the Seventies. After turning briefly to those accounts, I conclude with a look back at the four case studies that form the heart of this book.

## Historians in the Seventies Confront a Crisis in Their Discipline

At the very beginning of the decade, in a piece on "The Future of the Past" published in the *American Historical Review*, the leading journal of the history profession in the United States, Yale historian C. Vann Woodward saw difficult days ahead for American historians. Despite nearly two decades of growth in both student interest and faculty publication, enrollments in history courses at colleges and universities had already begun to dip precipitously in 1968. A recent poll showed that high school students considered history the most "irrelevant" of twenty-one subjects they were asked about. Even among fellow academic humanists and social scientists, Woodward argued, history was losing its prestige. Woodward saw much public interest in the past. But the past and history were not, in Woodward's estimation, the same thing. Drawing on British historian J. H. Plumb's use of the term, Woodward argued that "the past" was always instrumentalized by elites "to bemuse and coerce and exploit." History, on the other hand, in Plumb's words, "seeks to cleanse the story of mankind from the deceiving visions of a purposeful past." For Woodward, the problem was not so much that history was seen as "irrelevant" as that relevance had become the measure of its worth. In instrumentalizing history by searching for a "usable past," Woodward argued, even some historians had begun to confuse history and the past. The problem of the triumph of "the past" over history was made more serious by the fact that "ours is essentially an age of disjuncture, not of continuity." Usable pasts, so often based on asserting continuities with the present, were thus even less likely to be good history in the 1970s, according to Woodward.[2]

While Woodward warned of the dangers of putting the past entirely in service of the present, other historians worried that Americans' growing interest in the past constituted a form of escapism, a way of avoiding the problems of the present. The historian Philip D. Jordan devoted his "Editor's Page" column in the Fall 1974 issue of the journal *Minnesota History* to what had become, by the middle of that decade, a common source of anxiety among historians and cultural critics: "the neurosis of nostalgia."[3] The American people "who have always been proud of their get-up-and-go and confident they held the future in their hands seem to be turning more and more to memories and less and less to current realities," Jordan charged. The "cuts and wounds and the bewilderments of contemporary problems—economic, social, religious, political" have destroyed the nation's self-confidence and apparently sent "ever-increasing numbers of Americans subconsciously searching for a time when things were good and life was fun by retreating into yesteryears." For Jordan, the then current craze in collecting historical knickknacks represented a dangerous attitude to the past. Americans in the 1970s, he felt, were trying to escape to the past, but did not have any interest in understanding it. People rushed to collect "pewter, pretty china, and souvenir plates . . . reflecting a real or imagined image of the gone-before" but had no interest in reading serious books about the past. Like most historians, Jordan believed that studying history could help Americans navigate the present crises that he felt led to this wave of nostalgia. But the wave of interest in the past among Americans in the 1970s was the opposite of such a study, an effort to evade the present, not to understand it. As we saw in chapter 1, this idea that America culture was becoming dangerously obsessed with nostalgia for (often poorly understood) pasts was common in the 1970s. And the idea that the 1970s was an unusually nostalgic decade lives on in American popular culture.

Other historians tried to rework the professional study of the past in light of both demands for relevance and the collapse of the academic job market in history. Toward the end of the decade, graduate programs in public history began to appear. *The Public Historian* journal began publication in 1978, and the professional society that would go on to host the journal, the National Council on Public History, was formed the next year.[4] The newly formalized subdiscipline of public history sought to professionalize the role of academically trained historians outside the academy. Early issues of *The Public Historian* were enthusiastic about the promises of public history both for the larger historical profession and for the institutions employing public historians. Public history could bridge the gap between the public enthusiasm for the past and the declining fortunes of the historical profession. "As we traipsed through the bicentennial era," noted Larry Tise, then executive director of the North Carolina Division of Archives and History in a piece published in the summer of 1979, "we found ourselves in an ironic situation in which there was greater interest in history than at any time in the American past, but in which it seemed that historians, historical agencies, and historical societies were unable to benefit appreciably from the spate of enthusiasm for the past." For Tise, building the subfield of public history was a necessary part of reasserting the role of professional historians in a country fascinated by the past but largely uninterested in academic history. Tise's view, and that of his fellow public historians more generally, was almost the reverse of Woodward's from the start of the decade. Far from avoiding the instrumentalization of history, historians and their professional organizations, in Tise's view, needed to embrace it: "We must become greatly more concerned that [sic] we are at present with the economies, practicalities, and the usefulness of history."[5]

But some pieces in the very first issue of *The Public Historian* expressed concerns that doing public history necessarily altered the practice of history in ways that might raise serious ethical questions. Robert Kelley of the University of California, Santa Barbara, who, at that institution, founded one of the first graduate programs in public history, noted that the most significant difference between traditional academic history and public history was "who is posing the question to which the historian is seeking to give an answer." Public historians, unlike academic historians, always had to answer questions posed by others.[6] Todd Shallatt, who had worked as public history intern for the City of Fresno, California, noted that "public historians must be salespeople and entertainers as well as scholars."[7] And Bob McKenzie of the University of Alabama suggested that working for government or business raised new challenges to the goal of maintaining historical objectivity.[8]

But despite these potential challenges, the essays in the early issues of *The Public Historian* were overwhelmingly positive about the future of the new subfield. It would benefit professional historians by creating a whole new set of jobs for them. The public and private institutions that public historians would serve would benefit from the wisdom of the field. And, in making history relevant in entirely concrete ways, public history might go a long way toward convincing a public already fascinated with the past to engage in the formal study of history.

The historian and critic John Lukacs, on the other hand, was simply less troubled by historical thinking in America essentially leaving the academy behind. In a paper delivered in April 1980, Lukacs suggested that a new, potentially fruitful form of historical consciousness was emerging in America. Like both Woodward and Jordan, Lukacs noted that the arrival of "an appetite for history—more exactly for physical and mental reminders of the past—which in the entire history of this country has had no precedent" was unaccompanied by an interest in formal historical study, though Lukacs blamed "those responsible for [the teaching of history]" for this latter phenomenon. "Professional historianship in America," he declared, "has become gnarled and ossified." But despite this failure of professional historians to rise to the occasion, the public's "new appetite for history" indicated "a slow and profound development of the maturation of the American spirit, an emergence from adolescent habits of mind."

Lukacs was hopeful that, from this interest, new literary approaches to the past would emerge in American culture. But he was unsure of what these approaches might be. "Some time in the twenty-first century, after the passing of the American Century in the history of the world," Lukacs predicted, "it is through a new kind of history that the American Dante or the American Cervantes or the American Shakespeare may appear."[9] In an earlier review, in which he had panned not only E. L. Doctorow's popular historical novel *Ragtime* (1975) but its approach to history more generally, Lukacs had similarly declared that, despite his misgivings about the novel, he "continue[d] to believe that others may come to create a more perfect model of a genre that may be the genre of the near future, perhaps eventually dominating all forms of narrative literature."[10] For all his optimism about history's future in American culture, even Lukacs could be perturbed by many of the ways in which Americans were engaging with the past in the 1970s present.

## Looking Back on the Past in the Seventies

With the benefit of hindsight, historians in the twenty-first century, have begun to paint their own portraits of the place of the past in Seventies American culture. M. J. Rymsza-Pawlowska places interactivity at the center of her account of how the past changed for Americans in that decade. Through museums, television programs, and other forms of public history, Americans, she argues, sought new ways to place themselves into the past, not to escape from the present, but rather to better understand the past in individual, experiential ways.[11] Daniel Rodgers also suggests that, in the last quarter of the twentieth century, a new understanding of the past emerged in American thought and culture that emphasized its immediacy. Rodgers uses the metaphor of time folding in on itself to describe this emergent view of history. However, Rodgers is considerably less sanguine about this development than Rymsza-Pawlowska is. For Rodgers this vision of history brought with it a sense of fragmentation, which fed the culture wars of the late twentieth century. And the new sense of accessibility of the past was, for Rodgers, largely illusory. Unlike the 1970s critics of nostalgia like Philip D. Jordan, Rodgers does not think that the new place of the past in late twentieth-century American culture constituted a form of escapism. But he shares Jordan's and Woodward's concern that it distorts the complexity of history.[12]

Focusing on four case studies, this book has explored the diversity of the intense Seventies cultural engagement with the American past. Though there were elements of nostalgia in Seventies representations of Fifties greasers and mid-century hard-boiled private investigators (PIs), these figures were never simply repositories of longings for the past. Crucially, these representations tended to be designed to be put in dialogue with perceived problems of the present. Even a text like the musical *Grease*, which has frequently been labeled, often dismissively, as a nostalgia piece, is quite self-conscious in its critique of the sexual politics of the world it depicts and of present-day, misplaced nostalgia for that world. Though critics have tended to see Seventies' attitudes toward the Fifties as nostalgic and fundamentally conservative, the image of the greaser was much more culturally flexible than such accounts suggest. As rebels from the past, greasers could be domesticated in ways that trivialized the rebellion they once represented. Or their rebellion could be reaffirmed, their image adopted by groups, from leathermen to punks, who challenged the dominant cultures of the day.

The explosion of interest in film noir and the emergence of the genre of neo-noir, though certainly marked by nostalgia for Hollywood's past, were, from the start, concerned about the American present. Paul Schrader's essay "Notes on Film Noir" (1971), which in many ways marked the beginning of this growth in both critical and filmmaking interest in noir, suggested the very complicated relationship of noir to the past. First, Schrader drew analogies between the political situation of the 1940s, in which noir first appeared, and that of the 1970s. Noir would be relevant in the Seventies because the post-Vietnam present resembled the grimmer aspects of the post–World War II past that had fed the creation of classic film noir. But, just as crucially, Schrader saw a fascination with the burden of the past as a foundational component of noir itself from its beginnings in the 1940s. Schrader's ideas found expression, too, in the neo-noir films made later in the decade. Neo-noirs like Robert Altman's *The Long Goodbye* and the Schrader-scripted *The Yakuza* were thus doubly engaged with the past. They drew on the classic noir concerns about the inescapability of the past in order to ask questions about the relationship of the moral universe of mid-century noir to the world of the Seventies.

Nostalgia did not much mark the celebration of the Bicentennial. Despite a history full of scandal, redirection, and downsizing, the federal effort to mark the nation's two-hundredth birthday was judged to be an emotional success by most observers in the summer of 1976. A number of decisions by the American Revolution Bicentennial Administration (ARBA), the federal agency eventually responsible for coordinating the celebration, contributed to that success. First, the celebration was extraordinarily diffuse. Abandoning the idea of a single national event akin to the Philadelphia Centennial Exhibition of 1876, ARBA instead emphasized that each American could and should celebrate the event as they saw fit. Second, ARBA's own discussions of the Revolution focused on a series of founding documents: the Declaration of Independence, the Constitution, and the Bill of Rights. ARBA head John Warner spoke of these documents—two of which were, of course, written well after 1776—as sacred and eternal texts without elaborating on their meanings. The Bicentennial celebrations, thus framed, managed to emphasize a vision of national unity and common purpose in a time otherwise marked by often bitter political and social divisions. But that vision of unity was based on a refusal to present the concrete grounds of that unity.

Many in the African American community felt excluded from such anodyne attempts to ground national unity in a shared past that tended to systematically ignore or distort the place of African Americans in it. But during the Bicentennial year, Alex Haley's runaway bestseller *Roots* successfully established a compelling narrative of Black history that proved appealing to both Black and white readers. Focusing on the experience of slavery, Haley's book did not shy away from the horrors of the past. But it told a story of individual, familial, and, at least by implication, communal triumph over those horrors. *Roots* suggested that the key to the survival and prosperity of Haley's forebears had been the preservation and celebration of the family's roots in Africa before their ancestor, Kunta Kinte, had been kidnapped into slavery. For Haley and his family, knowledge of the past was itself the key to overcoming oppression and establishing an authentic African American identity. If there was any nostalgia in *Roots*, it was for Kunta Kinte's idyllic life in Africa prior to being enslaved.

While *Roots* focused on what was distinctive about the African American experience, it also suggested that African American identity was less unlike European American identities than had been conventionally thought. Slavery did not erase the past. Black family histories, Haley suggests, are recoverable, especially with the help of distinctly African forms of knowledge and storytelling. As a result, Black Americans, like white Americans, can form a meaningful relationship to the culture of the "old country" from which their ancestors came. And embracing those roots can help them succeed in a diverse, multicultural America. While grappling with elements of the American past that were often left out of dominant narratives, in *Roots* Haley managed to craft an ultimately affirmative story about America and the place of Black people within it.

Octavia Butler, on the other hand, presented a very different picture of the relationship between African American lives in the present and the experience of slavery in the past, one utterly shorn of nostalgia. Even more than Haley's *Roots*, Butler's *Kindred* suggests the past is inescapable. But far from providing a lifeline to an Edenic world before slavery, as the story of Kunta Kinte does for his descendants in *Roots*, *Kindred*'s Dana Franklin experiences slavery and her family's relationship to it in ways that implicate her in the oppression in disturbing ways. Trying to understand the past is absolutely necessary for *Kindred*'s protagonist. But doing so feels anything but liberating.

These intense Seventies explorations of the past call to mind much of what critics and historians have written about Americans' relationship to the past in that decade. They show Americans grappling with the past in ways that seem to indicate that the past is immediate and experientially accessible. But they show little interest in the formal study of history. The urgency of these explorations of the past reflected the discontinuities and disruptions that, already in the Seventies, Americans associated with the Sixties. C. Vann Woodward, writing in 1970, proved wrong to worry, at the start of the decade, that, in an "age of disjuncture," a fascination with the past, unguided by formal historical study, would necessarily flatten that past to emphasize continuities over discontinuities. But while Americans in the Seventies looking backward sometimes found continuities—in American perseverance and quasi-sacred documents during the Bicentennial or in Haley's family's attachment to its African past—they found discontinuities just as, if not more, often. Although Paul Schrader grounded his interest in noir, at least in part, in similarities he saw between the Forties and the Seventies, his and others' neo-noir screenplays often explored what had changed between then and now—how the values embodied by the mid-century figure of the hard-boiled PI no longer quite functioned in the Seventies, if they ever had in the past. Even the various popular explorations of the Fifties like *Grease*, *American Graffiti*, and *Happy Days* were as much about understanding what had changed since then as they were about a nostalgic desire to return to an imagined past. Like Joan Didion, on the first day of the Seventies, looking back to the Fifties and measuring what had changed, Americans in the Seventies looked back to understand their present. The crises and divisions that would come in that decade only intensified these searches.

# ACKNOWLEDGMENTS

At the time I began this book, I had recently set aside an entirely different project that, after years of work, I realized was never going to get finished. Before even finding a new direction, I needed to simply start writing again. The Society for U.S. Intellectual History's *U.S. Intellectual History Blog*, which I was then editing and writing for weekly, provided me with a time and place to do that. I am incredibly grateful to my fellow bloggers and the community of regular commenters for their criticism and encouragement. As I note in this book's introduction, this project itself eventually grew out of some of my work at the blog. Quite separate from the blog, a conversation that I had with Tom Lacquer at around this time also proved crucial in nudging me toward this project.

In the early days of working on *Happy Days* I happened to meet, in person, an old online friend, Claire Potter. She was enthusiastic about this project from the moment I mentioned it to her. And over the years she provided invaluable advice about it. This book would never have happened without her.

I am grateful for the incredible archivists and staff at the University of Tennessee, where I consulted the Alex Haley Papers; at the National Archives, where I delved into the records of the American Revolution Bicentennial Commission and its successor organization, the American Revolution Bicentennial Administration; and at the Huntington Library, where I worked with the Octavia E. Butler Papers. The enthusiastic curators and staff of the Alex Haley Museum and Interpretive Center in Henning, Tennessee, also deserve mention. Though I do not discuss the materials I encountered there in this book, my visit to Henning affected my thinking about Haley and *Roots*.

My colleagues and students at the Honors College at the University of Oklahoma, which has been my institutional home for nearly a quarter century, were an important influence on this manuscript. Teaching seminars on film noir and on America in the Seventies, the latter of which I co-created with my colleague Bob Lifset, had a profound impact on the growth of this project. I also presented drafts of a number of these chapters at our Faculty Research Seminar, where I received insightful feedback from my wonderful colleagues.

The other intellectual community that was crucial for this project was the Society for U.S. Intellectual History, whose blog I have already mentioned. Many pieces of this manuscript were presented as papers at their annual conference. And the intellectual companionship and human support that I received over the years from dozens of colleagues in the society was of immeasurable importance. I simply cannot express enough gratitude for all that they have given me.

My participation in two writing groups bookended this project. At its beginning, the Academic Muse online writing boot camp proved incredibly useful to me. And during my final semester working on it, the University of Oklahoma's Faculty Writing Group was similarly helpful.

I am deeply grateful to the anonymous readers of my manuscript, whose careful assessments of it and excellent suggestions for revision have made this a better book, and to Nicole Solano at Rutgers University Press, whose enthusiasm, guidance, and patience helped bring this project home.

Financial support was provided from the Office of the Vice President for Research and Partnerships and the Office of the Provost, University of Oklahoma. Research funds from the University of Oklahoma's Honors College also helped make this book possible.

Last, but certainly not least, I'd like to thank my family. My wife, Karin Schutjer, and my mother, Svetlana Alpers, are both brilliant scholars in their own rights. In addition to their love and support, at various times in this project, their intellectual advice was also crucial. Over the course of writing this book, my two kids grew into extraordinary young adults, both of whom are themselves budding humanists. Finally, I want to mention our late dog Abbey, who passed away at the age of twelve in early 2022. Karin called her a "healing presence." Especially during the difficult COVID years, having her in our lives was vital.

# NOTES

### Introduction

1 Joan Didion, *The White Album*, 205.
2 Clive Barnes, "'No, No, Nanette' Is Back Alive."
3 Gerald Clarke, "The Meaning of Nostalgia."
4 Benjamin L. Alpers, "*American Graffiti* and the Sixties in the Seventies."
5 Roger Ebert, Review of *American Graffiti*.
6 Daniel Rodgers, *Age of Fracture*, 221–229.
7 Peter N. Carroll, *It Seemed Like Nothing Happened: America in the 1970s*, 71–72, 297–301.

### Chapter 1   "Where Were You in '62?"

1 The scholar Daniel Marcus notes that the word "greaser" was not, in fact, a Fifties term at all, but rather a Seventies one. Somewhat tendentiously, Marcus argues that figures who in the Seventies were called "greasers" would have been called "hoods" in the Fifties. The *Oxford English Dictionary* traces the term "greaser" back to the middle of the Sixties, when it emerged as California slang for a leather-clad member of a biker gang. Throughout this chapter I use the word "greaser" to designate these figures because that was, in fact, the overwhelmingly dominant term for them in the Seventies. Daniel Marcus, *Happy Days and Wonder Years: The Fifties and Sixties in Contemporary Cultural Politics*, 12; "greaser, n.," *OED Online*, Oxford University Press, March 2022, https://www.oed.com/view/Entry/81098.
2 Johnathan Rodgers, "Back to the '50s"; "The Nifty Fifties."
3 Clive Barnes, "Stage: 'No, No, Nanette' Is Back Alive."
4 Gerald Clarke, "The Meaning of Nostalgia."
5 Wayne King, "The Boom in Nostalgia Turns Junk into Junque."
6 "Man and Woman of the Year: The Middle Americans," 13.
7 Roger Ebert, Review of *The Great Gatsby*.
8 Vincent Canby, "A Lavish 'Gatsby' Loses Book's Spirit."
9 Vincent Canby, "They've Turned 'Gatsby' to Goo."
10 Rick Perlstein, *The Invisible Bridge: The Fall of Nixon and the Rise of Reagan*, 166.

11 Douglas T. Miller and Marion Nowak, *The Fifties: The Way We Really Were*, 1–7.
12 Marcus, *Happy Days and Wonder Years*, 9–35.
13 Marley Brant, *Happier Days: Paramount Television's Classic Sitcoms, 1974–1984*, 18–20.
14 "The Nifty Fifties"; Rodgers, "Back to the '50s."
15 "The Nifty Fifties."
16 Rodgers, "Back to the '50s."
17 Harris Green, "'Grease'? Groovy."
18 Clive Barnes, "Theater: 'Grease,' 1959 as Nostalgia."
19 Michael Feingold, "Introduction: Goodbye to Sandra Dee."
20 Some of this section appeared, in slightly different form, as blog post on the U.S. Intellectual History blog: Benjamin L. Alpers, *American Graffiti* and the Sixties in the Seventies."
21 John Baxter, *Mythmaker: The Life and Work of George Lucas*, 93–116.
22 Larry Sturhahn, "The Filming of *American Graffiti*," 19.
23 Baxter, *Mythmaker*, 112.
24 Sturhahn, "Filming," 22–23.
25 Pauline Kael, "The Current Cinema: Un-People."
26 Sturhahn, "Filming," 24.
27 Jim Smith, *George Lucas*, 32, 29–40.
28 Sally Kline, ed., *George Lucas: Interviews*, 22.
29 Kline, *George Lucas*, 22.
30 Kline, *George Lucas*, 23.
31 Kline, *George Lucas*, 23–24.
32 Roger Ebert, Review of *American Graffiti*.
33 Quoted in Rodgers, "Back to the '50s," 82.
34 "The Nifty Fifties," 42.
35 Brant, *Happier Days*, 28.
36 David Kehr, "A Star Is Made," 10.
37 Gayle Rubin, "Old Guard, New Guard."
38 Guy Baldwin, "The Old Guard (The History of Leather Traditions)."
39 Legs McNeil and Gillian McCain, *Please Kill Me: The Uncensored Oral History of Punk*, 205–207.
40 On the importance of Punk magazine to the naming of punk rock, see Nicholas Rombes, *A Cultural Dictionary of Punk: 1974–1982*, 153–155. Rombes suggests that the term "New Wave," a term later applied to the pop-ier successor genre to punk, had been a more common term used by those in the scene prior to 1976.
41 O'Brien quoted by John Holmstrom in Jed Lipinski, "John Holmstrom Talks about Founding and Editing 'Punk,' the Chronicle of Late-'70s New York."
42 Rombes, *A Cultural Dictionary*, 86.
43 Rombes, *A Cultural Dictionary*, 24.
44 Legs McNeil and John Holmstrom, "Robert Gordon."

45 Paul Nelson, Review of "Ramones."

46 Ken Tucker, Reviews of *Blondie* and *Marquee Moon*.

47 Nicholas Rombes, *Ramones*, 20.

48 Quoted in Rombes, *Ramones*, 21.

49 Rombes, *Ramones*, 98–99.

50 Quoted in Clinton Heylin, *From the Velvets to the Voidoids: A Pre-Punk History for a Post-Punk World*, 159–160.

51 Quoted in Rombes, *Ramones*, 16.

52 James Wolcott, "A Conservative Impulse in the New Rock Underground."

53 Ellen Willis and Nona Willis Aronowitz, *Out of the Vinyl Deeps: Ellen Willis on Rock Music*, 114–115.

54 Fred Davis, *Yearning for Yesterday: A Sociology of Nostalgia*.

55 Davis, *Yearning*, 122–124.

56 Davis, *Yearning*, 129–132.

57 Davis, *Yearning*, 132–134.

58 Davis, *Yearning*, 136.

59 Davis, *Yearning*, 126.

60 Christopher Lasch, "The Politics of Nostalgia: Losing History in the Mists of Ideology."

61 Centers for Disease Control and Prevention, "Population by Age Groups, Race, and Sex for 1960–97," accessed May 5, 2023, https://www.cdc.gov/nchs/data/statab/pop6097.pdf.

62 Smith, *George Lucas*, 43–44.

## Chapter 2   Rip Van Marlowe

1 Some material in this chapter appeared, in a different context, in Benjamin J. Alpers, "Culture as Intellectual History: Broadening a Field of Study in the Wake of the Cultural Turn."

2 An excellent account of the origins of the term "film noir" can be found in James Naremore, *More Than Night: Film Noir in Its Contexts*.

3 Paul Schrader, "Notes on Film Noir," *Film Comment* 8, no. 1 (1972): 8–13, reprinted in Silver and Ursini, *Film Noir Reader*, 53–63, here 53. Page references to this work will be to the *Film Noir Reader*.

4 Raymond Durgnat, "Paint It Black: The Family Tree of the Film Noir," reprinted in Alain Silver and James Ursini, eds., *Film Noir Reader*, 37–51.

5 Paul Schrader and Kevin Jackson, *Schrader on Schrader and Other Writings*, 1–15.

6 Schrader and Jackson, *Schrader*, 30–32.

7 Paul Schrader, "Notes on Film Noir."

8 Schrader, "Notes," 58.

9 Schrader, "Notes," 59.

10 Schrader, "Notes," 53. Schrader had lost his job as film critic for the *Los Angeles Free Press* following his negative review of *Easy Rider*.

11  More recent scholarship on film noir has borne out Schrader's emphasis on the relationship between wartime conditions in Hollywood and the birth of film noir. See, for example, Sheri Chinen Biesen, *Blackout: World War II and the Origins of Film Noir*.

12  Paul Arthur, "Murder's Tongue: Identity, Death, and the City in Film Noir," 162–193. For more on World War II veteran characters in film noir, see also Elizabeth D. Samet, *Looking for the Good War*, 153–177.

13  Naremore, *More Than Night*, 33.

14  Arthur, "Murder's Tongue," 172.

15  Richard Jameson, "Son of Noir," *Film Comment* 10, no. 6 (1974): 30–33, reprinted in Alain Silver and James Ursini, eds., *Film Noir Reader 2*, 197–205.

16  Robert J. Emery, *The Directors: Take Two*, 121–123.

17  Emanuel Perlmutter, "Head of Building Trades Unions Here Says Response Favors Friday's Action."

18  J. Hoberman, *The Dream Life: Media, Movies and the Myth of the Sixties*, 281–283.

19  Reprinted in Harlan Ellison, *Harlan Ellison's Watching*, 73–75. Judith Crist, reviewing the movie for *New York* magazine, had a similar positive reaction, seeing it as accidentally, but extraordinarily, topical; reprinted in Norman Wexler, *Joe*, 9–13.

20  Mark Goodman, "Jonah in a Hard Hat."

21  Penelope Gilliat, "The Current Cinema; God Save the Language, at Least."

22  Stanley Kauffmann, "Stanley Kauffmann on Films."

23  Vincent Canby, "Playing on Our Prejudices."

24  David Denby, "New York Blues."

25  Denby, "New York Blues," 124–125.

26  Larry Powell and Tom Garrett, *The Films of John G. Avildsen*: Rocky, *The Karate Kid and Other Underdogs*, 16–25.

27  David A. Cook, *Lost Illusions: American Cinema in the Shadow of Watergate and Vietnam, 1970–1979*, 1–7.

28  Cook, *Lost Illusions*, 159.

29  James Paris, "How Hollywood's Memory Plays Tricks on Us." The term first appeared in Roger Greenspun, "Screen: Mike Hodges's 'Pulp' Opens," a negative review of a film that, in the critic's view, was unsuccessfully "parodying a genre that more or less lived by the grace of self-parody even in the classical noon of its warmest heyday."

30  Foster Hirsch, *Detours and Lost Highways: A Map of Neo-Noir*, 4.

31  Paul Schrader's insistence, following most French critics, that classic film noir was limited to a particular, short period was echoed by later American critics who wrote about noir in the Seventies like Robert Porfirio and James Damico. Silver and Ursini, *Film Noir Reader*, 77, 99–100.

32  Schrader, "Notes," 58.

33 Woody Allen's play *Play It Again, Sam*—later made into a movie—exemplifies this tendency in the late 1960s and early 1970s.

34 Robert Altman and David Thompson, *Altman on Altman*, 75, 81; Mitchell Zuckoff, *Robert Altman: The Oral Biography*, 244–245.

35 "Elliott Gould: The Urban Don Quixote."

36 Del Harvey, "Elliott Gould: Seventies Everyman."

37 Quoted in Zuckoff, *Robert Altman*, 244.

38 Altman and Thompson, *Altman on Altman*, 75.

39 Altman and Thompson, *Altman on Altman*, 81.

40 Altman and Thompson, *Altman on Altman*, 76.

41 Harvey, "Elliott Gould: Seventies Everyman."

42 Harvey, "Elliott Gould: Seventies Everyman."

43 Harvey, "Elliott Gould: Seventies Everyman."

44 Altman and Thompson, *Altman on Altman*, 81.

45 Arthur, "Murder's Tongue," 160.

46 George Anderson, "Elliott Gould Stars in 'Long Goodbye' at Forum, Encore."

47 Pauline Kael, "The Current Cinema: Movieland—The Bums' Paradise."

48 Andrew Sarris, "Living the Private-Eye Genre." See also the first half of his review: Andrew Sarris, "In the Public and Private Eye."

49 Elizabeth Ward, "*The Long Goodbye* and *Hickey and Boggs*: The Private Detective in Despair," Associated Students of UCLA Program Notes, 1974, reprinted as "The Post-Noir P.I.: *The Long Goodbye* and *Hickey and Boggs*," in Silver and Ursini, *Film Noir Reader*, 237, 239–241.

50 Reprinted in Silver and Ursini, *Film Noir Reader 2*, 201.

51 Schrader and Jackson, *Schrader on Schrader*, 116.

52 Schrader and Jackson, *Schrader on Schrader*, 119.

53 Schrader and Jackson, *Schrader on Schrader*, 111–113.

54 Stuart Byron, "'I Can't Get Jimmy Carter to See My Movie!': Robert Aldrich Talks with Stuart Byron," 50; Richard Thompson, "Paul Schrader / Richard Thompson Interview"; Schrader and Jackson, *Schrader on Schrader*, 113; Elaine Lennon, "A Question of Authorship: *The Yakuza*."

55 Schrader, "Notes," 59.

56 Robert Towne's screenplay for *Chinatown* is famously full of doubles and doubling. Director Roman Polanski calls attention to the structural importance of doublings to that film's story by making visual doublings a critical part of *Chinatown*'s mise-en-scène. Sydney Pollack, on the other hand, does no such thing in *The Yakuza*, which never visually connects Tanner and Tono and visually links Ken and Kilmer only in ways that the screenplay absolutely demands (i.e., the two dismemberments and the farewell at the airport).

57 Lawrence van Gelder, "'The Yakuza,' a Cinematic Hybrid about Obligation."

58 Roger Ebert, Review of *The Yakuza*.

59 Negative critical assessments of the film include "Review: 'The Yakuza,'";
   Charles Higham, "When I Do It, It's Not Gore, Says Writer Paul Schrader";
   Pauline Kael, "Revivals: *The Yakuza*."

60 Guy Flatley, "For Film Makers, Horror Stories Are a Supernatural."

61 "Hollywood Tackles the Vietnam War."

62 Louise Sweeney, "Studio Boss Who Called It Quits."

63 Norman Dresser, "'Rolling Thunder' Falls Prey to Excessive Gore, Cliches."

64 "Plenty of Violence in 'Rolling Thunder.'"

65 C. Michael Potter, "'Rolling Thunder': First of New Wave Vietnam War
   Flicks."

66 John Duvoli, "'Rolling Thunder' Violent for Sake of Violence."

67 Vincent Canby, "'Rolling Thunder' Film, Few Claps."

68 Schrader and Jackson, *Schrader on Schrader*, 121.

69 Paul Schrader, "Yakuza-Eiga: A Primer."

70 Schrader, "Yakuza-Eiga," 17.

71 Schrader, "Notes," 55.

### Chapter 3   "A Committee of 215 Million People"

1 Max Lerner, "This Isn't Right Time to Hold Bicentennial."

2 Sherman Edwards and Peter Stone, *1776: A Musical Play (Based on a
   Conception of Sherman Edwards)*, 153.

3 Clive Barnes, "Theater: Spirited '1776.'"

4 Hans Rosenhaupt, "A Bridge at Generation Gap."

5 Roger Ebert, Review of *1776*.

6 Pauline Kael, "Foundering Fathers."

7 Mark Carnes, *Past Imperfect: History according to the Movies*, 92.

8 Carnes, *Past Imperfect*, 90.

9 Edwards and Stone, *1776*, 90–91.

10 Peter Hunt and Peter Stone, "Commentary."

11 Jeremy Rifkin and Jeffrey St. John, *The Great Bicentennial Debate: History as a
   Political Weapon*.

12 Quoted in Milton M. Klein, "Commemorating the American Revolution,"
   260.

13 "Private Sector Active in Bicentennial" (*Bicentennial News* press release),
   April 26, 1976, RARBA, "1976–77 P.R." Folder, Box 175.

14 Untitled *Bicentennial News* press release, January 12, 1976, RARBA, "1976–77
   P.R." Folder, Box 175.

15 Klein, "Commemorating the American Revolution," 261.

16 Vincent Canby, "Nashville."

17 Pauline Kael, "Coming: 'Nashville.'"

18 Andrew Sarris and Molly Haskell, "A Critics' Duet on 'Nashville.'"

19 Kael, "Coming: 'Nashville,'" 82.

20  More details of the history of ARBC and ARBA are covered in Tammy S. Gordon, *The Spirit of 1976: Commerce, Community, and the Politics of Commemoration.*

21  Anthony E. Neville, "Bicentennial Blues"; James Ridgeway, "'We Deserve a Break Today.'"

22  Gordon, *The Spirit of 1976*, 38–39; ARBC press release, August 2, 1972, RARBA, "Press Releases Issued by the American Revolution Bicentennial Commission" Binder, Box 175.

23  Neville, "Bicentennial Blues."

24  Gordon, *The Spirit of 1976*, 34–35.

25  Neville, "Bicentennial Blues."

26  Martin S. Goldman, Briefing of Trip to Indiana State University, Terre Haute, Indiana, RARBA, Martin S. Goldman to John Warner, "Goldman's Briefing for Warner" Folder, Box 311.

27  Goldman, Briefing of Trip to Indiana State University.

28  Goldman, Briefing of Trip to Indiana State University.

29  Goldman, Briefing of Trip to Indiana State University.

30  Goldman, Briefing of Trip to Indiana State University.

31  Goldman, Briefing of Trip to Indiana State University.

32  RARBA, "Warner: Indiana State University May 11, 1974" Folder, Box 177.

33  John Warner, "The American Revolution Bicentennial" (Speech), June 24, 1974, RARBA, "California, San Diego. U.S. Conference of Mayors (6/24/74)" Folder, Box 177.

34  Robert Miller, "America's Retailers and the Bicentennial: Obligation and Opportunity" (Speech), January 6, 1975, RARBA, "Miller; Nat'l Retail Merchants Assoc. 1/6/75" Folder, Box 178.

35  John Scholzen, *Bicentennial News* memorandum enclosing Warner testimony, February 4, 1976, RARBA, "1976–77 P.R." Folder, Box 175.

36  Untitled *Bicentennial News* press release, July 2, 1976, RARBA, "1976–77 P.R." Folder, Box 175.

37  "Cultural Revolution Gains Momentum in America" (*Bicentennial News* press release), June 12, 1974, RARBA, "1974 P.R." Folder, Box 175.

38  "America's Youth and the Bicentennial" (*Bicentennial News* press release), November 5, 1974, RARBA, "1974 P.R." Folder, Box 175.

39  John Warner, "The American Revolution Bicentennial" (Speech), June 24, 1974, RARBA, "California, San Diego. U.S. Conference of Mayors (6/24/74)" Folder, Box 177.

40  "Bicentennial Planners in Error on Madison." See also "ARBA Issues Correction on Youth Brochure" (*Bicentennial News* press release), November 19, 1974, RARBA, "1974 P.R." Folder, Box 175.

41  Letter from John W. Warner to Ronald W. Van Nostrand, stamped April 29, 1974, RARBA, "Declaration of Americans (Scroll)" Folder, Box 317.

42  "Carl Byoir Selected as PR Counsel for US Government Bicentennial Program" (*Bicentennial News* press release), October 9, 1975, RARBA, "1975 P.R." Folder, Box 175.

43  Gordon, *The Spirit of 1976*, 47–67, 86–89; Klein, "Commemorating the American Revolution."

44  Israel Shenker, "Bicentennial Stirs Book Deluge; Some Say It's a Bit Too Much."

45  Michael Kammen, "The American Revolution Bicentennial and the Writing of Local History."

46  Richard E. Shalhope, "Toward a Republican Synthesis: The Emergence of an Understanding of Republicanism in American Historiography."

47  Laurence Veysey, "The "New" Social History in the Context of American Historical Writing."

48  In 1973, the historian Jack P. Greene called for such a comprehensive view of the Revolution's social origins. Jack P. Greene, "The Social Origins of the American Revolution: An Evaluation and an Interpretation."

49  Letter from Stephen Kurtz to David Hansen, June 25, 1971, RARBA, "Library of Congress" Folder, Box 312.

50  RARBA, "1972 Biographies" Folder, "Heritage General" Tab, Box 311.

51  "Heritage '76 Committee Members," n.d., RARBA, "Presentation for Warner" Folder, "Briefing Materials" Tab, Box 311.

52  Memorandum from Martin Goldman to Hugh Hall, May 14, 1974, RARBA, "Historical Societies" Folder, Box 320.

53  Edmund S. Morgan, "A Loyal Un-American."

54  Rick Perlstein, *The Invisible Bridge: The Fall of Nixon and the Rise of Reagan*, xv.

55  Gordon, *The Spirit of 1976*, 148.

56  M. J. Rymsza-Pawlowska, *History Comes Alive: Public History and Popular Culture in the 1970s*, 4–8.

57  Daniel Rodgers, *Age of Fracture*, 221–255.

58  Rogers, *Age of Fracture*, 228.

### Chapter 4    Family Stories and the African American Past in Alex Haley's *Roots* and Octavia Butler's *Kindred*

1  Untitled *Bicentennial News* press release, August 2, 1972, RARBA, "Press Releases Issued by the American Revolutionary Bicentennial Commission" Binder, Box 175.

2  Letter from Barbara J. Diggs to Jean Hutson, February 12, 1973, RARBA, "Colleges—Ethnic and Minority Participation" Folder, Box 317.

3  "Report on the First Planning Conference of the Afro-American Humanities Bicentennial Celebration," RARBA, "Hurray for Black Women" Folder, Box 269. See also Tammy S. Gordon, *The Spirit of 1976: Commerce, Community, and the Politics of Commemoration*, 83–85.

4  Richard Pryor, "Bicentennial N——"; Gordon, *The Spirit of 1976*, 85.

5 "The Story of Us All," AHP, Box 76, Folder 12.

6 Robert J. Norrell, *Alex Haley and the Books That Changed a Nation*, 3–4.

7 Norrell, *Alex Haley*, 82.

8 Letter from Alex Haley to Paul Reynolds, January 30, 1965, AHP, Box 3, Folder 10.

9 Letter from Alex Haley to Paul Reynolds, August 24, 1965, AHP, Box 3, Folder 10.

10 Letter from Maurice Ragsdale to Alex Haley, January 25, 1967, AHP, Box 3, Folder 10.

11 Alex Haley, *Roots: The Saga of an American Family*, v.

12 James Baldwin, "How One Black Man Came to Be an American [Review of *Roots*]."

13 Norrell, *Alex Haley*, 150–151.

14 Theodore Solotaroff, Review of *World of Our Fathers*.

15 Norrell, *Alex Haley*, 151–152, 166–169; Harry Castleman and Walter J. Podrazik, *Watching TV: Six Decades of American Television*, 255–256.

16 Ruth A. Protinsky and Terry M. Wildman, "Roots: Reflections from the Classroom."

17 See, for example, Herb Boyd, ed., Roots: *Some Student Perspectives*.

18 Quoted in Matthew F. Delmont, *Making* Roots: *A Nation Captivated*, 205.

19 Norrell, *Alex Haley*, 225–226.

20 These controversies are covered in Norrell, *Alex Haley*, 175–202. See also Adam Henig, *Alex Haley's Roots: An Author's Odyssey*.

21 Norrell, *Alex Haley*, 199–202.

22 Philip Nobile, "Uncovering Roots."

23 Norrell, *Alex Haley*, 221–225.

24 Haley, *Roots*, 18–19.

25 Haley, *Roots*, 19–20.

26 Haley, *Roots*, 31–32.

27 Haley, *Roots*, 437.

28 Haley, *Roots*, 459.

29 Haley, *Roots*, 464.

30 Haley, *Roots*, 480–481.

31 Haley, *Roots*, 481–483, 492–494.

32 Haley, *Roots*, 547.

33 Haley, *Roots*, 559.

34 Haley, *Roots*, 560.

35 Haley, *Roots*, 570–572.

36 Haley, *Roots*, 582.

37 Haley, *Roots*, 653.

38 Haley, *Roots*, 661–663.

39 Haley, *Roots*, 672.

40 Haley, *Roots*, 747.

41 Haley, *Roots*, 795–796.

42 Haley, *Roots*, 799.

43 Haley, *Roots*, 808.

44 Haley, *Roots*, 849.

45 Haley, *Roots*, 856–860.

46 Haley, *Roots*, 864–888.

47 Ulrich Bonnell Phillips, *American Negro Slavery: A Survey of the Supply, Employment and Control of Negro Labor as Determined by the Plantation Régime.*

48 Stanley Elkins, *Slavery: A Problem in American Institutional and Intellectual Life.*

49 For the relationship between Bettelheim's work and Elkins's, see Kirsten Lise Fermaglich, *American Dreams and Nazi Nightmares: Early Holocaust Consciousness and Liberal America, 1957–1965*, 24–57.

50 Daniel Patrick Moynihan, *The Negro Family: The Case for National Action.*

51 Norrell, *Alex Haley*, 146.

52 Donald Wright, Review of *Roots.*

53 Norrell, *Alex Haley*, 146.

54 Dierdre Carmody, "Haley Gets Special Pulitzer Prize; Lufkin, Tex., News Takes a Medal"; Norrell, *Alex Haley*, 181.

55 Norrell, *Alex Haley*, 148–149.

56 Delmont, *Making* Roots, 188–190.

57 Letter from Leo Charles Pochinkas Jr. to Alex Haley, June 5, 1978, AHP, Folder 10, Box 3.

58 M. J. Rymsza-Pawlowska, *History Comes Alive: Public History and Popular Culture in the 1970s*, 31.

59 Delmont, *Making* Roots, 200.

60 Gerry Canavan, *Octavia E. Butler*, chap. 1, locs. 367–368 (Kindle).

61 Quoted in Canavan, *Octavia E. Butler*, chap. 1, locs. 386–387.

62 Canavan, *Octavia E. Butler*, chap. 1.

63 Octavia Butler, *Kindred*, 98.

64 Butler, *Kindred*, 101.

65 Butler, *Kindred*, 177, 182.

66 Butler, *Kindred*, 229, 186.

67 Octavia Butler, Note (undated; possibly for a talk), OEBP, Box 162, OEB 329.

68 Letter from Octavia Butler to Marjorie Rae Nadler, July 20, 1979, OEBP, Box 213, OEB 4182.

69 On Haley's patriarchal understanding of Black history, see Delmont, *Making* Roots, 46.

70 I thank my University of Oklahoma Honors College colleague Julia Ehrhardt for this observation.

71 Octavia Butler, "Prologue" to *Switchback* (undated), OEBP, Box 61, OEB 1188.

72 Folder 2 ("Alex Haley and *Roots*"), OEBP, Box 296.

73 Octavia Butler, Note dated June 19, 1976, OEBP, Box 162, OEB 3213.

74 Octavia Butler, Notecard (undated), OEBP, Box 61, OEB 1191.

75 Butler, *Kindred*, 264.
76 Delmont, *Making* Roots, chap. 3.
77 Norrell, *Alex Haley*, 123.
78 Delmont, *Making* Roots, 72.
79 Canavan, *Octavia E. Butler*, chap. 1, loc. 649.
80 Quoted in Canavan, *Octavia E. Butler*, chap. 3, locs. 1266–1270.
81 Canavan, *Octavia E. Butler*, chap. 3, loc. 1280.

**Afterword**

1 Robert B. Townsend, "Precedents: The Job Crisis of the 1970s."
2 C. Vann Woodward, "The Future of the Past," 716–717.
3 Philip D. Jordan, "Editor's Page: The Neurosis of Nostalgia."
4 "National Council on Public History Records, 1977–2002."
5 Larry E. Tise, "State and Local History: A Future from the Past."
6 Robert Kelley, "Public History: Its Origins, Nature, and Prospects."
7 Todd Shallatt, "We Who Would Sell History?"
8 Bob McKenzie, "Objectivity and the Public Historian."
9 John Lukacs, "American History? American History."
10 John Lukacs, "Doctorwurlitzer or History in *Ragtime*."
11 M. J. Rymsza-Pawlowska, *History Comes Alive: Public History and Popular Culture in the 1970s.*
12 Daniel T. Rodgers, *Age of Fracture*, 221–255.

# BIBLIOGRAPHY

AHP    Alex Haley Papers (MS-1888), University of Tennessee Libraries, Special
        Collections, Knoxville, TN.
OEBP   Octavia E. Butler Papers, Huntington Library, San Marino, CA.
RARBA  Records of the American Revolution Bicentennial Administration,
        Record Group 452, National Archives, College Park, MD.

Alpers, Benjamin L. "*American Graffiti* and the Sixties in the Seventies." *U.S.
    Intellectual History Blog*, November 11, 2013. https://s-usih.org/2013/11/american
    -graffiti-and-the-sixties-in-the-seventies/.
———. "Culture as Intellectual History: Broadening a Field of Study in the Wake of
    the Cultural Turn." In *American Labyrinth: Intellectual History for Complicated
    Times*, edited by Raymond Haberski and Andrew Hartman, 271–284. Ithaca,
    NY: Cornell University Press, 2018.
Altman, Robert, and David Thompson. *Altman on Altman*. London: Faber and
    Faber, 2006.
Anderson, George. "Elliott Gould Stars in 'Long Goodbye' at Forum, Encore."
    *Pittsburgh Post-Gazette*, November 15, 1973.
Arthur, Paul. "Murder's Tongue: Identity, Death, and the City in Film Noir." In
    *Violence and American Cinema*, edited by J. David Slocum, 153–175. New York:
    Routledge, 2001.
Baldwin, Guy. "The Old Guard (The History of Leather Traditions)." Accessed
    December 23, 2014. http://www.hawkeegn.com/bdsm/oldgd.html.
Baldwin, James. "How One Black Man Came to Be an American [Review of *Roots*]."
    *New York Times*, September 26, 1976.
Barnes, Clive. "Stage: 'No, No, Nanette' Is Back Alive." *New York Times*, Janu-
    ary 20, 1971.
———. "Theater: 'Grease,' 1959 as Nostalgia." *New York Times*, February 15, 1972.
———. "Theater: Spirited '1776.'" *New York Times*, March 17, 1969.
Baxter, John. *Mythmaker: The Life and Work of George Lucas*. New York: Spike, 1999.
"Bicentennial Planners in Error on Madison." *New York Times*, November 22, 1974.
"'Bicentennial Schlock' Spoofs Tradition." *New York Times*, October 11, 1976.
Biesen, Sheri Chinen. *Blackout: World War II and the Origins of Film Noir*.
    Baltimore: Johns Hopkins University Press, 2005.

Biskind, Peter. *Easy Riders, Raging Bulls: How the Sex-Drugs-and-Rock 'n' Roll Generation Saved Hollywood*. New York: Simon and Schuster, 1999.

Boyd, Herb, ed. Roots: *Some Student Perspectives*. Detroit: Wayne State University, 1977.

Brant, Marley. *Happier Days: Paramount Television's Classic Sitcoms, 1974–1984*. New York: Billboard Books, 2006.

Butler, Octavia. *Kindred*. Boston: Beacon Press, 2003.

Byron, Stuart. "'I Can't Get Jimmy Carter to See My Movie!': Robert Aldrich Talks with Stuart Byron." *Film Comment* 13, no. 2 (1977): 46–52.

Canavan, Gerry. *Octavia E. Butler*. Champaign-Urbana: University of Illinois Press, 2016. Kindle.

Canby, Vincent. "A Lavish 'Gatsby' Loses Book's Spirit." *New York Times*, March 28, 1974.

———. "'Nashville.'" *New York Times*, June 12, 1975.

———. "Playing on Our Prejudices." *New York Times*, August 2, 1970.

———. "'Rolling Thunder' Film, Few Claps." *New York Times*, October 15, 1977.

———. "They've Turned 'Gatsby' to Goo." *New York Times*, March 31, 1974.

Carmody, Dierdre. "Haley Gets Special Pulitzer Prize; Lufkin, Tex., News Takes a Medal." *New York Times*, April 19, 1977.

Carnes, Mark C., ed. *Past Imperfect: History according to the Movies*. New York: Henry Holt, 1995.

Carroll, Peter N. *It Seemed Like Nothing Happened: America in the 1970s*. New Brunswick, NJ: Rutgers University Press, 2000.

Castleman, Harry, and Walter J. Podrazik. *Watching TV: Six Decades of American Television*. 2nd ed. Syracuse, NY: Syracuse University Press, 2010.

Centers for Disease Control and Prevention. "Population by Age Groups, Race, and Sex for 1960–97." Accessed June 5, 2023, https://www.cdc.gov/nchs/data/statab/pop6097.pdf.

Chandler, Raymond. *The Big Sleep*. New York: Vintage Books, 1988.

Clarke, Gerald. "The Meaning of Nostalgia." *Time*, May 3, 1971.

Cook, David A. *Lost Illusions: American Cinema in the Shadow of Watergate and Vietnam, 1970–1979*. New York: C. Scribner, 2000.

Davis, Fred. *Yearning for Yesterday: A Sociology of Nostalgia*. New York: Free Press, 1979.

Delmont, Matthew F. *Making Roots: A Nation Captivated*. Oakland: University of California Press, 2016.

Denby, David. "New York Blues." *Atlantic Monthly*, November 1970.

Didion, Joan. *Slouching towards Bethlehem*. New York: Farrar, Straus and Giroux, 1968.

———. *The White Album*. New York: Farrar, Straus and Giroux, 1979.

Dresser, Norman. "'Rolling Thunder' Falls Prey to Excessive Gore, Cliches." *Toledo Blade*, October 24, 1977.

Duvoli, John. "'Rolling Thunder' Violent for Sake of Violence." *Evening News,*
    October 23, 1977.
Ebert, Roger. Review of *1776. Chicago Sun-Times,* December 26, 1972.
———. Review of *American Graffiti. Chicago Sun-Times,* August 11, 1973.
———. Review of *The Great Gatsby. Chicago Sun-Times,* January 1, 1974.
———. Review of *The Yakuza. Chicago Sun-Times,* January 1, 1975.
Edwards, Sherman, and Peter Stone. *1776: A Musical Play (Based on a Conception of
    Sherman Edwards).* New York: Viking Press, 1970.
Elkins, Stanley M. *Slavery: A Problem in American Institutional and Intellectual
    Life.* Chicago: University of Chicago Press, 1976.
"Elliott Gould: The Urban Don Quixote." *Time,* September 7, 1970.
Ellison, Harlan. *Harlan Ellison's Watching.* Los Angeles: Underwood-Miller, 1989.
Emery, Robert J. *The Directors: Take Two.* New York: Allworth Press, 2002.
Feingold, Michael. "Introduction: Goodbye to Sandra Dee." In *Grease: A New 50's Rock
    'n Roll Musical* by Jim Jacobs and Warren Casey. New York: Winter House, 1972.
Fermaglich, Kirsten Lise. *American Dreams and Nazi Nightmares: Early Holocaust
    Consciousness and Liberal America, 1957–1965.* Waltham, MA: Brandeis
    University Press, 2007.
Flatley, Guy. "For Film Makers, Horror Stories Are a Supernatural." *New York
    Times,* July 16, 1976.
Gilliat, Penelope. "The Current Cinema: God Save the Language, at Least." *New
    Yorker,* August 15, 1970.
Goodman, Mark. "Jonah in a Hard Hat." *Time,* July 27, 1970.
Gordon, Tammy S. *The Spirit of 1976: Commerce, Community, and the Politics of
    Commemoration.* Amherst: University of Massachusetts Press, 2013.
Green, Harris. "'Grease'? Groovy." *New York Times,* June 4, 1972.
Greene, Jack P. "The Social Origins of the American Revolution: An Evaluation and
    an Interpretation." *Political Science Quarterly* 88, no. 1 (1973): 1–22.
Greenspun, Roger. "Screen: Mike Hodges's 'Pulp' Opens." *New York Times,*
    February 9, 1973.
Haley, Alex. *Roots: The Saga of an American Family.* Boston: Da Capo Press, 2014.
Harvey, Del. "Elliott Gould: Seventies Everyman." *Film Monthly,* June 15, 2000.
    https://web.archive.org/web/20210126134414/http://www.filmmonthly.com
    /Profiles/Articles/EGould/Elliott%20Gould.html.
Henig, Adam. *Alex Haley's Roots: An Author's Odyssey.* CreateSpace Independent
    Publishing Platform, 2014.
Heylin, Clinton. *From the Velvets to the Voidoids: A Pre-Punk History for a
    Post-Punk World.* New York: Penguin Books, 1993.
Higham, Charles. "When I Do It, It's Not Gore, Says Writer Paul Schrader." *New
    York Times,* February 5, 1978.
Hirsch, Foster. *Detours and Lost Highways: A Map of Neo-Noir.* New York:
    Limelight Editions, 1999.

Hoberman, J. *The Dream Life: Media, Movies and the Myth of the Sixties.* New York: New Press, 2005.

"Hollywood Tackles the Vietnam War." *New York Times,* August 2, 1977.

Hunt, Peter, and Peter Stone. "Commentary." *1776, Director's Cut.* Dir. by Peter Hunt. Culver City, CA: Sony Pictures Home Entertainment, 2015. Blu-ray Disc.

Jameson, Richard. "Son of Noir." In *Film Noir Reader 2,* edited by Alain Silver and James Ursini, 197–205. New York: Limelight Editions, 1999.

Jordan, Philip D. "Editor's Page: The Neurosis of Nostalgia." *Minnesota History* 44, no. 3 (1974): 113–114.

Kael, Pauline. "Coming: 'Nashville.'" *New Yorker,* March 3, 1975.

———. "The Current Cinema: Movieland—The Bums' Paradise." *New Yorker,* October 23, 1973.

———. "The Current Cinema: Un-People." *New Yorker,* October 29, 1973.

———. "Foundering Fathers." *New Yorker,* November 25, 1972.

———. "Revivals: *The Yakuza.*" *New Yorker,* September 4, 1995.

Kammen, Michael. "The American Revolution Bicentennial and the Writing of Local History." *History News* 30, no. 8 (1975): 179–190.

Kauffmann, Stanley. "Stanley Kauffmann on Films." *The New Republic,* August 22, 1970.

Kehr, David. "A Star Is Made." *Film Comment* 15, no. 1 (January–February 1979): 7–12.

Kelley, Robert. "Public History: Its Origins, Nature, and Prospects." *The Public Historian* 1, no. 1 (1978): 16–28.

King, Wayne. "The Boom in Nostalgia Turns Junk into Junque." *New York Times,* August 8, 1970.

Klein, Milton, M. "Commemorating the American Revolution: The Bicentennial and Its Predecessors." *New York History* 58, no. 3 (1977): 257–276.

Kline, Sally, ed. *George Lucas: Interviews.* Jackson: University of Mississippi Press, 1999.

Lasch, Christopher. "The Politics of Nostalgia: Losing History in the Mists of Ideology." *Harper's,* November 1984.

Lennon, Elaine. "A Question of Authorship: *The Yakuza.*" *Sense of Cinema,* no. 37 (October 2005). http://sensesofcinema.com/2005/37/yakuza/.

Lerner, Max. "This Isn't Right Time to Hold Bicentennial." *Eugene Register-Guard,* April 10, 1975.

Lipinski, Jed. "John Holmstrom Talks about Founding and Editing 'Punk,' the Chronicle of Late-'70s New York." *Politico,* December 19, 2012. https://www.politico.com/states/new-york/albany/story/2012/12/john-holmstrom-talks-about-founding-and-editing-punk-the-chronicle-of-late-70s-new-york-073812.

Lukacs, John. "American History? American History." *Salmagundi* 50–51 (1980–1981): 172–180.

———. "Doctorwurlitzer or History in *Ragtime.*" *Salmagundi* 31–32 (1975–1976): 285–295.

"Man and Woman of the Year: The Middle Americans." *Time,* January 5, 1970.

Marcus, Daniel. *Happy Days and Wonder Years: The Fifties and the Sixties in Contemporary Cultural Politics*. New Brunswick, NJ: Rutgers University Press, 2004.

McKenzie, Bob. "Objectivity and the Public Historian" [Letter]. *The Public Historian* 1, no. 1 (1978): 12–13.

McNeil, Legs, and John Holmstrom. "Robert Gordon." *Punk*, January 1978.

McNeil, Legs, and Gillian McCain. *Please Kill Me: The Uncensored Oral History of Punk*. New York: Grove Press, 1996.

Miller, Douglas T., and Marion Nowak. *The Fifties: The Way We Really Were*. Garden City, NY: Doubleday, 1977.

Morgan, Edmund S. "A Loyal Un-American." *New York Review of Books*. March 21, 1974.

Moynihan, Daniel Patrick. *The Negro Family: The Case for National Action*. Washington, DC: Office of Policy Planning and Research, U.S. Department of Labor, March 1965. https://www.dol.gov/general/aboutdol/history/webid-moynihan.

Naremore, James. *More Than Night: Film Noir in Its Contexts*. Berkeley: University of California Press, 2008.

"National Council on Public History Records, 1977–2002." Archives Online. Indiana University. https://archives.iu.edu/catalog/mss021 (accessed May 22, 2023).

Nelson, Paul. Review of "Ramones." *Rolling Stone*, July 29, 1976.

Neville, Anthony E. "Bicentennial Blues." *Harper's*, July 1972.

"The Nifty Fifties." *LIFE*, June 16, 1972.

Nobile, Philip. "Uncovering Roots." *Village Voice*, February 23, 1993.

Norrell, Robert J. *Alex Haley and the Books That Changed a Nation*. New York: St. Martin's Press, 2015.

Paris, James. "How Hollywood's Memory Plays Tricks on Us." *New York Times*, November 23, 1975.

Perlmutter, Emanuel. "Head of Building Trades Unions Here Says Response Favors Friday's Action." *New York Times*, May 12, 1970.

Perlstein, Rick. *The Invisible Bridge: The Fall of Nixon and the Rise of Reagan*. New York: Simon and Schuster, 2014.

Phillips, Ulrich Bonnell. *American Negro Slavery: A Survey of the Supply, Employment and Control of Negro Labor as Determined by the Plantation Régime*. New York: D. Appleton, 1918.

"Plenty of Violence in 'Rolling Thunder.'" *Palm Beach Post*, April 18, 1978.

Potter, C. Michael. "'Rolling Thunder': First of New Wave Vietnam War Flicks." *Michigan Daily*, October 22, 1977.

Powell, Larry, and Tom Garrett. *The Films of John G. Avildsen: Rocky,* The Karate Kid *and Other Underdogs*. Jefferson, NC: McFarland, 2013.

Protinsky, Ruth A., and Terry M. Wildman. "*Roots*: Reflections from the Classroom." *Journal of Negro Education* 48, no. 2 (1979): 171–181.

Pryor, Richard. "Bicentennial Nigger." Track #9 on *Bicentennial Nigger*. Warner Bros., 1976. LP.

"Review: 'The Yakuza.'" *Variety*, December 31, 1974.

Ridgeway, James. "'We Deserve a Break Today.'" *Village Voice*, October 26, 1972.

Rifkin, Jeremy, and Jeffrey St. John. 1976. *The Great Bicentennial Debate: History as a Political Weapon: A Record of the Debate between Jeremy Rifkin and Jeffrey St. John, Held at St. Olaf's College, Minnesota, 1976*. Washington, DC: Heritage Foundation.

Rodgers, Daniel T. *Age of Fracture*. Cambridge, MA: Harvard University Press, 2011.

Rodgers, Johnathan. "Back to the '50s." *Newsweek*, October 16, 1972.

Rombes, Nicholas. *A Cultural Dictionary of Punk: 1974–1982*. New York: Continuum, 2009.

———. *Ramones*. New York: Continuum, 2005.

Rosenhaupt, Hans. "A Bridge at Generation Gap." *Journal of Higher Education* 41, no. 4 (1970): 256–263.

Rubin, Gayle. "Old Guard, New Guard." *Cuir Underground* 4, no. 2 (1998). http://www.black-rose.com/cuiru/archive/4-2/oldguard.html.

Rymsza-Pawlowska, M. J. *History Comes Alive: Public History and Popular Culture in the 1970s*. Chapel Hill: University of North Carolina Press, 2017.

Samet, Elizabeth D. *Looking for the Good War: American Amnesia and the Violent Pursuit of Happiness*. New York: Farrar, Straus, and Giroux, 2021.

Sarris, Andrew. "In the Public and Private Eye." *Village Voice*, November 1, 1973.

———. "Living the Private-Eye Genre." *Village Voice*, November 8, 1973.

Sarris, Andrew, and Molly Haskell. "A Critics' Duet on 'Nashville.'" *Village Voice*, June 9, 1975.

Schrader, Paul. "Notes on Film Noir." *Film Comment* 8, no. 1 (1972): 8–13.

———. "Yakuza-Eiga: A Primer." *Film Comment* 10, no. 1 (1974): 9–17.

Schrader, Paul, and Kevin Jackson. *Schrader on Schrader and Other Writings*. London: Faber, 2004.

Shalhope, Richard E. "Toward a Republican Synthesis: The Emergence of an Understanding of Republicanism in American Historiography." *William and Mary Quarterly* 29, no. 1 (1972): 49–80.

Shallatt, Todd. "We Who Would Sell History?" *The Public Historian* 1 no. 1 (1978): 81–82.

Shenker, Israel. "Bicentennial Stirs Book Deluge; Some Say It's a Bit Too Much." *New York Times*, November 11, 1975.

Silver, Alain, and James Ursini, eds. *Film Noir Reader*. New York: Limelight Editions, 1996.

Silver, Alain, and James Ursini, eds. *Film Noir Reader 2*. New York: Limelight Editions, 1999.

Smith, Jim. *George Lucas*. London: Virgin, 2003.

Solotaroff, Theodore. Review of *World of Our Fathers*. *New York Times*, February 1, 1976.

Sturhahn, Larry. "The Filming of American Graffiti." *Filmmakers Newsletter* 5, no. 5 (1974): 19–27.

Sweeney, Louise. "Studio Boss Who Called It Quits." *Christian Science Monitor*, February 7, 1980.

Thompson, Richard. "Paul Schrader / Richard Thompson Interview." *Film Comment* 12, no. 4 (1976). http://www.filmcomment.com/article/paul-schrader-richard-thompson-interview.

Tise, Larry E. "State and Local History: A Future from the Past." *The Public Historian* 1, no. 4 (1979): 14–22.

Townsend, Robert B. "Precedents: The Job Crisis of the 1970s." *Perspectives on History*, April 1, 1997. https://www.historians.org/publications-and-directories/perspectives-on-history/april-1997/precedents-the-job-crisis-of-the-1970s.

Tucker, Ken. Reviews of Blondie, "Blondie," and Television, "Marquee Moon." *Rolling Stone*, April 7, 1977.

van Gelder, Lawrence. "'The Yakuza,' a Cinematic Hybrid about Obligation." *New York Times*, March 20, 1975.

Veysey, Laurence. "The 'New' Social History in the Context of American Historical Writing." *Reviews in American History* 7, no. 1 (1979): 1–12.

Wexler, Norman. *Joe.* Chicago: Avon, 1970.

Willis, Ellen, and Nona Willis Aronowitz. *Out of the Vinyl Deeps: Ellen Willis on Rock Music*. Minneapolis: University of Minnesota Press, 2011.

Wolcott, James. "A Conservative Impulse in the New Rock Underground." *Village Voice*, August 18, 1975.

Woodward, C. Vann. "The Future of the Past." *American Historical Review* 75, no. 3 (1970): 711–726.

Wright, Donald. Review of *Roots. Social Education* 41, no. 6 (October 1977): 547.

Zuckoff, Mitchell. *Robert Altman: The Oral Biography*. New York: Vintage Books, 2010.

# INDEX

## ABOUT THE AUTHOR

BENJAMIN L. ALPERS is Reach for Excellence Associate Professor of History in the Honors College at the University of Oklahoma. He is the author of the book *Dictators, Democracy, and American Public Culture: Envisioning the Totalitarian Enemy, 1920s–1950s.*